THE PRESENT IN PERSPECTIVE

the Present

in

Second Edition /

Perspective

A LOOK AT
THE WORLD SINCE 1945

by Hans W. Gatzke

The Johns Hopkins University

RAND McNALLY & COMPANY : Chicago

RAND McNALLY HISTORY SERIES

Fred Harvey Harrington, Advisory Editor

BORDEN:
America's Ten Greatest Presidents

GATZKE:
The Present in Perspective

JONES:
Ancient Civilization

MOSSE:
The Culture of Western Europe

MOSSE, CAMERON, HILL, PETROVICH:
Europe in Review

PALMER:
Atlas of World History

STARR, NOWELL, LYON, STEARNS, HAMEROW:
A History of the World (2 vols.)

TREADGOLD:
Twentieth Century Russia

WILLIAMS:
The Shaping of American Diplomacy

WRIGHT:
France in Modern Times

THE AUTHOR AND PUBLISHER WISH TO THANK THE COUNCIL ON FOREIGN RELATIONS, INC., NEW YORK, FOR PERMISSION TO QUOTE FROM *Foreign Affairs.*

Printed in the U.S.A. by Rand McNally & Company
Library of Congress Catalogue Card Number 61-6578
Second Printing, March, 1962

Preface

THE PURPOSE OF THIS SMALL BOOK IS TO present, in a minimum of space, the most important events that have occurred since World War II. The book is primarily written for students, to whom the earlier happenings here described will seem quite remote. But even older readers may welcome this brief recapitulation, since it will help them gain a clearer perspective on current problems. More than at any other time in history, the very survival of our civilization may depend on an understanding of the vital issues we face. It is hoped that this book will contribute to such an understanding.

The trouble with writing "current history" is that its subject matter does not stand still. A first edition of this book, published in 1957, is already incomplete and out of date. Instead of making only a few changes and additions, it seemed preferable to bring out a complete revision. Only the title and a fraction of the text have been kept from the first edition. The rest of this second edition is sufficiently different to make it a substantially new book. Anyone patient enough to compare the two editions will be struck by the many important changes that have taken place in so short a time. History always quickens its pace in time of war. This certainly holds true for the cold war in the midst of which we are living today.

To present the recent past in all its complexity, events have been left largely to speak for themselves. Trends have been pointed out only where they are clearly discernible, and conclusions have been drawn where they appear truly valid. The temptation of making predictions has been avoided. Crystal gazing is a risky business at best and is done better by news analysts than by historians. Because the book is so brief, its treatment has to be selective. Nevertheless, it is hoped that nothing vital has been overlooked or neglected.

H.W.G.

CONTENTS

Preface v

Introduction: The Present in Perspective 1

1/THE SEARCH FOR PEACE 3

The Yalta Conference • Organizing the United Nations • The Potsdam Conference • The Surrender of Japan • The Satellite Treaties • Dissension among the Victors • The East-West Split over Germany • The Cold War in Europe • The United Nations in the Cold War • The Cold War in the Far East

2/THE ECLIPSE OF EUROPE 37

Great Britain — Recovery through Self-Discipline • France — Political Instability Retards Recovery • Germany — Recovery through

Hard Work • Italy — Poverty Prevents Recovery • The Small Nations of Western Europe • The Quest for European Unity

3/THE UNITED STATES AND ITS GOOD NEIGHBORS 67

The Search for a Postwar Policy • The Growing Fear of Communism • The War in Korea • The First Eisenhower Administration • The Second Eisenhower Administration • The United States and Canada • Latin America in Transition • The United States and Latin America • The United States and Cuba

4/THE SOVIET UNION AND ITS SATELLITES 99

Russia under Stalin • Eastern Europe under Stalin • "Collective Leadership" • The Khrushchev Era • Soviet Foreign Policy under Khrushchev • Revolt among the Satellites • The Satellites under Khrushchev

5/THE END OF COLONIALISM 129

The Independence of India and Pakistan • Communist China • Nationalism in Southeast Asia • Nationalism in the Middle East • Turbulent Africa • The Afro-Asian Bloc

6/COMPETITIVE COEXISTENCE 163

The Climax of the Cold War • The Search for Coexistence • The First "Meeting at the Summit" • The Cold War Continues • The Summit Meeting that Failed • The Cold War in the United Nations • Aid to Underdeveloped Lands • Competition for Arms and Outer Space • Atoms for War or Peace? • The Future in Perspective

Epilogue: Grave New World 193

Index 199

MAPS by Willis R. Heath

Central and Eastern Europe After World War II 16
Communism in Latin America 90
Underdeveloped Economies 91
Asia in 1960 136-37
The Middle East in 1960 150
Africa in 1960 156

Introduction: The Present In Perspective

LOOKING BACK FROM OUR VANTAGE POINT in the sixties, we see the two great wars of our century as the birth pangs of a new age. We do not know as yet what the age holds in store for us, but we do know its general trends. Some of these trends were already evident during the years after World War I: the eclipse of Europe's predominance and the rise of two superpowers, the United States and Russia, as determining factors in world affairs; the decline of colonial imperialism and the emergence of the nonwhite peoples as a significant political force; and the split of much of the world into conflicting Communist-totalitarian and liberal-democratic camps. Other characteristics of our age have become clear only since World War II: the utilization of atomic power in peace and war; the alarming increase of the world's population; and man's first probes into outer space. Taken together, these changes justify the feeling that mankind has entered a major new phase in its development.

The Present in Perspective

Despite the revolutionary changes of recent years, however, the basic issues before us today are not too different from those faced by our forebears. The "three scourges"—pestilence, famine, and war—so gruesomely depicted by artists through the ages, are still very much with us. Pestilence—that is, sickness—has been much alleviated by medical discoveries, many of them made in our own day. But while some scientists are trying to eradicate the last traditional killers of man, other scientists are creating new and perhaps greater dangers to human life by poisoning the atmosphere through atomic tests. Medical science, meanwhile, by enabling more people to live and live longer, is helping to perpetuate the threat of famine. Population growth in the past was often checked by war. But in our age of hydrogen bombs carried by guided missiles, war does more than merely check population, it threatens to extinguish mankind altogether. If, on the other hand, the world could be freed from the dread of war, the unprecedented resources now at our disposal could be used to eradicate both sickness and hunger forever. To change the wasteful and suicidal preparation for war into peaceful economic development remains the foremost task of our generation.

We have been speaking here of mankind and the world rather than of our own people and country. This in itself is significant. The economic interdependence of peoples in an age of advanced industrialization, the rise to independence and influence of the former colonial regions, and the ideological struggle between East and West are some of the factors that have forced us to widen our outlook. The narrow study of national history has become meaningless in an age of world-wide problems and issues. Not only are constant improvements in means of transportation and techniques of communication making the globe a much smaller place, but our scientists have also begun raising their sights from the conquest of terrestrial distances to the conquest of outer space. The fact that interplanetary travel has become an imminent reality is perhaps the clearest indication that man is in the midst of a major breakthrough in his technical development.

Most of the developments just outlined are quite obvious to us today, but we must remember that they have become so only since World War II. They were certainly not foreseen while the war was still in progress. This fact we must keep in mind as we take a look at the often inadequate plans made during the war to cope with the problems of the postwar world.

MEN OF GOOD WILL

Dag Hammarskjold (l.), UN Secretary General, and his Assistant, Ralph Bunche (r.), on one of their many missions of peace. WIDE WORLD PHOTO.

It is not so difficult to keep unity in time of war since there is a joint aim to defeat the common enemy, which is clear to everyone. The difficult task will come after the war when diverse interests tend to divide the Allies.

STALIN at Yalta

THE SEARCH FOR PEACE

IT IS SURPRISING, IN RETROSPECT, HOW LITTLE attention was given to the planning for peace by Western statesmen (we know nothing, of course, of Russia's planning). Prime Minister Churchill and President Roosevelt, it seems, were too preoccupied with winning the war to give much thought to preparations for peace. We do have one early version of their peace aims in the Atlantic Charter, which was issued in August, 1941, before the United States entered the war. It was subsequently endorsed by most of the countries at war with Germany, including Russia. The postwar world, the Atlantic Charter stated, was to be free from want and fear. There were to be no territorial changes against the wishes of the people concerned; each nation was to have the right to choose its own form of government; there was to be equal economic opportunity with access to essential raw materials for all nations; aggressor nations were to be disarmed; and there was to be no more use of force in the settling of international conflicts. Unfortunately these idealistic aims were largely ignored in the later negotiations between the Western powers and Russia. But to this day the Atlantic Charter represents the kind of settlement that the free world should like to see realized, if it could have its way.

THE YALTA CONFERENCE

It was not until 1945 that the problem of peace again became the subject of top-level discussions. The occasions were the meetings of the Big Three at Yalta and Potsdam. There had been earlier conferences in 1943 between Roosevelt and Churchill at Casablanca and Quebec, and between these two Western leaders and Stalin at Teheran. But these talks had dealt primarily with immediate military matters and only incidentally with long-range political questions. An exception was the meeting between Churchill and Stalin in Moscow in October, 1944. It was on this occasion that Britain recognized Russia's pre-eminence in Romania, Bulgaria, and Hungary, in return for comparable British control over Greece. Influence in Yugoslavia was to be divided equally between the two powers. But these agreements, while of considerable subsequent importance, were not considered binding by the United States.

The conference which met at the Russian resort of Yalta in the Crimea in February, 1945, is an important landmark. Its major decisions concerned Germany, Poland, the Far East, and the United Nations. There had been little preliminary planning on the future of Germany. The Russians had made it plain all along that they would insist on a harsh settlement. The Western powers had gone along with this, and at their Quebec meeting in August, 1943, had endorsed the plan of United States Secretary of the Treasury Henry Morgenthau for the partition and deindustrialization of Germany. But since then Roosevelt and Churchill had begun to wonder if the "Morgenthau Plan" was really wise. To dismember Germany would leave a power vacuum and would greatly enhance Russia's influence in central and eastern Europe. At Yalta, therefore, the Western powers asked that final decisions on Germany's political and economic fate be postponed. Russia's demand for 10 billion dollars in reparations was referred to a Reparations Commission, which was to use Russia's figure "as a basis for discussion." Russia's request, finally, that Germany surrender to Poland the area east of the Oder and Neisse rivers was also left undecided. All that the Western Allies conceded was that Poland "must receive substantial accessions of territory in the North and West." As far as Germany was concerned, the Yalta meeting was thus notable for the postponement rather than the solution of issues. The only firm agreement was on the postwar division of the country into four occupation zones (including one for France) under an Allied Control Council. The capital of Berlin, situated within the Soviet occupation zone, was to be occupied and administered jointly; but no specific agreement was made guaranteeing Western access to the city.

Most of the time at Yalta was spent trying to establish Poland's postwar frontiers and to agree on her provisional government. The Soviet Union, for reasons of her own security, claimed a special interest in the Polish question. The fact that she was in actual possession of the country greatly strengthened her position. The problem of what territory Russia was to receive caused few difficulties. Prior to Yalta the Western leaders had already consented to the "Curzon Line" (drawn up after World War I, but subsequently ignored), and with some modifications this boundary was approved at Yalta. Russia thus received about 47 per cent of Poland's prewar territory. Her effort to compensate Poland at Germany's expense, as we have just seen, though recognized in principle, was postponed for the time being.

The real headache developed over the formation of Poland's future government. There were at the time two provisional governments, the Polish government-in-exile in London and the Soviet-sponsored Committee of National Liberation at Lublin. The Russians insisted that a new government be formed by enlarging the Lublin group. Despite protests from the London Poles, the Western powers finally gave way on this crucial point. Their decision was made easier because the new Polish government was to hold "free and unfettered elections on the basis of universal suffrage and secret ballot." A similar promise of free elections for the other liberated peoples in central and eastern Europe was embodied in a simultaneous "Declaration on Liberated Europe." Having already resisted Soviet aims in Germany and hoping to gain Russian participation in the Pacific war and in the United Nations, the Western powers obviously shrank from making too much of an issue over a region which was so clearly within the Russian orbit.

Of all the negotiations at Yalta, those concerned with the Far East went most smoothly at the time, yet have stirred up the most criticism since. Russia's aid against Japan had been desired by the American military since shortly after Pearl Harbor and had been pledged by Stalin on several earlier occasions. But it was only at Yalta that details were worked out and that Russia was granted the concessions she expected in return for such aid. Specifically, Roosevelt agreed that the *status quo* in Outer Mongolia, already within the Russian sphere as the "Mongolian People's Republic," would be preserved; that the Kurile Islands would be transferred to the Soviet Union; and that Russian losses in the Russo-Japanese War of 1904–5 would be restored. The latter involved the return of the southern part of Sakhalin Island, the lease of the Port Arthur naval base, internationalization of the port of Dairen, and joint Russo-Chinese operation of the Chinese Eastern and South Manchurian railroads. In return, the Soviet Union promised participation in the Pacific war and the negotiation of a pact of friendship and alliance with the Chinese government of Chiang Kai-shek.

The problem closest to the heart of the American delegation at Yalta was to get British and Russian agreement to final plans for a United Nations organization. The groundwork for such an organization had been laid in negotiations going back to 1941 and culminating in the Dumbarton Oaks Conference in 1944. But agreement had still to be reached on two important points: the extent of the great powers' veto in the Security Council, and the number of seats each of them was to hold in the UN Assembly. On the first of these points, the three powers had felt all along that questions involving security should be settled only by the unanimous vote of the permanent Council members, that is, the great powers. This would give each of them the power to veto any such question. The United States, in order to soften the absolute nature of such a veto, proposed that a power should not be allowed to vote in cases relating to the settlements of disputes to which it might be a party. After long deliberation the British and the Russians agreed to this American modification. The issue on the second point revolved around the Soviet Union's demand that some of her constituent republics be given separate seats in the Assembly, partly to balance the membership of the British dominions. This argument seemed plausible to Churchill, and it was agreed that at the forthcoming United Nations Conference in San Francisco the Western powers would second Russia's request for admission of the White

Russian (Byelorussian) and Ukrainian republics. The United States was promised similar support by Britain and Russia if she should desire two additional votes for herself.

These, then, were the main provisions of Yalta. They were certainly far removed from the idealistic pronouncements of the Atlantic Charter. But as Churchill reminded Roosevelt, the Charter was not "a law, but a star." There was some hard bargaining at Yalta, but on the whole proceedings were amicable. This, in some ways, was the culmination of the wartime era of good feeling between Russia and the West. The Yalta decisions, far from causing any indignation, were hailed at the time "as one of the most important steps ever taken to promote peace and happiness in the world." In the final analysis, of course, the success of Yalta depended on the adherence of the Soviet Union to its terms. And it was not long before the issues on which agreement had been reached at Yalta became the subject of heated controversy between East and West. But this circumstance certainly was not foreseen by the Western statesmen at Yalta. They and their peoples admired the Russians for their major contributions to the common war effort; and they expected the friendship born in war to facilitate the making of peace. In that connection, it seemed like a good omen that America's fondest hope, the founding of a United Nations organization, was realized little more than two months after the Yalta Conference adjourned.

ORGANIZING THE UNITED NATIONS

The San Francisco Conference, which convened on April 25, 1945, was attended by delegations from fifty nations. President Roosevelt, generally regarded as one of the main architects of the United Nations, had died on April 12, and the leadership of the American delegation was in the hands of Secretary of State Edward Stettinius. The British were led by Foreign Minister Anthony Eden, and the Russians by Foreign Commissar Vyacheslav Molotov. These were the same men who had worked together at Yalta, assisting their respective heads of government. But there were a great many other interests besides those of the great powers represented at San Francisco, with the result that two months were needed before the Dumbarton Oaks proposals and the Yalta modifications could be made into the official United Nations Charter. In the process, many amendments were added to the original draft to give expression to the wishes of the smaller nations. But none of these affected the preponderant influence reserved for the great powers. The United Nations, from the very start, fell short of being a true world government.

The Charter was signed on June 26 and went into effect on October 24, 1945. The main purposes of the United Nations, like those of the League of Nations before it, were to be the maintenance of peace and security, the development of friendly relations among nations, and the sponsorship of international co-operation in the solution of economic, social, and cultural problems. It was specifically stated, however, that the United Nations could not "intervene in matters which are essentially within the domestic jurisdiction of any state." Membership was to be open to all peace-loving states on recommendation by the Security Council and a two-thirds vote of the Assembly. During the first fifteen years of the United Nations' existence close to fifty new members were admitted. The only important nonmembers are Switzerland, the divided states of Germany, Korea, and Vietnam, and Communist China.

The center of UN power is vested in the Security Council. Five of its eleven seats are assigned permanently, one each to the United States, Great Britain, France, the Soviet Union, and Nationalist China. The other six members are elected, for two-year terms, by the General Assembly on recommendation of the Council. The main task of the Security Council, as the name implies, is the maintenance of peace and security. In all nonprocedural questions, unanimity of the five permanent members is required. The United Nations was founded on the assumption that the only way to prevent the recurrence of a major conflict was through continued co-operation among all the great powers. This assumption has gained much validity since the advent of nuclear warfare, which has made a major war almost certainly synonymous with world destruction. In settling an international dispute, the Security Council can recommend a wide range of peaceful methods: mediation, arbitration, judicial settlement, and others. If its recommendations are not followed, it can suggest measures short of war, such as economic sanctions; and it may even take "such action by air, sea, or land forces as may be necessary to maintain or restore international peace." For this purpose the Charter provides for an "international police force" supplied by member nations. But such a permanent

UN military force has yet to be created. On the three occasions when such an army was needed—during the Korean War, the Suez crisis, and in the Congo—it had to be formed on a temporary basis.

The effectiveness of the Security Council, as we shall see, was increasingly hampered by disagreements between Russia and the West. Up to 1949 the Council scored a few successes in areas such as Indonesia, Israel, and Kashmir, where interests of the major powers were not in conflict. But since then the incessant use of the veto by the Soviet Union has tied the Council's hands on most crucial issues. The role thus abdicated by this basic organ has on some occasions, such as the Korean War and the Suez crisis, been assumed by the UN General Assembly. The Assembly is the most universal body of the United Nations in which all states have equal representation and equal voting power. It holds regular annual meetings, and it may be called into special session. Its decisions on important matters require a two-thirds majority; otherwise a simple majority is sufficient. Initially the General Assembly's functions were largely advisory, concerned with the shaping rather than the making of policy. During the Korean War, however, American initiative led to adoption of the "Uniting for Peace" resolution of November 3, 1950. This resolution defined the Assembly's role in times when the Security Council is deadlocked because of the veto. But this attempt to strengthen the power of the United Nations has not been overly successful. In cases where the interests of the Soviet Union and the United States conflicted, as in the Hungarian revolution in 1956 and the Lebanon crisis in 1958, the UN Assembly proved little more effective than the Security Council. The Assembly's success during the Suez crisis, furthermore, was made possible only because the United States and Russia for once took a common stand on a major issue.

Still, the General Assembly has become a far more important force than the authors of the Charter ever envisaged. With the expanding membership of the United Nations, the composition of the General Assembly has changed, until today the largest bloc of votes is held by the newly independent and neutralist nations of Asia and Africa. As a result, the West no longer finds it easy to command a two-thirds majority in the United Nations, and both East and West have to listen more attentively to the opinions and wishes of the smaller powers. Because of the needs of these powers, the emphasis of UN activity in recent years has shifted increasingly from political concerns to programs of economic and social improvement.

The purpose of the United Nations went beyond the prevention of war. To get to the roots of conflict by studying "international economic, social, cultural, educational, health, and related matters," an Economic and Social Council was set up, composed of eighteen members elected for three-year terms by the General Assembly. This Council appoints its own commissions, such as the Commission on Human Rights, which in 1948 drafted the "Universal Declaration of Human Rights." The United Nations also has affiliated with it a dozen specialized agencies, such as the International Bank for Reconstruction and Development ("World Bank"), the International Labor Organization (inherited from the League), the World Health Organization, and the Food and Agriculture Organization. As their names indicate, most of the specialized agencies are concerned with economic matters. Beginning in 1950 the United Nations launched the very successful Expanded Program of Technical Assistance, to help economically backward countries learn new skills and make fuller use of their resources. Compared to the bilateral programs of the United States and even the Soviet Union, the aid provided by the United Nations is still insignificant. But its activities are constantly expanding.

In the cultural sphere, the United Nations Educational, Scientific, and Cultural Organization (UNESCO), with headquarters in Paris, attempts to bring about better international understanding in the arts, sciences, and education. A more limited but very useful organ of the United Nations has been the Trusteeship Council, which exercises authority over nonself-governing territories like the former League of Nations mandates. Finally, there is the International Court of Justice at The Hague, successor to the Permanent Court of International Justice established in 1919. Its purpose is the judicial arbitration of international disputes.

The day-to-day administrative work of the United Nations is handled by the Secretariat. It is directed by a Secretary General, who is elected by the General Assembly upon the recommendation of the Security Council. The first to hold this post was Norway's foreign minister, Trygve Lie. He was succeeded in 1953 by Dag Hammarskjold of Sweden. The latter's wisdom, patience, and dedication in settling international disputes have greatly enhanced the importance of his office. The headquarters of the United Nations are in New York City, but occasional meetings of the General Assembly have been held in Paris.

THE POTSDAM CONFERENCE

On May 8, 1945 (V-E Day), while the San Francisco Conference was still in session, the official surrender of Germany was ratified in Berlin. The common task that had kept the Grand Alliance between East and West intact over the past years had thus been accomplished, and another top-level conference was needed to put some order into the chaos that Hitler had left behind. But already there were signs that the earlier cordiality between the Western Allies and Russia had given way to a formal coldness bordering on hostility. This was chiefly due to certain Russian actions that indicated her intention of following a policy of her own in eastern Europe. Two weeks after Yalta the Soviet member of the Allied Control Council for Romania had pressured King Michael into forming a new government with strong pro-Russian leanings, a change that the United States refused to recognize. At the same time the Russians were trying to evade the reorganization of the Lublin government in Poland and showed no signs of preparing for the free elections in that country that had been agreed on at Yalta.

The atmosphere of the Potsdam Conference in July, 1945, therefore, was quite different from that of Yalta. The fact that the first successful explosion of an atomic bomb in the proving grounds at Los Alamos, New Mexico, coincided with the beginning of the conference considerably stiffened the back of the United States delegation, because it made Russian participation in the Pacific war no longer essential. With Harry S. Truman in place of Roosevelt, and Clement Attlee taking over from Churchill after the latter's defeat in Britain's parliamentary elections on July 23, Stalin remained as the only member of the original Big Three. The major item on the agenda concerned the future of Germany, and the agreements reached had a profound influence upon postwar developments in that country. The Potsdam Declaration on Germany stated that the victors had no intention "to destroy or enslave the German people" but that they did intend to provide them with "the opportunity to prepare for the eventual reconstruction of their life on a democratic and peaceful basis." The aims of Allied occupation policy were specified as (1) disarmament and demilitarization; (2) denazification and the trial of war criminals; (3) democratization of Germany's political, educational, and judicial systems; (4) decentralization of her political structure and emphasis on local self-government; and (5) deindustrialization of war and heavy industries and placement of primary emphasis on agriculture and peaceful domestic industries. Most of these aims had already been agreed on in principle at Yalta and were here merely restated.

There were two other subjects that had already caused much trouble at Yalta and that continued to do so at Potsdam. These were Germany's eastern frontier and the payment of reparations. Without notifying her allies, Russia, three months earlier, had entrusted Poland with the administration of German territory east of the Oder and Neisse rivers, and had herself taken over the northern part of East Prussia. Faced with this *fait accompli,* the Western powers had no choice but to recognize "in principle . . . the ultimate transfer to the Soviet Union of the city of Königsberg and the area adjacent to it." The West insisted, however, that the final delimitation of the German-Polish frontier should wait until a definite peace settlement was reached. This did not keep Poland from subsequently expelling most of the Germans from east of the Oder-Neisse line and from claiming that the term "delimitation" merely applied to details of the frontier. Poland thus acquired almost one-fifth of Germany's pre-1938 territory. The fate of this easternmost part of Germany, subsequently completely Polanized, has remained an important issue in the cold war between East and West.

No final decision was reached at Potsdam on the total amount of German reparations, although Russia continued to insist on her lion's share of 10 billion dollars. This amount was to be collected through removal of industrial equipment from the Russian zone of occupation and from German foreign assets. In addition the Russians were to get some of the industrial equipment in the western occupation zones that was not needed for Germany's own postwar economy. The powers agreed, however, that "the amount and character of the industrial equipment unnecessary for the German peace economy and therefore available for reparations shall be made by the Control Council under policies fixed by the Allied Commission on Reparations," and that during the period of occupation Germany should be treated "as a single economic unit." Here was ample material for subsequent friction among the powers.

In respect to other issues, the Potsdam Conference achieved very little. Russia denied Western charges that she was violating the Yalta agreements on eastern Europe and unsuccessfully tried to gain the trusteeship over one of Italy's former colonies and a voice in the control of the Turkish Straits. The only additional agreement was on the establishment of a Big Four Council of Foreign Ministers to draft the peace treaties for Germany's satellites and Finland.

THE SURRENDER OF JAPAN

Four days after the Potsdam Conference adjourned, the United States dropped an atomic bomb on the Japanese city of Hiroshima. Two days later Soviet Russia declared war on Japan and invaded Manchuria. On August 10, 1945, after a second bomb had been dropped, Japan offered her surrender, and on August 14 (V-J Day) the war in the Far East was over. Since the United States had carried the major burden of the war against Japan, she felt justified in claiming sole control over the defeated country, an arrangement that greatly facilitated the postwar administration of Japan. There were set up an Allied Council with headquarters at Tokyo, consisting of the Big Three powers and China, and a Far Eastern Commission located in Washington, composed of eleven powers primarily concerned with Far Eastern affairs. But the functions of these bodies were purely advisory. Supreme authority over Japanese affairs was vested in a Supreme Commander for the Allied Powers, a post filled for almost six years by General Douglas MacArthur.

The fact that Russia had entered the war against Japan, even though she did so at the last moment and did not materially affect its outcome, now entitled her to the rights and territories she had been promised at Yalta (see p. 8). In accordance with another Yalta provision, Russia concluded a treaty of friendship and alliance with the Nationalist government of China, in which the latter agreed to the Yalta concessions as far as they affected China's interests. To complete the Far Eastern settlement, Russia and the United States jointly occupied the Korean peninsula, pending the formation of a democratic Korean government.

THE SATELLITE TREATIES

With Japan defeated, the great powers now at last could devote their full attention to the making of peace. But a successful post-

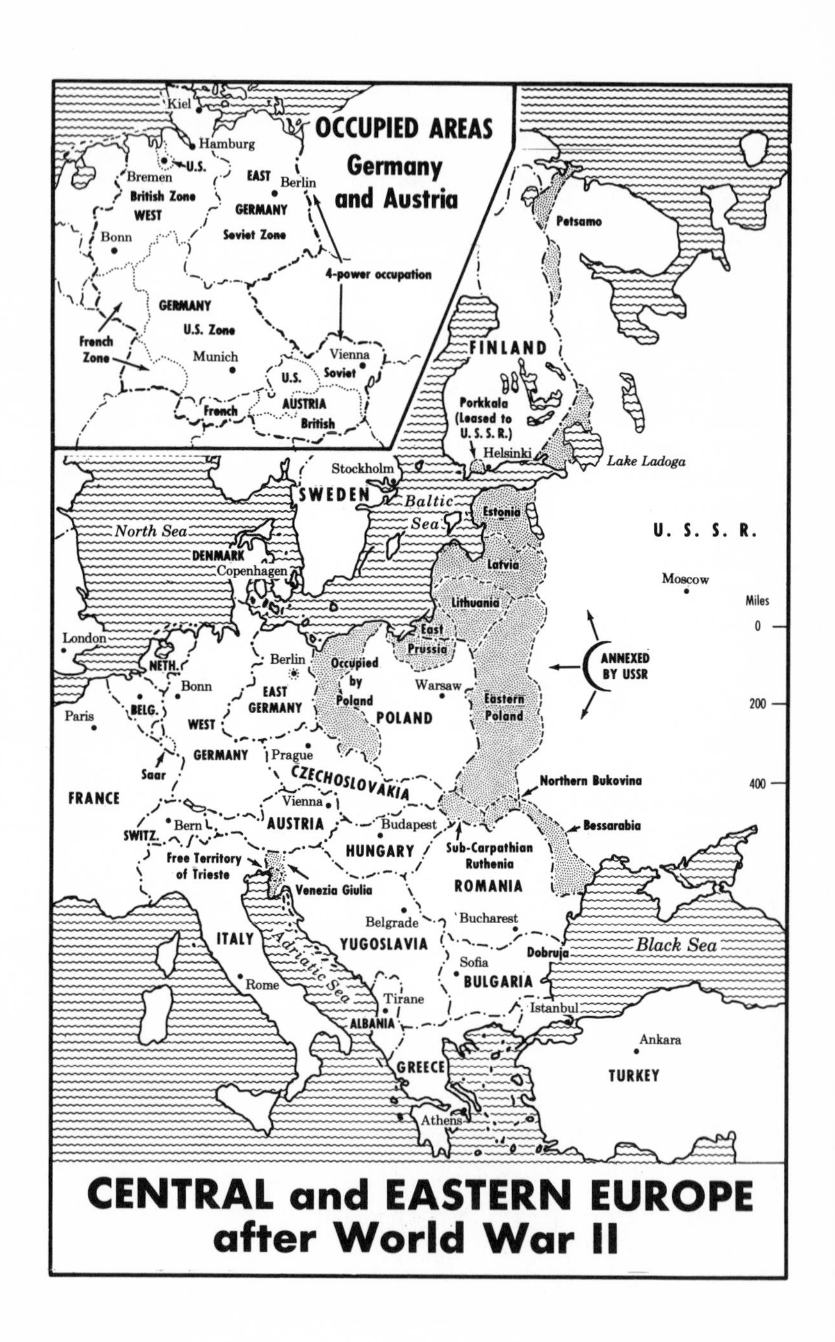

CENTRAL and EASTERN EUROPE after World War II

war settlement required above all a certain measure of harmony among the victors, and such harmony, as the previous months had shown, was rapidly disappearing. It is not surprising, therefore, that the attempts of the Big Four Council of Foreign Ministers to draw up peace treaties for the European powers other than Germany and Austria soon ran into a maze of difficulties. It is unnecessary here to go into the wranglings that lasted from September, 1945, until July, 1946. By that time sufficient agreement had been reached on the various treaty drafts to call a meeting at Paris of the twenty-one nations that had waged war against the European Axis. The Paris Conference lasted for more than two months. Like its predecessor in 1919, it was dominated entirely by the great powers; but unlike the earlier conference it gave the defeated countries an opportunity to plead their cause. Much of the time at Paris was spent in a tug of war between East and West. The dispute arose chiefly over Russia's efforts to impose a harsh treaty on Italy and to gain more favorable terms for those Axis satellites that were now within Russia's sphere. By the middle of December the task begun fifteen months earlier was finally completed. In view of the ever widening split between the Soviet Union and the West, it seems surprising in retrospect that any settlement was reached at all.

The peace treaties with Italy, Romania, Hungary, Bulgaria, and Finland were signed in the historic Clock Room of the Quai d'Orsay on February 10, 1947. Italy, in spite of her partnership-in-crime with Germany, got off remarkably easy, although the Italians did not think so. She lost some territories to France, Yugoslavia, and Greece. But more than these losses, Italy resented the transfer of her African colonies to the temporary trusteeship of Great Britain. Their ultimate status was to be determined later. The port of Trieste, which Yugoslavia, with Russian backing, was claiming for herself, was made into a free territory under the protection of the UN Security Council. Italy's armed forces were drastically reduced, and she agreed to pay 360 million dollars in reparations, of which Russia was to receive 100 million. The remaining Axis satellites, as well as Finland, had to pay substantial reparations, most of which went to Russia, and also had to cut their armed forces. With the exception of Finland, however, these countries were already so deeply under the influence of the Soviet Union that the details of these peace terms soon became meaningless.

Of greater interest were the territorial changes involving the smaller powers. In the Balkans Romania lost Bessarabia (which had been Russian from 1812 to 1918) and the northern Bucovina (inhabited largely by Ukrainians) to the Soviet Union; but she regained northern Transylvania, which Hungary had acquired during the war. Hungary was thus left with her 1938 frontiers, except for a minor rectification in favor of Czechoslovakia (the Bratislava bridgehead). Bulgaria returned her wartime gains to Yugoslavia, but she was allowed to retain the southern Dobruja, which Romania had taken from her in 1913 and which the Axis powers had restored to her in 1940. Another territorial change in this region, though not part of the satellite treaties, involved the cession by Czechoslovakia of the Ukrainian territory of Carpatho-Ruthenia to Russia. Most of these changes were based on ethnic principles. This does not mean, however, that the populations involved necessarily favored joining their brethren under Russian rule. In the north the Russians took the Petsamo district from Finland, thus regaining the common frontier with Norway that had existed for centuries prior to 1918. Finland also had to grant the Soviets a lease of the naval base at Porkkala, which Russia relinquished again in 1956. In addition, Finland lost territory along the central Russo-Finnish frontier and west of Lake Ladoga.

There were some other changes not covered by the satellite treaties that deserve mention. As far back as 1940 the Russians had incorporated the Baltic republics—Estonia, Latvia, and Lithuania—as member republics in the U.S.S.R. They were re-established as members of the Soviet Union after the Red Army reconquered the Baltic region in November, 1944, though the Western powers refused official recognition of this status. Russia's excuse was that the Baltic states had been part of the Russian Empire for two centuries before they became independent after World War I. In Europe, as in the Far East, Russia's immediate postwar aims thus appeared to be motivated by a desire to restore the territorial position she had enjoyed before the advent of communism.

More important in the long run, probably, than the territorial changes resulting from World War II, were the changes in the human geography of Europe that took place during and directly after the war. To find anything at all comparable in Western history, we have to go back to the early Germanic migrations in the days of the late Roman Empire. The modern version of this barbaric means of sorting out the ethnic confusion of eastern and central Europe dates from the large-scale resettlement programs devised by Hitler to gather the scattered German minorities of the eastern plains. By the middle of 1947, partly through Hitler's action, but mostly through expulsion after Germany's defeat, nearly ten million Germans had thus been moved or driven from regions that, in some cases, they had inhabited for centuries.

It was not only Germans who suffered this resettlement. There were also large numbers of "displaced persons" (DP's). These were eastern Europeans who had been moved to Germany under Hitler and who now could not or would not return to their former homes. In addition, there were the thousands of Poles expelled from the region east of the Curzon Line and resettled in eastern Germany. And there were at least three hundred thousand Esths, Letts, and Lithuanians who had fled before the Red Army. The total effect of these forced population transfers, according to Arnold Toynbee, "was to cancel the ethnic effects of a thousand years of German, Polish, and Lithuanian conquest and colonization, and to restore the ethnic map to something like the *status quo ante A.D.* 1200." As the Germans were driven from the cities they had founded centuries ago, these places were given Slavic names to obliterate their past. Together with the redrawing of the territorial frontiers, these population shifts have greatly simplified the ethnic picture in eastern Europe. But they have done so at a price of such human suffering and such glaring injustices that the hope to undo the postwar settlement in eastern Europe remains the aim of millions of people.

DISSENSION AMONG THE VICTORS

The signing of the satellite treaties ended, for the time being, the process of peacemaking. Several years were to pass before similar treaties were concluded with Japan and with Austria, and there has as yet been no settlement with Germany. The reason for this postponement of peace treaties lay in the ever increasing dissension among the victorious powers, which soon developed into an outright "cold war." It is a historical truism that alliances go to pieces once their objectives have been achieved; and in the light of prewar differences between the Soviet Union and the West, it should have been expected that the Grand Alliance would not survive the war. Yet there had been a general awareness on the part of all powers during the war that the peaceful reorganization of the world depended on their continued collaboration. It was this belief that had led to the founding of the United Nations. Why, then, despite such awareness, did this collaboration fail to be maintained?

To understand the genesis of the East-West split, we must consider briefly the basically different peace aims of the two superpowers whose policies were to determine the future course of world affairs. We have already seen the unfortunate tendency of American policy during the war to postpone major political decisions until the end of hostilities. Had some of the later issues been faced before 1943, when Russia was still on the defensive, the position of the United States in 1945 might easily have been much stronger. Part of America's indecisive attitude was no doubt due to the divergent aims among her leaders, which ranged anywhere from the noble sentiments of the Atlantic Charter to the hardheaded desire for military bases and economic expansion. But when all is said and done, the way in which most Americans, including their government, envisaged the postwar world was in prewar terms. They expected the restoration of a Europe balanced within itself, a United Nations as successor to the League of Nations, but without the latter's shortcomings, and a general adjustment among the victors, insuring to each an equitable sphere of political and economic influence in which some of the enlightened principles of the Atlantic Charter and the United Nations would gradually be realized.

But the defeat of the Axis, when it finally came, was such that it made a return to the past quite impossible. The complete collapse of Germany and Japan left a power vacuum in Europe and the Far East that had to be filled somehow. America's role in the Far Eastern war predestined her for a leading position in that part of the world, and the United States never hesitated about assuming this responsibility. In Europe, on the other hand, the situation was quite different. America's traditional aversion against involvement in the affairs of the old continent was still a strong factor in her immediate postwar policy. This aversion found popular expression in the general clamor for "getting the boys home" as soon as the fighting was over; and it was reflected in such governmental measures as the abrupt ending of Lend-Lease operations in the summer of 1945. There was to be continued American participation, of course, in the occupation of Germany and Austria, and America's role in the United Nations certainly was a radical departure from her isolationist retreat after World War I. But at first there was no clear understanding of the deep effect which the virtual disappearance of Germany and the emergence of Russia had upon the European balance of power. The obvious fact that Britain and France, while still given the courtesy title of "great powers," were really no match for the Soviet Union and needed the active support of the United States to maintain that balance, was only realized gradually, as the divergence of aims between Russia and the West became ever more obvious.

While America's immediate policy in Europe was one of partial withdrawal, the policy of the Soviet Union was the direct opposite. Russia's professed aims were economic reconstruction with the aid of large-scale reparations, and the creation of a security sphere in eastern Europe that would prevent the recurrence of the kind of invasion from the west which she had suffered twice within the last generation. These aims, the Russians felt, had been substantially recognized at Yalta and Potsdam. There was an additional requirement for Russian security, however, never clearly stated but nevertheless real, and that was the establishment of governments friendly to the Soviet Union along her western frontier. This was the real source of much of the subsequent trouble, because in Russian eyes a government to be friendly had to be pro-Communist. In retrospect, of course, this all seems quite obvious. But it did not appear so at the end of the war. It took the object lesson of Poland to drive home to the West the fundamental differences between its own and Russia's concept of what constituted a "democratic" government. And it soon became clear that the West was unwilling to recognize Russian predominance in eastern Europe if this was synonymous with the spread of communism in that area.

Here, then, was the basic issue: what the West looked upon as Communist expansion, Russia defended on grounds of national security. There is some doubt whether Stalin himself foresaw the extent to which the nations of eastern Europe ultimately became communized. It is certain that Stalin felt a clear delimitation of spheres of influence had been arrived at between the East and West. An example of this is his abstention from interfering with England's efforts to deal with the threat of communism in Greece (see p. 26). An example in the other direction is Stalin's refusal to tolerate interference with Russia's efforts to insure the victory of communism in Poland. But Russian desire for security, as events were soon to show, was not satisfied with the domination of eastern Europe. Since Russia was most deeply concerned over the resurgence of a powerful Germany, the establishment of a friendly, that is a Communist, regime in that country came to be the Soviet Union's basic aim in the extended negotiations with the Western powers over the future of Germany. It was largely over the German issue that the dissension among the victors developed into a cold war of ever widening dimensions.

THE EAST-WEST SPLIT OVER GERMANY

For purposes of occupation, the German Reich had been divided into four zones, with an Allied Control Council at Berlin to insure a certain uniformity of policy. But when the occupying powers tried to cope with Germany's economic and political problems, they soon discovered a considerable divergence of aims. The Russians, having suffered most heavily at the hands of the Germans, immediately began collecting large reparations in kind from their zone. They also insisted on an additional share of reparations from the rest of Germany. The Soviet zone was hermetically sealed against inspection by the Western powers, and its agriculture and industry were gradually nationalized. Politically, the Soviet zone was the first to see the revival of a German party system. To make sure of a pro-Russian majority, the Russians forced the large Socialist party to merge with the less numerous Communists into the "Socialist Unity Party" (SED). For the future, the Soviet Union favored a centralized German state, to facilitate its eventual communization.

The French, like the Russians, were determined to make the Germans pay for the war and to prevent Germany from ever again disturbing the peace. But unlike the Soviets, France saw the best guarantee for future security in a loose federal union rather than in a centralized state. Any early efforts of the Allied Control Council to treat the country as an economic or political entity were therefore vetoed by the Council's French representative. Only after the East-West split over Germany had become irreparable did the French gradually join the Anglo-American side.

Britain and the United States, while differing on some details, agreed on their basic principles in dealing with Germany. Since their zones were more heavily populated, they not only had to support their own occupation forces (while the French and Russians lived off the country) but also had to import large quantities of food to keep the Germans alive. Both England and America initially favored a considerable reduction of Germany's industrial potential. They accordingly ordered the dismantling of factories and the breaking-up (decartelization) of large enterprises such as the Krupp armament works and the I.G. Farben chemical combine. But in time both powers realized that the only way in which West Germany's large population could help support itself was by increasing, rather than decreasing, her industrial production and by treating Germany as the "single economic unit" that had been agreed on at Potsdam. The main exponent of this revised Western attitude towards Germany was General Lucius Clay, commander of the American zone during the most crucial postwar years until 1949. In the political sphere, the Western powers favored a federated, rather than a highly centralized, German state.

As this brief summary shows, there was considerable disagreement among the British and Americans on the one hand and the French as well as the Russians over the policies they advocated for Germany. A further disagreement arose over denazification. Each power soon began accusing the others of not doing enough to eliminate former Nazis from positions of influence. But considering the large number of persons who in some way had been involved in the activities of the Nazi party, complete denazification was a stupendous task. The United States made the most thorough attempt at denazification, but finally had to turn the job over to the Germans themselves, with not very satisfactory results. In all four zones Nazis who were not convicted of actual crimes gradually began to reassert themselves, without, however, ever constituting a real threat of neo-Nazism.

The first major showdown between the East and West came over the problem of German reparations. When the Russians refused to abide by the Potsdam terms governing the removal of industrial equipment, the British and Americans in May, 1946, stopped the delivery of reparations from their zones. At the same time Anglo-American leaders demanded that Germany be treated as an economic unit and that some general plan be devised for her economic future. When both the French and the Russians objected, Britain and the United States went ahead independently and in December, 1946, joined their zones into an economic "Bizonia." By early 1947 the four-power administration of Germany had come to a virtual standstill. In an effort to break this deadlock, the Big Four Council of Foreign Ministers met in Moscow in March, 1947. Just about this time American foreign policy, now under the direction of Secretary of State George C. Marshall, began taking a noticeably firmer line. The immediate occasion for America's stronger stand arose over a crisis in Greece, which led to the proclamation of the so-called Truman Doctrine (see p. 27). The effect of this proclamation upon the Moscow meeting was to make an already strained atmosphere still more tense. American and British efforts to reach agreement on German economic unity again ran into Russian and French opposition, and after six weeks of futile wrangling the conference adjourned.

The failure of the Moscow Conference and the proclamation of the Truman Doctrine are usually considered to have marked the beginning of the cold war. From now on actions and counteractions, not only in Germany but elsewhere, followed one another in rapid succession. And each such action further intensified the climate of mutual distrust between East and West. As far as Germany was concerned, the months following the Moscow meeting saw the Russian and Western zones drifting further and further apart. In June, 1947, Secretary Marshall announced his plan for the economic rehabilitation of Europe (see p. 27). To improve the economic situation of West Germany as part of western European recovery, the Anglo-American commanders raised the industrial level of Bizonia, especially the output of steel. This action brought forth a tirade of abuse from the East against the "imperialist" policy of the West. In October, 1947, the Russians founded the "Cominform" as a central organization of international communism, with a pronounced anti-Western platform. Three weeks later General Clay lifted the ban against attacks on communism in the West German press. When the Council of Foreign Ministers met again in London in December, 1947, the atmosphere was one of open hostility. The meeting broke up after three weeks of fruitless argument.

In the meantime, events in East and West Germany continued to move along their separate ways. It is unnecessary here to review the various steps by which the final division of Germany came about. In view of the split between the great powers, such a division was inevitable. In an effort to halt the creation of a West German state, the Soviet authorities in June, 1948, imposed a tight blockade on the western sectors of the city of Berlin. The Russians claimed that with the end of four-power government there was no further need for the Western powers to remain in the former German capital. The Americans replied with an unprecedented airlift and by imposing a counterblockade on East Germany. The duel over Berlin ended in the spring of 1949, when the Russians, realizing the impossibility of ousting the Western powers, lifted the blockade.

The division of Germany, meanwhile, had progressed further. A West German Parliamentary Council on May 8, 1949, adopted the Basic Law of the future "Federal Republic of Germany." Simultaneously, the East German People's Congress completed a constitution for the "German Democratic Republic." In mid-August, 1949, the first general elections were held in West Germany, and within a month the Federal Republic had been launched. In October, 1949, the Democratic Republic was established in the East, but without the benefit of popular elections. In November the newly-named "high commissioners" of the three Western powers, and the chancellor of West Germany, Konrad Adenauer, signed the Petersberg agreement, which defined the rights of the occupying powers and made further economic concessions to the Federal Republic. The struggle between East and West over Germany had thus developed into a stalemate—Germany was split in two.

THE COLD WAR IN EUROPE

Germany, because of her continued potentialities as a major power, had thus become the main battleground of the cold war. But she was not the only scene of East-West conflict. It was the creeping expansion of communism in eastern and southeastern Europe that caused the United States to take the lead in drawing together the nations of the West, first economically and later militarily. The communization of eastern Europe was a gradual process. Using her occupation forces to discourage movements unfriendly to her, the Soviet Union in the course of three years was able to weld the nations within her orbit into a solidly Communist bloc. By early 1947 this process had gone far enough to cause the deepest alarm among the leaders of the West. Romania, Poland, Yugoslavia, Albania, and Bulgaria all had either Communist or pro-Communist regimes; Czechoslovakia had a coalition government headed by a Communist; and in Hungary a purge against anti-Communists within the coalition government was under way. In addition, the Communists during 1946 had emerged as the strongest party in the French National Assembly and the third strongest in the Italian Constituent Assembly. The question was: What could the Western powers do to stem this rising Communist tide, without at the same time starting a third world war?

The partial answer had already been given in an address by Winston Churchill at Fulton, Missouri, in March, 1946. "From Stettin in the Baltic to Trieste in the Adriatic," its most memorable passage ran, "an iron curtain has descended across the continent." The former British prime minister strongly condemned "the police governments" of eastern Europe and recommended a policy of strength as the only attitude the Russians respected. Churchill's call for resistance to Russia was subsequently echoed in the American State Department. George F. Kennan, an expert on Russia and head of the department's policy-planning staff, declared that "the main element of any United States policy toward the Soviet Union must be that of a long-term, patient but firm and vigilant containment of Russian expansive tendencies . . . by the adroit and vigilant application of counter-force at a series of constantly shifting geographical and political points." The occasion for openly proclaiming the "containment" thesis as the basis of future American policy came in the spring of 1947, when Russian influence threatened to reach toward the Mediterranean by way of Greece and Turkey.

Greece, since the end of World War II, had been sharply divided between a militant left and a royalist right. Britain, concerned over her interests in the eastern Mediterranean, had tried to stabilize the situation by backing the rightists, who won the first postwar elections in March, 1946 (with the leftists abstaining). But the return of the monarchy did not end Greek unrest. The Communist contingent of the left, supported by Greece's Communist neighbors, started extensive guerrilla activities, which soon developed into a regular civil war. The only way for the government to hold its own was through continued British aid. But Britain was having her own economic difficulties at home. In addition, she had also been supporting Turkey's efforts to maintain a strong military force against Soviet demands for territorial concessions in the Caucasus and control of the Turkish Straits. In the spring of 1947, therefore, Britain felt that she could no longer afford aid to Greece and Turkey and announced its termination. At this point the United States stepped into the breach.

On March 12, 1947, President Truman, in a speech to Congress, declared that it should be the policy of the United States "to support free peoples who are resisting attempted subjugation by armed minorities or by outside pressures." He asked for the appropriation of 400 million dollars in economic and military aid to Greece and Turkey and for authorization to send American military and civilian personnel to those countries. "The free peoples of the world," the President concluded, "look to us for support in maintaining their freedom." Here was a wholly new concept in American foreign policy, soon to be known as the "Truman Doctrine." American help, President Truman said, was to be "primarily through economic and financial aid." This idea was elaborated upon in an address by Secretary of State Marshall, on June 5, 1947, at Harvard University. The "Marshall Plan," which was thus inaugurated, called for far-reaching economic assistance to European nations. It contained a strong element of humanitarianism, but its basic motive was national self-interest. By helping Europe to help itself, America hoped to bring about a general recovery that would banish the threat of communism.

The reaction of Europe to this imaginative American proposal clearly showed the extent to which the continent had already become divided along ideological lines. The nations of western Europe responded with enthusiasm. A central agency, the Organization for European Economic Cooperation (OEEC), was formed in the spring of 1948 to supervise what was called the European Recovery Program (ERP). Within the four years of ERP operation, thanks to Europe's energy and 13 billion American dollars, the Marshall Plan not only prevented the economic collapse of western Europe but raised production and living standards in many countries above prewar levels. As far as Russia was concerned, the plan was branded as merely another step in America's policy of establishing an anti-Communist, capitalist alliance. There was nothing in Secretary Marshall's proposal to exclude the nations of eastern Europe from participation. But Russian pressure soon forced any satellite that was attracted by America's generous offer back into line. In January, 1949, a Council for Mutual Economic Assistance ("Molotov Plan") was formed in Moscow, as an Eastern counterpart to ERP.

By this time, however, Russia had already taken other steps to tighten her hold over eastern Europe. Even before the end of the war she had concluded mutual assistance pacts with Yugoslavia, Poland, and Czechoslovakia. Since then the Soviets had signed similar treaties with Hungary, Romania, Bulgaria, and Finland. In September, 1947, at a conference in Warsaw, the Communist parties of eastern Europe, together with those of France and Italy, founded the Communist Information Bureau (Cominform). Its purpose (as was that of its predecessor, the Comintern, which had been dissolved in 1943) was to co-ordinate the activities of European communism and to combat "Anglo-American imperialism."

The most serious blow to the cause of freedom, however, was struck in February, 1948, when the Communists in a *coup d'état* seized the government of Czechoslovakia. That small republic had tried to steer a middle course between the East and West. In their foreign policy the Czechs had followed the lead of the Soviet Union, whose fear of Germany they shared. But in her domestic affairs Czechoslovakia had tried to maintain some of the personal freedoms that had made her an outpost of Western democracy in the interwar period. In the Czech elections of May, 1946, however, the Communists had polled 38 per cent of the vote, and the Communist leader Klement Gottwald had become head of a coalition government. By the spring of 1948 the Communists, through infiltration tactics and with Soviet support, had so strengthened their position that they could force President Beneš to agree to a predominantly Communist regime. In March, 1948, Foreign Minister Jan Masaryk, known for his Western leanings, was reported to have committed suicide. In June President Beneš resigned and was succeeded by Gottwald. Except for Finland, all of eastern Europe was thus in Communist hands.

The Communist seizure of Czechoslovakia, while not the only hostile act, certainly was the most blatant example of postwar Soviet expansionism. And there were signs, as in the continued civil war in Greece and the blockade of Berlin, that it might not be the last. The Western powers, therefore, began to face up to the fact that something more drastic than mere economic measures were needed to contain the Russians. In March, 1947, France and Great Britain had concluded a military alliance, the Treaty of Dunkirk. To widen its scope and effectiveness, these two powers, together with the Benelux countries—Belgium, the Netherlands, and Luxembourg—in March, 1948, signed the Treaty of Brussels. This treaty called for a fifty-year alliance against armed attack in Europe and established a Western Union for mutual co-operation in economic and military matters. It soon became clear, however, that western Europe, without American assistance, was no match for the military might of the Red Army. The United States was equally aware of this and in 1948 began discussions for a wider alliance.

The North Atlantic Treaty was signed in Washington on April 4, 1949, by the members of the Brussels pact plus Italy, Portugal, Denmark, Iceland, Norway, Canada, and the United States. These twelve powers were joined later by Greece and Turkey (1951) and by West Germany (1955). The gist of the treaty was contained in Article 5, which stated that "an armed attack against one or more" of its members, in Europe, North Africa, or North America, "shall be considered an attack against them all." A North Atlantic Council was set up to direct the formation of the North Atlantic Treaty Organization (NATO). General Dwight D. Eisenhower was appointed as NATO Supreme Commander in December, 1950, and established his headquarters at Rocquencourt, France, the following April. To provide the necessary financial aid, the American Congress approved a Mutual Defense Assistance Program which by 1959 had appropriated more than 10 billion dollars.

THE UNITED NATIONS IN THE COLD WAR

In the course of two years, from 1947 to 1949, America's foreign policy had thus undergone a major reorientation. The growing awareness of America's responsibility as the leading power of the West, however, was by no means shared by all Americans. Each step that involved the United States more deeply in the affairs of Europe was met with vociferous opposition in Congress and outside. Up to 1947 the United States had hoped that the system of collective security embodied in the United Nations would suffice to cope with international crises. Experience soon taught otherwise. Collective security was not very effective as long as one power, through use of the veto, could prevent the others from taking the necessary measures. This regrettable situation, however, did not mean that the West abandoned or ignored the United Nations. On the contrary, special care was taken that the regional pacts concluded among the Western powers did not conflict with but rather supplemented the UN Charter.

The United Nations had no sooner started its first session in January, 1946, when it received a complaint from Iran against the Soviet Union. To counteract German influence in that oil-rich Middle Eastern country, British and Russian forces had occupied Iran in 1941. Both powers had promised to withdraw their forces at the end of the war. When that time came, the British complied, but the Russians refused to leave. At this point the Security Council was asked to intervene. By putting pressure on the Soviet Union, the Council finally got Russia to withdraw. This was the first, though modest, achievement of the United Nations in settling an international issue.

There were other disputes that came before the United Nations during its early years. As long as such disputes did not involve the major powers, the United Nations, like the League of Nations before it, was quite effective. In 1947 the Security Council called for a cease-fire between Dutch and native forces in Indonesia and initiated negotiations that led to the independence of the Republic of Indonesia. In 1948 the Security Council helped stop the fighting between India and Pakistan over Kashmir. But when it came to settling conflicts between small powers that were backed by Russia or the United States, the United Nations found its work much more difficult.

This was shown in the case of Greece. As we have seen, that unhappy country had been plagued by civil war since 1946. In December of that year Greece complained to the United Nations that Yugoslavia, Bulgaria, and Albania were aiding the Greek Communists. The Security Council appointed a special Balkan Commission to investigate, and the Greek charges were found to be correct. But Russia used her veto to prevent the Council from taking any further action. To break the deadlock, the Greek question was referred to the General Assembly in October 1947. The Assembly then called upon Greece's neighbors to cease their interference. But it was chiefly due to American aid and the defection of Yugoslavia from the Communist camp in early 1948 that the Greek government finally gained the upper hand in its fight against communism.

In the Greek crisis the role of the United Nations had been greatly overshadowed by the actions of the major powers. But in the solution of the Palestine problem, where Russia and the United States saw eye to eye, the United Nations played a much more decisive part. The idea of making Palestine a Jewish state goes back to the Zionist movement at the end of the nineteenth century. During World War I Great Britain, in the "Balfour Declaration," had favored Zionist aspirations, as long as they did not "prejudice the civil and religious rights of existing non-Jewish communities in Palestine." After World War I Palestine became the mandate of Great Britain under the League of Nations. Encouraged by the Balfour Declaration, large numbers of Jews migrated to the Holy Land, especially after the advent of Hitler in 1933. This influx alarmed the Arabs, who had inhabited the region for centuries. To prevent losing Arab support in the vital Middle East, Britain in 1939 imposed restrictions on Jewish migration to Palestine and in 1945 prohibited immigration altogether. But large-scale illegal immigration continued, and the British found it increasingly difficult to keep order between Jews and Arabs. Various proposals for a compromise satisfied neither side. In April, 1947, Britain in desperation referred the matter to the United Nations and announced her withdrawal from the Palestine mandate as of May, 1948.

The United Nations decided that the most feasible solution would be the partition of Palestine into independent Jewish and Arab states. But while this was acceptable to the Jews, it did not satisfy the Arabs. When the British withdrew, a Jewish provisional government under David Ben-Gurion proclaimed the independent state of Israel. Both the United States and Russia immediately recognized the new regime. But soon the sporadic fighting between Jews and Arabs developed into a full-scale war. The Israeli forces gained the upper hand and cleared their new country of Arab armies. United Nations efforts to secure an armistice did not succeed until July, 1949. But the armistice remained an uneasy one, with constant border clashes threatening to flare up into a new war. The Arab countries refused to recognize Israel, and more than eight hundred thousand Arab refugees, driven from their homes as a result of the Arab-Israeli war, helped keep the Palestine issue alive.

Among the major problems facing the United Nations from the beginning was disarmament. A Commission for Conventional Armaments was formed to discuss this question. But it decided that the international situation, for the time being at least, made any control of traditional weapons impossible. The chief concern of the United Nations was over the atomic bomb. To discover ways and means of controlling atomic energy and restricting atomic weapons, an Atomic Energy Commission was created in January, 1946. At its first session the United States representative on the Commission, Bernard M. Baruch, presented his country's plan for atomic control. It called for the establishment of an International Atomic Development Authority with a monopoly over all raw materials and processes connected with atomic energy. The plan provided the Authority with the right of inspection, in order to insure the use of atomic energy for peaceful purposes only. The United States promised to hand over to the Authority its atomic knowledge and facilities and to destroy its supply of atomic weapons once the system of control and inspection had become effective. Since America still held a monopoly in the atomic field, this offer was most generous. But the Soviet Union opposed any inspection by the proposed Authority and suggested instead inspection by the Security Council, whose actions were subject to the veto. The Russians also demanded that the United States destroy its stockpile of atomic bombs before any control system went into effect. Despite the subsequent endorsement of the "Baruch Plan" by an overwhelming majority of the General Assembly, the Soviet veto in the Security Council prevented its adoption. In July, 1949, the Atomic Energy Commission voted to end its deliberations until a basis for agreement among the major powers could be found. Two months later the world was startled by reports of an atomic explosion inside the Soviet Union. With both sides now in possession of this deadly weapon, agreement on atomic control had become more imperative but also much more difficult.

Taken as a whole, the efforts of the United Nations during its early years to maintain peace and security were not very successful. The main achievements of the United Nations were in the less spectacular fields of social and economic reform. These absorbed the main energy of its three thousand staff members and its many special agencies. In December, 1948, the General Assembly passed a resolution providing for a long-range program of technical assistance to the world's underdeveloped areas. To be effective, however, such a plan needed the help of the richest and technically most advanced nation, the United States. In his inaugural address in January, 1949, President Truman rose to the occasion. He outlined four points of future policy, the last of which called for "a bold new program for making the benefits of our scientific advances and industrial progress available for the improvement and growth of underdeveloped areas." This was the beginning of the Point Four program. It was aided substantially by American money and personnel. The U.S.S.R. and her satellites, on the other hand, refused to participate in Point Four, but in time began to advance their own aid to underdeveloped countries.

Despite these positive achievements, it was by no means certain that the United Nations would be able to perform its primary function: the prevention of war and the punishment of aggressor nations. The General Assembly repeatedly discussed the possibility of modifying the veto as the major cause of UN weakness, but it always met with resistance from the great powers. To test the effectiveness of the United Nations, a major international incident was needed. Such an incident arose in the summer of 1950 with the sudden invasion of South Korea by North Korean forces.

THE COLD WAR IN THE FAR EAST

In dealing with the cold war in the Far East, we must keep in mind the radical changes taking place in Asia since World War II: the emergence of most of Asia's former colonial peoples into political independence (see Chapter 5). The international effects of this transformation were not really felt until the cold war was well under way. When these effects did appear, it soon became clear that most of the new nations of Asia were unwilling to be drawn into the East-West conflict. They preferred instead to remain neutral.

The first problem facing the victors in the Far East concerned the future of Japan. As we have seen, the United States claimed a dominant voice in settling that country's affairs. For this reason the tensions that arose in Europe over the joint occupation of Germany were avoided in the Far East. The occupation of Japan was directed by General Douglas MacArthur as Supreme Commander for the Allied Powers. He approached his task with firmness and tact and achieved a remarkable degree of success in a short time. The directive given him called for complete disarmament and demilitarization, the development of democratic institutions, and the creation of a viable economy. In pursuing these objectives, MacArthur was to work through the emperor and his government rather than through a hierarchy of military government, as was done in Germany. This arrangement, too, facilitated matters.

As a result of the war, Japan was reduced from an empire of 3 million square miles and 500 million people to the 142,000 square miles she had ruled a century ago, when Japan was first brought into contact with the outside world. But while at that time there were only about 28 million Japanese, today the Japanese number more than 85 million. To support this large population in an area about the size of California is Japan's major problem. In the early days of occupation, attempts were made to break up the large family combinations of industrial and financial power (*zaibatsu*) and to divide the large landholdings of absentee landlords. Also, the right of collective bargaining was recognized and labor unions were organized. But the breaking-up of large corporations was slowed down when its effects were felt to be detrimental to Japan's recovery, and for the same reason the right to strike was curbed. The redistribution of land, on the other hand, proceeded, and by 1952, 90 per cent of the arable acreage was owned by former tenants. Despite these reforms, however, Japan required close to 2 billion dollars of American aid in the first six years after the war. It was only with the demand for strategic goods during the Korean War that Japan's economy began to show any marked improvement.

The problems of demilitarization and democratization proved much simpler. The Japanese imperial army and navy were dissolved, patriotic organizations were banned, and education was purged of its militaristic elements. Emperor Hirohito disclaimed the divinity attributed to him by his people and denied the idea of Japanese racial superiority. To aid the democratization of Japan, a new constitution was proclaimed in 1947. It was closely modeled on the democratic institutions of Great Britain. Sovereignty was transferred from the emperor to the people, individual rights were safeguarded, and women were given equal status with men. Early postwar elections brought large Socialistic returns, but by 1948 a swing to the right set in, paralleling a similar trend in economic affairs.

By 1950 the occupation had accomplished most of its aims, and the time had come to conclude a peace treaty. The rift between the United States and Russia, however, made a peace conference impracticable. Instead, the United States took matters into its own hands, preparing a peace treaty which was signed on September 8, 1951. The treaty restored Japanese sovereignty, but only over the four main islands. There were no military or economic restrictions, except that the United States was permitted to maintain military bases in Japan. The United States also gained trusteeship over the Ryukyu and Bonin islands and over Japan's former Pacific mandates. Japan relinquished the Kurile Islands and southern Sakhalin (already occupied by Russia), as well as Formosa, but their future disposition was left open. It was a purposely generous treaty, which recognized the value of Japan as an ally against communism. It was for this reason chiefly that the Soviet Union refused to sign it. Some of Japan's other neighbors, especially the Philippines, Australia, and New Zealand, also felt apprehensive about a possible military revival of Japan. To allay the fears of these countries, the United States signed a mutual security treaty with the Philippines and a similar pact with Australia and New Zealand (ANZUS Treaty). In addition, the United States and

Japan signed a bilateral defense agreement which in 1952 was broadened into a mutual security pact. Japan thus became America's main bastion in the struggle with Russia for influence in the Far East.

If in Japan matters went largely according to American wishes, in China developments were much less favorable. The end of the war found China still divided between the Nationalist forces of Chiang Kai-shek and the Communist forces of Mao Tse-tung. Chiang had the support of powerful Chinese business and banking circles. Mao Tse-tung's program of land reform gave him the backing of China's landless millions. Both groups embarked on a campaign for the regions liberated from the Japanese. In this contest the Communists were the more successful. Various attempts to end the Chinese civil war by mediation proved fruitless. In the course of 1948 the decline of Chiang Kai-shek's forces, already evident in 1947, proceeded rapidly, and by the end of the year most of northern China was in Communist hands. The Nationalists by now had lost most of their best troops. Corruption among their provincial leaders had led to surrender or sale to the Communists of vast amounts of equipment that had been supplied by the United States. The Nationalist economy, badly in need of reform, had long depended on American aid, which since V-J Day had exceeded 2 billion dollars. But as time went on and the Nationalist government failed to reform itself, American aid was drastically curtailed and finally, in August, 1949, completely cut off. A few months earlier Chiang Kai-shek had begun the withdrawal of his forces to the island of Formosa. The Nationalist capital, Nanking, fell in April, 1949, Shanghai in May, and Canton in October. By early 1950 the whole mainland of China was in Communist hands. On October 1, 1949, the People's Republic of China was officially proclaimed at Peiping. The new regime was immediately recognized by the Soviet Union, but not by the United States. In February, 1950, Mao Tse-tung signed a thirty-year pact of friendship and mutual assistance with Soviet Russia.

The victory of communism in China was a major setback for the United States. Its importance was brought home almost immediately as developments in Korea transformed the hitherto cold war in that country into an armed conflict, involving not only the United States, but ultimately Communist China as well. The great powers had agreed that Korea, originally part of China, but in Japanese hands since 1910, should be given her independence after the war. At Yalta and Potsdam it was decided to divide the

Korean peninsula, for purposes of temporary occupation, along the thirty-eighth parallel. The United States was to assume responsibility for the southern half, and the U.S.S.R. for the northern half. The result of this partition for Korea, as for Germany, was the creation of two widely different native regimes. The Russians set up a Communist-dominated Provisional People's Committee, which catered to the poor peasants. In their zone the Americans favored the propertied, conservative elements. American efforts to bring about a merger of the two zones on the basis of free elections were countered by Russian proposals for the withdrawal of all occupation forces. When no agreement was reached, the matter was referred to the United Nations in early 1948, where the American proposal for elections was adopted. Since the Russians refused to let their zone participate, the elections were limited to the south, where they resulted in a conservative, rightist victory. After continued refusal by North Korea to join the National Assembly in the south, a Republic of Korea was proclaimed in August, 1948, with Dr. Syngman Rhee as president. A month later the North Koreans formed their own People's Democratic Republic. In December, 1948, the Soviet Union announced the withdrawal of its forces from North Korea. Six months later America followed suit in the south. A UN commission continued its efforts to mediate between the two Korean regions, but with negative results. In September, 1949, the commission warned of a possible civil war in Korea.

On June 24, 1950, North Korean troops suddenly crossed the thirty-eighth parallel in order to "liberate" South Korea. The UN Security Council immediately called upon North Korea to cease hostilities and withdraw her invasion forces. When the North Koreans refused to comply, the Council asked members of the United Nations to give assistance to the Republic of Korea. The United States had already decided to intervene, and was subsequently joined by token forces from other UN members. The United Nations had thus passed a major landmark. For the first time in its brief history, it had decided to use force. This move was made possible only because of Russia's temporary boycott of the Security Council, due to the United Nations' refusal to admit Communist China in place of Nationalist China. The Soviet Union consequently called the UN action illegal. Together with Communist China, Moscow accused the United States of aggression against North Korea. The issue was joined—the cold war had turned hot.

2

EUROPEAN UNITY

President Charles de Gaulle of France (l.), welcomes Chancellor Konrad Adenauer of West Germany (r.) to his private residence. WIDE WORLD PHOTO.

In World War II, which was decided by the participation of the Soviet Union and the United States, the collapse of the traditional European system became an irrevocable fact. What is commonly called the "historic Europe" is dead and beyond resurrection.

HAJO HOLBORN, *The Political Collapse of Europe* (New York: Alfred A. Knopf, 1951)

THE ECLIPSE OF EUROPE

ONE OF THE MOST SIGNIFICANT RESULTS OF World War II has been the decline of Europe's pre-eminence in world affairs. This has gone so far that some contemporary historians have spoken of "the political collapse of Europe," and have bid "farewell to European history." Europe's fate in our day has come to be determined more and more by two superpowers, originally descendent, but by now quite independent, from Europe. This decline of Europe's importance had actually set in during World War I, which would have taken quite a different course if it had not been for the intervention of the United States. But with America's withdrawal into her traditional isolation after 1919, a semblance of the old European system of great powers was resurrected and survived for a brief spell between the wars. It was during this period that the second of the superpowers, the Soviet Union, came to exploit the great potentialities inherent in her vast

Eurasian land mass. Russia thus emerged as the giant of the East, balancing the American giant of the West. As a result of Communist expansion since World War II, the political and cultural sphere of Europe today no longer corresponds to its geographic boundaries, which reach as far east as the Ural Mountains. When we speak of Europe now, we mean the region west of the "iron curtain," that is, free western Europe. The territory east of this line has become so closely integrated into the Soviet system that it can no longer lay claim to many of the cultural values that we associate with the term "European."

This territorial shrinkage helps to explain Europe's declining influence. Europe, as we use the term here, comprises only about one-fourth of the old continent and slightly more than one-third of the area of the United States. Upon this highly civilized region, two world wars have left their deep marks. But the effect of these wars has not been quite so disastrous and lasting as one might have expected. Western Europe's more than three hundred million people, her wealth of raw materials, and her highly developed industries still leave her the most valuable region for its size in the world. Western Europe today produces almost as much coal and steel as the United States and still outproduces the Soviet Union. We must, therefore, not exaggerate the decline of European influence. It has been a relative decline, as Russia and the United States have assumed the determining roles in world affairs. But as a potential "third force" in the global balance of power, Europe, at least for the present, remains far more important than the underdeveloped regions of Asia and Africa that have so recently become emancipated from European control.

The postwar problems facing the nations of free Europe differed in each case. There were few territorial and political changes, except in Germany and Italy. The threat of communism was greater in some countries, notably France and Italy, than in others. The one issue confronting all the powers, big and small, was to recover from the economic effects of the war and to regain the place that they had held in the world economy before the war. The governments differed in the methods they employed to bring about economic recovery, ranging from the socialist measures of Britain's Labor government to the free-enterprise economy of the German Federal Republic. In their efforts to find a solution to their economic troubles, the nations of western Europe were brought face to face with the necessity of modifying their traditional nationalism in the direction of some form of European union. As we shall see, this movement towards integration has not yet gone very far. For the time being, the history of Europe continues to be the history of its major powers, Great Britain, France, Germany, and Italy.

GREAT BRITAIN— RECOVERY THROUGH SELF-DISCIPLINE

Great Britain had fought longer than any other power against the Fascist aggressors, and her losses had been accordingly heavy. Yet these losses were not the main factor that retarded Britain's post-war recovery. The chief problem facing the British government was a perennial one, dating back to before the war: how to support a population of over fifty million on an island that produces less than half of the necessary food and hardly any of the needed raw materials, except coal. In the past, Britain had met this challenge in three ways—through income from foreign investments, through proceeds derived from merchant shipping, and through vast exports. But the heavy costs of war drastically reduced Britain's foreign holdings; the loss of half her merchant tonnage made it impossible to resume her leading role in shipping; and Britain's exports were only 30 per cent of what they had been before the war. The outlook for the future, therefore, was bleak, and most of Britain's efforts had to be concentrated upon regaining her economic health.

In July, 1945, the British electorate, for the first time since 1935, went to the polls again. The coalition cabinet of Winston Churchill was replaced by a Labor government headed by Clement R. Atlee. The Labor Party had campaigned on a platform of far-reaching socialization as a remedy for Britain's economic ills, and its resounding victory gave it a free hand to put its plans into operation. During the war a detailed report prepared by Sir William Beveridge had outlined an extensive program of social insurance for every citizen "from the cradle to the grave." It was along the lines of this report that the Labor government between 1946 and 1948 extended the already existing social insurance system. Outstanding among the new measures were the Education Act, providing free education to the age of sixteen, and the National Health Service Act which introduced free medical care for all. During the same period such key industries and utilities as the

Bank of England, the overseas cable and wireless services, the coal mines, the transport system, the gas industry, and the electricity supply industry were put under public ownership. Finally, in 1949, after much debate, a bill nationalizing the iron and steel industries passed both houses of Parliament, but it was not to go into effect until 1951. In their totality, the socialization measures of the Labor government affected some 20 per cent of Britain's industry and amounted to nothing less than a social and economic revolution.

As far as Great Britain's immediate economic difficulties were concerned, however, this transformation from free enterprise to limited socialism, in the opinion of the Conservative opposition at least, was a hindrance rather than a help. To solve the basic problem of achieving a positive balance of exports over imports, the government tried a number of remedies. To start Britain on her road to recovery, the United States in 1945 granted a loan of 3.75 billion dollars, and when the Marshall Plan began operating in 1949, Britain became its major beneficiary. Most of the funds thus made available were used to modernize British industry. At the same time an austerity program of continued rationing, long working hours, and reduction of luxury imports made the life of the average Britisher one of unrelieved drabness. Taxation, already high, was increased until only sixty people retained a net yearly income of six thousand pounds or more. As a result of these various efforts, Britain's economy by 1948 began to show marked improvement. Yet it was still so delicately balanced that a drop in American purchases during the following spring immediately reversed this upward trend. To master this new crisis the British government tightened its belt still further and in August, 1949, devalued the pound from $4.03 to $2.80. This was done in the hope that lower prices would mean increased exports. Improvement did follow, but it was interrupted again by the Korean War, which raised the cost of raw materials on the world market and thus undid much of Britain's earlier progress.

The slowness of Britain's economic recovery was thus chiefly due to causes beyond the control of the Labor government. But the British people had hoped for more from the party they had swept into office in 1945. Their disappointment was reflected in the outcome of the elections in October, 1951, which turned out the Labor government and returned a Conservative majority under Winston Churchill. The change in government, however, did not bring the complete reversal of Labor's radical program that many people expected. The only major socialist measure that was repealed was the nationalization of the steel industry. Britain's continued economic crisis required some further austerity measures. But beginning in mid-1952 things began looking up. Government controls were removed, taxes were cut, and rationing, that last reminder of the grim days of war, was gradually reduced and finally, in 1954, completely abolished. In June, 1953, the British and their Commonwealth cousins celebrated the coronation of Queen Elizabeth II, who had succeeded her father upon his death in February, 1952. Britain's recovery received temporary checks from a number of major strikes in 1954 and 1955. Yet with production booming, with a merchant fleet second only to that of the United States, and with ambitious building programs, the country, after ten years of hard work, finally regained its economic equilibrium. In April, 1955, Sir Winston Churchill, now in his eighty-first year, resigned as prime minister. He was succeeded by Sir Anthony Eden, longtime foreign minister. In the May elections of 1955 the electorate expressed its satisfaction with the way things were going by returning an increased Conservative majority to the House of Commons.

Britain was temporarily diverted from domestic issues by the government's futile intervention in the Suez crisis in the fall of 1956. But except for causing the resignation of Prime Minister Eden, who was succeeded by Harold Macmillan, the events in Egypt had no lasting effect at home. On the contrary, when the time for another election came in 1959, the Conservatives won their largest postwar parliamentary majority on a platform of "peace and prosperity." The government's pledge that it would double the British standard of living within one generation seemed borne out by the greater abundance of consumer goods now available. The Labor Party, since 1955 under the leadership of Hugh Gaitskell, had nothing to match these Conservative achievements, and Labor's program of further socialization apparently held little appeal for the British voter. Nor did the majority of the British people favor a more neutralist course in foreign policy, as advocated by a radical group within the Labor Party.

Many of Britain's initial postwar difficulties were due to the fact that her once mighty empire was undergoing a rapid and drastic shrinkage. Wherever after 1945 colonial peoples became restive and demanded concessions or independence, British interests were involved. From India, Burma, and Malaya, to Egypt, the Suez Canal, and Cyprus, Britain either was defeated or found herself on the defensive. Most of the newly independent native states, however, did not completely sever their ties with Great Britain. Instead they joined the United Kingdom and her older dominions—Canada, Australia, New Zealand, and South Africa—in that elusive organization of autonomous states known since 1948 as the "Commonwealth of Nations" (without the former designation of "British"). The accession since 1945 of India, Pakistan, Ceylon, Ghana, Malaya, Cyprus, and Nigeria to membership in the Commonwealth has presented Britain with a number of new problems and challenges. Three of the new members—India, Pakistan, and Ghana—are republics and thus no longer recognize the British sovereign as the "mystical link which unites this family of nations" (Winston Churchill), but look upon her as merely the "Head of the Commonwealth." The size of the Commonwealth, with more than a quarter of the world's surface and population, is truly impressive. But now, more than in the past, this loose federation has to justify its usefulness, which has been chiefly economic. The majority of Commonwealth people since 1947 are nonwhite and as such highly critical of the colonialism which their former mother country exercises in what is left of the British Empire. Great Britain, on the other hand, hopes not only to maintain but to enlarge the Commonwealth by admitting to membership, as in the past, those regions within her empire that desire and are ready for self-government. The next candidate for dominion status is the Federation of Rhodesia and Nyasaland.

It is quite natural that Great Britain, in view of her great past, her world-wide colonial interests, and her prominent position within the Commonwealth, should want to continue playing a leading role in world affairs. For this reason she has remained cool toward any projects for closer economic or political integration among western European states. She has broken precedent, however, by entering into a series of peacetime continental alliances. Britain's hope is that some day the Commonwealth may become a force similar in strength and influence to Russia and the United States. British influence in the world was given a substantial boost with the detonation of the first British hydrogen bomb in May, 1957. At the same time Great Britain continues to be deeply dependent on the United States for reasons of economic and military security. Anglo–United States relations since World War II have by necessity been very close, though as far as Britain is concerned not always too cordial. Britain at times has resented her dependence upon the United States and has followed a course different from that of her ally. Yet about the fundamental solidarity of Anglo-American interests there can be no doubt.

FRANCE–POLITICAL INSTABILITY RETARDS RECOVERY

France, like Great Britain, suffered acutely from problems of postwar economic readjustment. But unlike Britain, France's efforts at recovery were seriously hampered by political instability. The French political picture at the end of the war looked encouraging. After the liberation in 1944 a provisional government was formed by merging the wartime Committee of National Liberation with various resistance groups. This new regime was headed by General Charles de Gaulle, hero of the Free French Movement. It was chiefly under De Gaulle's direction that the transition from the Vichy regime of the past to the future Fourth Republic was accomplished. The most urgent tasks of the provisional government were economic. Under pressure from its leftist members, the government in 1945 embarked on a program of extensive nationalization of key industries. Simultaneously a planning council, under the direction of the brilliant economist Jean Monnet, worked out a set of production goals to rehabilitate and modernize French industry. It was at this critical point that the confusion of French politics interfered with the beginnings of economic recovery.

In October, 1945, elections were held for a National Constituent Assembly. There was the usual multiplicity of parties, but more than three-quarters of the seats were almost equally divided among the Socialists, the Communists, and the Popular Republicans, a new party advocating moderate social reform. The Communists received the largest single vote. In January, 1946, General de Gaulle, who had found co-operation with the leftists increasingly difficult, resigned the provisional presidency. In October, 1946, a new constitution was adopted by popular referendum. It closely resembled that of the Third Republic, with an all-powerful National Assembly, a primarily consultative Council of the Republic (the former Senate), and a weak executive.

The root of France's difficulties under the Fourth Republic, as under the Third, continued to be the innumerable divisions among its electorate. A system of proportional representation enabled even small splinter groups to elect delegates to the National Assembly, thus making the formation of viable coalition governments practically impossible. In the course of ten years the Fourth Republic saw more than twenty cabinets come and go, lasting anywhere from a few days to slightly over a year. Until May, 1947, a leftist majority kept matters relatively stable, but from then on confusion again became the order of the day. In April, 1947, General de Gaulle re-entered the political arena with a new party, the "Reunion of the French People." Its purpose was to serve as a counterweight to the Communists, who had the best-organized political force and commanded a large following among the working class. The parties between these two extremes desperately tried to steer a middle course. Yet they found it extremely difficult to agree on the continuation or abolition of social reforms and nationalization. If France somehow managed to continue functioning despite incessant domestic crises, this was due to her centralized bureaucracy and excellent system of municipal government as well as to the fact that a number of unusually able men—Robert Schuman, Georges Bidault, René Pleven, Jules Moch, René Mayer, and others—served the nation in different positions under various cabinets, thus insuring a certain continuity of policy.

The instability of France's domestic affairs was enhanced by the serious problems she faced abroad. Many of these problems were similar to those of Great Britain. But while the British had emerged from the war a cut below the two superpowers, the French suffered an even greater loss of prestige. Any independent international policy, for the time being at least, seemed out of the question. Some French politicians hoped to bolster their country's influence through closer affiliation with her British neighbor across the Channel. But as we have already seen, the British were reluctant to tie their hands in any way. The basic element of French foreign policy during the first years after the war was its dependence on American support, a relationship that was obnoxious to French pride. To regain some measure of initiative in foreign affairs, the French in the spring of 1950 became the chief advocates of a program of European union (see pp. 60-66). Such a policy immediately raised another question on which most Frenchmen had very strong feelings—the future of Franco-German relations. Events elsewhere, especially in Korea, hastened the integration of Germany into the Western camp. But most Frenchmen found it difficult to admit their recent enemy into a partnership that might some day become German-dominated. Yet without German participation, any kind of European union was incomplete and its security seriously weakened. This dilemma continued to plague France for some time.

One of the headaches France had in common with Great Britain concerned the future of the French colonial empire, the second largest in the world. To counteract the disruptive effects of native unrest, the constitution of the Fourth Republic called for the establishment of the French Union. This Union was "composed, on the one hand, of the French Republic, which comprises Metropolitan France and the Overseas Departments and Territories, and on the other hand, of the Associated Territories and States." It was headed by the President of the Republic and a High Council made up of representatives of the Union's members. The purpose of the Union was to preserve France's empire through greater administrative centralization. Thus the French Union differed markedly from Britain's Commonwealth with its emphasis on decentralization. Since France's overseas possessions demanded a greater degree of independence, the French Union was not very effective. Like Great Britain, France had been plagued since the war by almost continuous nationalist revolts in her colonies, notably in Indochina and in North Africa. The war in Indochina, which lasted until 1954, cost France more than thirty-five thousand lives and more than twice the amount of money she had received under the Marshall Plan. Despite these sacrifices, part of Indochina was lost to the Communist world, and the rest of France's former dependencies—Laos, Cambodia, and South Vietnam—after a brief stay in the French Union, declared their independence. A similar fate overtook most of France's holdings in the Middle East and in North Africa. The only territory where she decided to stand firm was Algeria, France's oldest possession in North Africa and part of Metropolitan France. It was the continued unrest in Algeria that led to the French crisis of 1958 which ended the Fourth Republic.

In view of France's political problems at home and abroad, it is not surprising that her economic recovery was extremely slow. French financial burdens after World War II were staggering. There were first of all the costs of the war itself, not only for the repair of war damage, which was heavier than in World War I, but also for pensions and annuities, some of which even dated back to the earlier war. Then there was the continued financial drain from the fighting in Indochina and the contribution to European rearmament. Added to these military expenses were the costs of the new social security system. And finally, in order to compete successfully on the world market, French industry required vast sums for the replacement of antiquated equipment and improvement of inefficient production methods. To meet these manifold obligations an effective system of taxation and a sound currency were needed. Efforts to reform the tax structure met with the traditional opposition of the French taxpayer, and the creeping inflation of the franc served to discourage saving and investment and thus further increased economic instability. Economic aid, chiefly under the Marshall Plan, did much to improve France's economy, and by 1949 the prewar level of industrial production had been regained. But by the middle of 1950 the trading crisis caused by the Korean War, the intensification of the war in Indochina, and the increased need for defense spending in Europe combined to undo much of the earlier progress. The situation was made still worse by an almost uninterrupted series of strikes, most of them led by the pro-Communist General Federation of Labor (CGT).

It was only after 1953 that the French economic picture began to brighten. Every possible method was tried to aid recovery—price control, reduction of government spending, curtailment of imports, export subsidies, public works, tax reform, building loans, and currency devaluation. By 1958 these combined efforts had resulted in a noticeable improvement. France's foreign trade came close to striking a balance, industrial production had risen by more than 50 per cent, wages were up, and the cost of living showed a slow downward trend. But the French economy was still far from sound. Much of the recovery had been due to continued foreign aid, principally from the United States. And what changes for the better there were had been won only against the bitter resistance of the many interest groups entrenched in the National Assembly. Here was the basic cause of France's troubles: the tenacity with which the French people clung to their individual, group, and regional interests, suspicious of concentrated political power and averse to any purposeful direction of national affairs. The resulting political instability not only retarded economic development, it also prevented the solution of France's most burning political problem: the future of Algeria.

Fighting in Algeria between an Arab independence movement

led by the National Liberation Front and the French army had been going on since 1954. By 1958 it had cost the lives of five thousand Frenchmen and fifty thousand Algerians. Efforts of the government to reach a compromise were fought by right-wing groups in Paris and by the more than one million persons of French extraction in Algeria. It was over rumors of another such compromise in May, 1958, that the colonists staged a riot in Algiers. They were joined by army units, embittered over France's previous futile colonial campaigns and over the government's indecisiveness. A "Committee of Public Safety," headed by the French commander in Algeria, called on General de Gaulle to form a French government "capable of restoring the grandeur and independence of the mother land." To avoid the outbreak of civil war at home, the government and De Gaulle collaborated on a legal and orderly transfer of power. On June 1, 1958, De Gaulle was made premier with full power to revise the constitution. In September the new constitution of the Fifth Republic was adopted by popular referendum. Its outstanding characteristic was the increased power it gave to the president. Thus it was hoped to insure greater political stability. On December 21, 1958, General de Gaulle was elected president of the republic.

Since then the French political scene has been dominated by the towering figure of Charles de Gaulle. His powers and functions are similar to those of the American chief executive. He has used these powers to gain stability at home and to increase French prestige abroad. The National Assembly, shorn of its arbitrary powers and with a majority of De Gaullist supporters, has passed a broad austerity program that has imposed sacrifices upon each and every Frenchman: higher taxes, currency devaluation, reduction of veterans' pensions and social security payments, a freeze on wages and sharp cuts in subsidies that have brought higher prices. Such sacrifices are needed, according to De Gaulle, to rescue France from economic stagnation and to make her once again a self-sustaining nation capable of fulfilling her international obligations. Only a France thus strengthened could support her claim to "grandeur" in the international sphere.

De Gaulle's concern over French power and influence abroad has been manifested in his intransigence on certain issues concerning NATO—such as the withdrawal of the French Mediterranean fleet from NATO control—as well as in his insistence upon an independent nuclear policy for France. After a long series of defeats in colonial wars and many real or imagined rebuffs by her allies, this assertion of French independence found the warm support of the French people and helped to offset some of the discontent arising from the austerity program. De Gaulle's ultimate aim is to have his country join Great Britain and the United States in the leadership of the free world. To strengthen France's position, he has followed a policy of close co-operation with West Germany. With respect to French overseas possessions, De Gaulle has taken a hand in transforming the former French Union into the present French Community. As constituted in 1958 the Community consists of the French Republic and the fourteen new republics that formerly made up French Equatorial and West Africa. Each of these republics at that time was given full autonomy except in matters of foreign policy, defense, and common economic questions. Two years later even these remaining restrictions were lifted and the onetime colonies became fully sovereign states within the French Community.

The most important issue before De Gaulle has been the solution of the Algerian question. Here, too, some progress was made. In an effort to come to terms with the Algerian nationalists, De Gaulle in September, 1959, announced that lasting peace could only be won on the basis of self-determination. The people of Algeria were to decide by referendum whether they wanted to remain with France, gain autonomy, or win complete independence. De Gaulle's proposal aroused violent protests among rightists at home and French settlers and the army in Algeria. But the majority of Frenchmen applauded the prospect of ending a costly war that has been noted for its "dirty" tactics on both sides. Negotiations for a cease-fire were begun in the summer of 1960, but soon broke down. The pacification of Algeria, if it succeeds, will be one of the greatest services De Gaulle has rendered his country.

GERMANY— RECOVERY THROUGH HARD WORK

When we speak of Germany here, we mean West Germany, just as when we refer to Europe, we mean western Europe. We have already seen how the division of Germany came about in the course of the cold war. Today the Federal Republic is recognized by the West as the only legitimate German government. The so-called

German Democratic Republic in the east is merely another Russian satellite and in Western eyes is still regarded as the Soviet zone of occupation. In size and resources the Federal Republic is by far the more important of the two Germanies. It is more than twice the size and has three times the population of East Germany, and it produces more than twice as much coal and almost ten times as much steel.

Of all the major powers of Europe, Germany has shown the most spectacular rise from rubble to riches. The key event that set this recovery in motion was the reform of West Germany's currency in July, 1948. The establishment of the sound and solid *Deutsche Mark* revived, almost overnight, the Germans' confidence in their country's future and thus helped to unleash the tremendous energy that is characteristic of the disciplined and industrious German people. The "German miracle," therefore, was due first and foremost to the hard work of the Germans. But Germany's recovery would have been impossible without material and technical aid from the West, and in particular from the United States.

The economic problems faced by Germany as a result of the war were overwhelming. The destruction from Allied bombing was not as serious for German industry as had been expected. But the postwar dismantling of factories and the separation of the western industrial from the eastern agricultural regions made economic revival seem quite hopeless at first. The influx of some ten million refugees into the already crowded west, the lack of essential raw materials except coal, and the severance of all international economic relations further aggravated the situation. The first three years after the war until 1948 were chiefly devoted to keeping the German people from starving. In this task American aid proved decisive. On the eve of the currency reform in 1948 the German index of production was only slightly more than 40 per cent of its 1936 level. More than two million Germans were unemployed. Exports, which offered the only hope for Germany's economic survival, were at a mere trickle.

Then the economic "miracle" happened. The direction of Germany's reconstruction was in the hands of Minister of Economics Dr. Ludwig Erhard. He was a firm believer in a "free-market economy," that is, free enterprise at home and free trade abroad. This approach, fundamentally different from the nationalization policies of France and Great Britain, turned out to be a great success. There were other factors contributing to Germany's rapid recovery. Among them was the fact that the German worker was satisfied at first with only a small share of the nation's growing wealth. This made possible the reinvestment of profits for further expansion. As a result, Germany's industrial output by 1950 had regained its 1936 level and by 1957 it had more than doubled. In 1959 the gross national product was close to 60 billion dollars and was growing at a rate of 6 per cent yearly. Germany in 1960 held second place in the world's manufacture of automobiles, third place in steel production, and fourth place in coal mining. Germany's foreign trade was again successfully competing in regions where she had traded in the past and was taking an increasing share in supplying underdeveloped countries. In 1959 German exports totaled almost 10 billion dollars. With a favorable trade balance, Germany has managed to build up a sizeable reserve of gold and foreign currency, some of which is now being used for foreign aid. The postwar trend toward centralization of industry was halted in 1953 and since then has been reversed. The motive behind this return to centralization of productive capacity has been the need for greater efficiency. As protection against the abuses of industrial concentration, the government has enacted an anticartel law similar to America's antitrust legislation. There is virtually no unemployment in Germany. On the contrary, there is a shortage of labor, necessitating the employment of foreign labor.

It is quite fitting that in dealing with postwar Germany we should begin by discussing her economic recovery, since this was her major problem and achievement. But it is doubtful if this recovery would have proceeded so smoothly if it had not been for the political stability of the new republic. This stability was largely due to the firm and able leadership of Germany's first chancellor, Konrad Adenauer, a poker-faced septuagenarian from the Catholic Rhineland. The Federal Republic, with Bonn as its capital, came into existence in May, 1949. Its constitution called for a legislature of two houses, the *Bundestag* and the *Bundesrat*. The *Bundestag* is elected by universal suffrage on the basis of proportional representation. The *Bundesrat* is appointed by, and represents, the governments of the various federal states. The first elections in August, 1949, pretty well set the political pattern that has existed since. Adenauer's middle-of-the-road Christian Democratic Union (CDU) received the largest number of votes. But to form a workable government, the CDU had to enter into a coalition with the right-wing liberal Free Democratic Party and one or two smaller groups. Subsequent elections in 1953 and 1957 gave the CDU an absolute majority. The opposition has been led by the Social Democratic Party (SPD). Until his death in 1952 the SPD was led by the dynamic Kurt Schumacher. Since then the more easygoing Erich Ollenhauer has taken over. The Socialists command the second largest number of votes, and their program, having lost its Marxist dogmatism, is similar to that of the British Labor Party. There are several smaller parties, but the trend in recent years has been in the direction of a two-party system. Communist strength in West Germany has been negligible. Only fifteen Communists won seats in the first *Bundestag*, and none was elected to the second. In 1956 the Communist Party was outlawed altogether. A similar fate befell the neo-Nazi German Reichs Party, which never gained more than 1.2 per cent of the popular vote.

Aside from economic questions, the two most important issues before the German government have been reunification and rearmament. The first of these has been on the agenda of most major conferences between the East and West since 1949, but the powers have been unable to reach any agreement. The insistence of the Western powers on free general elections as the only peaceful method of achieving a united Germany has run into consistent Soviet opposition, since such elections would doubtless spell the end of communism in East Germany. The problem of reunification became more complicated as Germany in 1952 prepared to join the defensive alliance of the West. Russia asserted that such a step would make reunification impossible. The majority of Germans followed Chancellor Adenauer in his undeviating adherance to the Western line; but a strong minority, centered on the Social Democrats, advocated a neutralist position for Germany to facilitate negotiations with the Russians on such questions as reunification and closer economic ties. As the fruitlessness of such negotiations became obvious, however, the Socialist opposition relented in its criticism of Adenauer's policy and finally, in 1960, officially accepted the Western alliance "in words and deeds." Similar unanimity among all Germans exists in their refusal to recognize as final the annexation by Poland and Russia of the German provinces east of the Oder and Neisse rivers.

On the question of rearmament more progress has been made.

First among the aims of the victorious powers had been the complete disarmament and demilitarization of Germany. The Germans, with the memory of the war fresh in their minds, found little fault with such a policy and voluntarily included a provision in their new constitution forbidding conscription and outlawing a German national army. But future events changed the powers' viewpoint on German disarmament. As the threat of Communist aggression in Europe increased, as Russia began training a German military force in East Germany, and as war broke out in Korea, the Western powers thought it desirable to have Germany participate in the security system of the West, even though this would mean a reversal of their earlier policy. German rearmament took five years, from 1950 to 1955, to materialize. At first events moved rather swiftly. To overcome the fears of Germany's western neighbors, notably the French, against the revival of German militarism, Germany's contribution to Western defense was envisaged within the framework of a supranational European Defense Community (EDC). The necessary agreements for EDC were signed in 1952. But French apprehension of Germany continued to be too strong, and by August, 1954, the EDC treaty still had not been ratified by the French National Assembly. At this point Great Britain took the lead and proposed a revision of the Brussels Treaty of 1948 so as to include Germany in the Western European Union and in NATO. Final agreement on this plan was reached at Paris in October, 1954, and ratified by the French Assembly the following December.

But opposition to German rearmament was not restricted to the French. There also were strong forces in Germany who, from genuine pacifism or from a desire for neutralism, tried to block the constitutional amendments necessary to make Germany part of NATO. Due to the skill and perseverance of Chancellor Adenauer, these obstacles were gradually overcome, and the Paris treaties of October, 1954, were finally ratified by Germany in May, 1955. Under the provisions of these treaties, Germany was to have an armed force of 500,000 men. This figure was later modified to 350,000, to be realized by 1961. Germany renounced the right to produce atomic, biological, or chemical weapons as well as long-distance guided missiles. In 1957, however, Chancellor Adenauer asked that West Germany be given tactical atomic weapons in view of similar developments in other countries. The granting of this request by the United States lead to a heated but futile Social Democratic "campaign against atom death." In March, 1958, the

Bundestag approved a resolution stating that the new German army, or *Bundeswehr*, was to be armed with the "most modern weapons."

Germany did not assume these military burdens without getting substantial concessions in return. Most of her economic and other restrictions had already been lifted after 1950, but she still had to regain full sovereignty. This she obtained under the Paris treaties. The only restriction remaining on Germany's sovereignty concerns the right of the three former occupying powers to keep their military forces on German soil. The Germans also agreed voluntarily to inspection of their armament industries by the Western powers. Ratification of the Paris treaties was completed on May 5, 1955, and on that day the Federal Republic became a sovereign state. The Allied high commissioners henceforth served as ambassadors, and on May 9, 1955, Germany became a full-fledged member of NATO.

Even though Germany did not regain her full independence until 1955, she had for several years been conducting a quite independent foreign policy. Both by necessity and by conviction, that policy had been immutable in its support of the West, despite the exposed position in which Germany finds herself vis-à-vis the Soviet Union, and despite the desire of many Germans for a more neutral course. Having lost their colonial empire after World War I, the Germans share none of the overseas difficulties of the French and British and actually have been able to use their freedom from the taint of colonialism to establish profitable economic contacts with the emancipated colonial peoples. Within Germany plans for some kind of European union have found the warmest support, especially among the young people. The constitution of the Federal Republic specifically permits the German government to yield its sovereignty to such a union, should it ever become a reality. Any such scheme, however, depends first and foremost on good relations between France and Germany, and the attainment of such relations has been Chancellor Adenauer's chief goal.

The beginnings of the rapprochement between France and Germany go back to the early 1950's, when the two nations decided to bury their "traditional enmity" and to collaborate in the economic unification of western Europe. We will discuss the results of this collaboration below (see pp. 60–66). Its early advocate, on the French side, was Robert Schuman, French foreign minister from 1948 to 1952. More recently the idea of Franco-German co-operation has found the warm support of General de Gaulle. For a while disagreement over the Saar, a coal-rich region on the French-German border, kept the two nations apart. The French after World War II had attached the area to France, hoping to gain a permanent hold over it. But since most of the Saar's inhabitants were German, this policy did not work. In 1955 the majority of the population voted to return to Germany. The political reunion with the Federal Republic came about on January 1, 1957, and the economic transfer was effected in July, 1959. Since then the Saar has been wholly German again. Collaboration between France and Germany in the last few years has been closest in economic matters. But the two have also supported each other diplomatically. Chancellor Adenauer is known to be genuinely pro-French; and President de Gaulle, while not exactly pro-German, has shown great personal respect for the German chancellor. By standing united, the two hope to eradicate past enmities that have done neither country any good and to assert the influence of continental Europe against the predominance of the United States and Great Britain.

The pro-Western policy of the Adenauer government is generally seen as a sign that Germany is making sincere efforts to break with her recent Nazi past. But there have also been signs—neo-Nazi demonstrations, anti-Semitic incidents, and leniency towards former Nazis—that all traces of the Nazi virus have not disappeared. There is little feeling of responsibility among the Germans for the horrors their nation committed during the twelve years of Nazi rule, and there is only a perfunctory recognition of the generosity that the Western powers have shown since the war. In their feverish preoccupation with material concerns, the Germans show little of the give-and-take in their dealings with each other and with outsiders that is part of the democratic way of life. The government, together with a highly responsible press, is trying to educate the German people in the ways of democracy; but this is a slow process. It will take time and continued peace and prosperity before the effects of these efforts at self-education can be felt.

ITALY—POVERTY PREVENTS RECOVERY

In a world where major decisions are reserved for superpowers and where even the traditional great powers are relegated to secondary positions, the weight of the smaller nations counts for very little, except as allies or pawns in the game of international politics. Even a country like Italy, in the past a member of the major league, does not have the potential strength to approximate anything like the astounding comeback of her former German ally. Italy is heavily overpopulated, short of capital and basic raw materials, and without enough good soil to produce sufficient food. Her economy has long been, and continues to be, in a most precarious position. Large-scale emigration, which in the past helped relieve some of the population pressure, is no longer possible due to foreign restrictions. Industrial production for export has made some headway since the war, but such production thus far has failed to cut the high rate of unemployment or to correct Italy's invariably adverse balance of trade. There has been a further expansion of hydroelectric resources, and the discovery of large amounts of natural gas since World War II has helped to reduce the imports of coal. Some long-range development programs, such as the land-reform act of 1950 and the simultaneous efforts to improve the economy of southern Italy, require both time and huge investments to become effective. The West has supplied substantial funds. Without the constant flow of such aid Italy would long since have fallen victim to communism and would have become a "people's democracy."

Italy's economic calamity has been reflected in the uneasy balance between moderation and extremism in her political life. In June, 1946, a popular referendum abolished the monarchy and established a republic. For a while the chief anti-Fascist parties—Christian Democrats, Socialists, and Communists—collaborated under the leadership of Alcide de Gasperi to insure a certain degree of stability. But with the coming of the cold war the co-operation among Italy's leading parties came to an end. In the crucial elections of 1948 communism was the main issue. De Gasperi's Christian Democrats received a majority, but the Communists emerged as the second largest party. Together with the left wing of the Socialists, the Communists now embarked on a vigorous campaign of obstructing Italy's alignment with the West. Communist domination of Italy's largest labor union, the General Confederation of Labor, led to an uninterrupted series of strikes. On the extreme right a neo-Fascist party, the Italian Social Movement, while never becoming a real threat, added further to the general instability. The gradual drift from center to left continued in the elections of 1953, which brought the Christian Democrats and their allies a very slim majority and gave more than a third of the popular vote to the left. The strength of the left increased further in the 1958 elections, but the major gains were made by the moderate parties of the center, chiefly at the expense of the extreme right. Despite their majority, however, the center parties have been unable to insure stable government. Proportional representation in Italy, as in France, has given rise to a multiplicity of parties and to intense interparty rivalry. The Christian Democrats, furthermore, while the dominant group, are themselves divided, especially on the issue of whether to form a coalition with the right or the left. In the spring of 1960 Italy's crisis became so acute that it was almost impossible to form a workable government. The Communists took advantage of the crisis and in July, 1960, staged the most serious riots Italy had known in ten years. The situation in Italy was not unsimilar to that in France two years earlier. The only difference was that Italy had no De Gaulle.

In her foreign affairs Italy has been a staunch supporter of the West, as a member both of NATO and since 1955 of the United Nations. We have already seen her disappointment over the peace settlement of 1947. The problem of Trieste, which had remained unsettled at that time and had led to much tension with Yugoslavia, was solved in 1954 by the partition of the region between Italy and Yugoslavia. In her role as a former colonial power, Italy has tried to mediate between the Western and Arab powers in the Middle East. Her resentment over the loss of her own colonies has subsided as native nationalism almost everywhere has put an end to colonialism.

THE SMALL NATIONS OF WESTERN EUROPE

Next to Italy, the most important among the smaller powers of western Europe are the three "Benelux" countries—Belgium, the Netherlands, and Luxembourg. All three of them are constitutional monarchies. Belgium changed rulers in 1951 when King Leopold III, unpopular because of his surrender to the Germans and marriage to a commoner, abdicated in favor of his eldest son, King Baudouin I. In the Netherlands Queen Juliana succeeded her mother, Queen Wilhelmina, in 1948. Political leadership in all three countries is exercised by Catholic and Socialist parties that, on the whole, have worked together successfully. Both Belgium and Luxembourg, after a brief period of transition, soon regained their prewar prosperity, while it took Holland several years and a rigid deflationary austerity program to regain her economic balance. The three nations are quite dependent on economic exchange with France and particularly Germany and have played a leading role in the economic integration of western Europe. As a first step they formed the Benelux Union in 1948, which called for a common customs barrier against other nations and envisaged the free exchange of commodities among its three members.

Both Belgium and Holland still had substantial colonial empires at the end of the war, but most of these have now been lost. Of the Netherlands' prize holdings in the East Indies, only New Guinea remains, and its possession by the Dutch is being challenged by the Republic of Indonesia. The rest of Holland's overseas colonies, situated in the Caribbean, have been given limited autonomy. Belgium, after granting independence to the Congo in 1960, no longer has an empire. In their foreign relations the Benelux countries have been firmly in the Western camp.

In discussing some of the remaining small powers of western Europe we can be brief. Spain had managed to stay out of World War II, but her benevolent neutrality toward Hitler and the repressive regime of Fascist dictator Francisco Franco left her an outcast among the democratic nations of the West. These nations, together with Russia, refused to admit Spain to the United Nations when that organization was founded. With the coming of the cold war, however, the strategic importance of the Iberian Peninsula somewhat modified Western coldness. Opposition to Spain remained strong enough to prevent her participation in the Marshall Plan and in NATO. Instead, the United States and Spain in 1953 concluded a bilateral agreement that permitted American use of Spanish air and naval bases in return for economic aid. This collaboration with a Fascist regime, considered necessary for military reasons, has been criticized by the opponents of fascism. Spain won a further diplomatic victory in 1955, when she was at long last admitted to the United Nations. Portugal, which was admitted at the same time, has been under a similar cloud because of the authoritarian regime of Premier Salazar. Her readiness to permit Allied use of the Azores as an air base during World War II, however, and her long-standing alliance with Great Britain have made Portugal somewhat more acceptable to the West. This acceptance was evidenced by her participation in the founding of NATO.

The three Scandinavian countries—Denmark, Sweden, and Norway—are constitutional monarchies with ruling houses that enjoy great popularity. Denmark suffered less than any other country from German occupation. Sweden, because of her neutrality, actually prospered during the war. All three nations have made satisfactory economic recovery and, like the Benelux countries, have moved toward closer economic integration. Sweden continues in her traditional policy of neutrality, maintaining close, though not always very satisfactory, economic relations with the Soviet Union. Both Denmark and Norway, on the other hand, have from the very beginnings of NATO placed their forces behind that defensive alliance of the West.

The small republic of Austria, finally, is in a category by itself. Although considered a "liberated" rather than a defeated country, Austria was placed under four-power occupation in 1945. The Western Allies did everything they could to aid Austria's recovery; but their efforts were nullified by the Russians, who insisted on payment of large reparations. The Austrian government was eager for a final peace settlement, and the Austrian question was discussed at every East-West conference. For ten years after the war Austria remained one of the major issues in the cold war. It was not until 1955 that the Soviet Union relented in its obstructionist attitude and it was possible to make peace. The Austrian State Treaty of May 15, 1955, recognized the independence of Austria and prohibited any future *Anschluss* (union) with Germany. Austria was allowed to retain the former German assets which Russia had been clamoring for, and the Austrians were given back the industries Russia had seized. Occupation troops were withdrawn in October, 1955, and two months later Austria was admitted to the United Nations. Russia's good will had to be bought at the price of large financial compensations as well as an Austrian promise of strict neutrality between East and West. But Austria's sympathies, like those of neutral Switzerland, are firmly with the West. Austria's economic recovery, thanks to Western aid, has been remarkable and she enjoys a stable prosperity unprecedented in the history of the republic.

THE QUEST FOR EUROPEAN UNITY

Our brief survey of recent events in western Europe clearly shows that the old continent has lost none of its traditional diversity. In their attempts to solve their postwar difficulties most of its nations have used widely varying solutions. Yet the difficulties themselves have shown great similarity. The need for economic recovery and the search for military security have been the foremost problems faced by each European government since 1945. It has become increasingly clear that neither problem is capable of unilateral solution. If Europe is to survive and play an important role in world affairs, she will have to overcome her national antagonisms and work toward some form of European integration. The quest for European unity, of course, had preoccupied the minds of statesmen for centuries. But thus far only in times of emergency, as under Napoleon or Hitler, has some measure of unity been achieved. Today there is again such an emergency. For the first time in European history efforts are now underway to create a united Europe, not from above by force of conquest, but from below, through voluntary collaboration among the different members of the European family.

The story of European efforts at integration since World War II is a complicated and at times frustrating one. The need for collaboration was first felt in the economic field. We have already seen how the Marshall Plan helped to set up an extensive European Recovery Program under the direction of an Organization for European Economic Co-operation. The purpose of OEEC was to promote economic recovery through co-operative action among the countries of western Europe. This step was certainly important, but it originated outside of Europe with the United States. The first indication that Europe itself understood the necessity to unite and was ready to act came with the Brussels Treaty of March, 1948. The immediate purpose of this treaty was to establish a defensive alliance against the threat of Soviet expansion; but it also called for collaboration among its members in economic, social, and cultural matters. For this purpose the treaty established a Western Union with a Council and an Assembly as governing bodies. The initial influence of this organization, however, was not very great. The Western Union was an international, rather than supranational, body, with only five members (Great Britain, France, and the Benelux countries), none of whom gave up any of their sovereign rights. Its chief military function, moreover, was gradually merged after 1949 with that of NATO. Despite its limitations, however, the Western Union opened the way for the discussion of more far-reaching projects, some of which began taking shape in the early 1950's.

The only one of these projects that materialized as originally conceived was an economic one, the famous Schuman Plan. It originated with the French economist Jean Monnet, one of the leading advocates of a united Europe. The plan was guided through its complicated stages of negotiations by French Foreign Minister Robert Schuman. Its main purpose was to establish a truly supranational authority over the coal and steel industries of western Europe, insuring the free flow of these vital raw materials among the plan's six member nations—France, Germany, Italy, and the Benelux countries. The European Coal and Steel Community (ECSC), as the organization set up under the Schuman Plan is officially called, was established by treaty on April 18, 1951, and was formally launched in 1952. ECSC has full power in fixing prices, setting export and import quotas, and allocating materials, unhampered by any interference on the part of a member state. It has its own governing body, the High Authority, with headquarters in the city of Luxembourg. Major policy decisions are made by the ECSC Common Assembly, elected by the parliaments of the member states. Disputes among members are settled by the Community's own Court of Justice. This is a momentous innovation. The economic interdependence of France (rich in iron ore) and Germany (rich in coal) had been recognized for almost a century. Previous efforts of France or Germany to control the whole rich industrial region, with the Rhine as its main artery, had led to much tension and even war. Some of these tensions, of course, will continue as long as there are national governments, and differences among the member states of the Community in the granting of industrial subsidies, tax structures, wage levels, and social insurance policies at first interfered with the smooth functioning of ECSC. But in time these differences were ironed out, and by 1957 the aim of a common market for coal and steel among the six nations of "Little Europe" had been achieved.

But this was only the beginning. The next steps to broaden European integration were taken on March 25, 1957, when the members of the Coal and Steel Community signed two further treaties, one of which established the European Economic Community (EEC) or Common Market, and the other established the European Atomic Energy Community (Euratom). The moving spirit behind these treaties again was Jean Monnet. EEC calls for the elimination of all tariff barriers among member states (including their overseas territories) and the adoption of a common tariff on imports from outside the Common Market. Ultimately labor and capital as well as goods are to move freely within the European Economic Community; there is to be standardization of wages and social security systems; and there will be a common investment pool with contributions from each member state. Euratom has created an agency for the common development of atomic energy within the six-nation community, including the sharing of atomic information, joint research, and a common market for fissionable materials and equipment. Both EEC and Euratom are administered by joint institutions—an Assembly, a Council, a Commission, an Economic and Social Committee, and a Court of Justice—some of which are identical with institutions of the Coal and Steel Community.

MEMBERSHIP IN EUROPEAN ORGANIZATIONS

	OEEC	*ECSC EEC Euratom*	*FTA*	*WEU*	*Council of Europe*	*NATO*
Austria	yes	no	yes	no	yes	no
Belgium	yes	yes	no	yes	yes	yes
Denmark	yes	no	yes	no	yes	yes
France	yes	yes	no	yes	yes	yes
Germany	yes	yes	no	yes	yes	yes
Greece	yes	no	no	no	yes	yes
Iceland	yes	no	no	no	yes	yes
Ireland	yes	no	no	no	yes	no
Italy	yes	yes	no	yes	yes	yes
Luxembourg	yes	yes	no	yes	yes	yes
Netherlands	yes	yes	no	yes	yes	yes
Norway	yes	no	yes	no	yes	yes
Portugal	yes	no	yes	no	no	yes
Sweden	yes	no	yes	no	yes	no
Switzerland	yes	no	yes	no	no	no
Turkey	yes	no	no	no	yes	yes
United Kingdom	yes	no	yes	yes	yes	yes
Canada	no	no	no	no	no	yes
United States	no	no	no	no	no	yes

The nations of Little Europe have been busy since 1957 making their Economic Community a reality. An investment bank and social security fund have been set up, the movement of capital inside the Common Market has been freed, and studies have been started on the free movement of labor. The most important aim of EEC, the abolition of internal tariff barriers, was originally intended to take some twelve to fifteen years. But here, too, much progress has been made, and if it continues, internal tariffs will be cut almost in half by the end of 1961. The move toward a common tariff against outsiders, on the other hand, has been slowed down, partly because it is complicated to work out, but chiefly because it has run into considerable opposition from the European countries that are not members of EEC.

The leader of this opposition is Great Britain. Together with some of the small nations on the periphery of western Europe—Austria, Switzerland, Portugal, Denmark, Norway, and Sweden—the British in 1960 launched the Free Trade Association (FTA). The aim of this association, as the name implies, is to establish free trade among its members. But in contrast to the European Economic Community of the "Inner Six," the Free Trade Association of the "Outer Seven" is a less formal arrangement, in which each country maintains its own tariff level with the outside world. Great Britain had been reluctant all along to become involved in continental affairs, especially since such involvement might affect her relations with the other members of the Commonwealth. There is a danger, however, that rivalry between the two groups of powers may retard rather than further European unity. It is for that reason that Jean Monnet, as head of the "Action Committee for a United States of Europe," urged Britain and the other European countries in July, 1960, to join the organizations of the European Community (ECSC, EEC, and Euratom). These organizations, according to Monnet, "are three aspects of a single reality, the economic unity of Europe in the process of formation, which tends towards a political unity whose exact nature it is still too early to foresee."

European unity outside the economic sphere, as this statement shows, has not as yet made much progress. There were proposals at the time the Schuman Plan was being negotiated for the military as well as the economic integration of western Europe. Again they came from France. In May, 1952, representatives of the ECSC nations met in Paris to sign a treaty establishing a European Defense Community (EDC). Under its provisions each signatory agreed to place its national military contingents under a single supranational command. But this military counterpart of ECSC failed to take into account the deeply rooted fears of the French people against the resurgence of a powerful Germany. These fears were increased when it became clear that Germany insisted on full equality within EDC, and that Great Britain was unwilling to become a member of any such supranational body. After two years of indecisive wrangling the French Assembly in 1954 still refused to ratify the EDC treaty. The problem of German rearmament was finally solved within the framework of the Western Union, or Western European Union (WEU) as it is now called, which has thus gained renewed importance. With Germany and Italy added to the original Brussels Treaty nations, and with its own Council and Assembly, the Western European Union serves a valuable purpose in regulating and co-ordinating the military forces and arms production of its member states. But the Union falls far short of establishing the integrated European army that EDC had envisaged.

Still more disappointing has been the lack of progress made toward European political unity. In May, 1949, under the sponsorship of Europe's most illustrious elder statesman, Winston Churchill, a Council of Europe was set up at Strasbourg, France, for the express purpose of promoting the development of European unity. This Council has a more inclusive membership than either the European Economic Community or the Western European Union. Like those two bodies, it has its own Community of Ministers and Consultative Assembly. But the Council's accomplishments thus far, other than serving as a sounding board, have been negligible. While the EDC treaty was still under discussion, hopes ran high in Strasbourg that some supranational political structure might be the next step. In 1953 a constitutional committee actually worked out a draft treaty for a European Political Community that was unanimously adopted by the Strasbourg Assembly. But the failure of EDC upset, for the time being, any hope for political integration. Still, the Council of Europe remains as the largest exclusively European body concerned with problems of future unity and the most suitable agency for co-ordinating already existing efforts in this direction.

Taken as a whole, then, Europe's quest for unity has not been overly successful. National differences and traditions are still too powerful to be forgotten overnight. The blame for the limited progress of European integration is usually laid at the door of Great Britain. Considering herself still primarily a world power rather than a European power, Britain hesitates to submit to the restrictions of a United States of Europe. But France, too, bears a share of responsibility for the failure to achieve a greater measure of European unity. It has been said that French demands at times "have been such as to make the 'Europe' in prospect appear as an extension of France." The only ones among the major powers who have wholeheartedly favored integration have been Germany and Italy. In the case of the Germans, the advantages to be derived from a large, free market may explain their enthusiasm. But despite British aloofness and French claims for leadership, the trend toward European integration is unmistakable. More progress has been made toward European unity since World War II than during the whole previous century. There is a general awareness, especially among Europe's youth, that the only way in which their continent can hope to become a "third force" in the world is by pooling its material and intellectual resources and by forgetting the divisive issues of the past that seem so insignificant before the larger issues of the present.

3

PRESIDENT JOHN F. KENNEDY

During the election campaign of 1960. NEW YORK TIMES PHOTO.

Can a nation organized and governed such as ours endure? That is the real question. Have we the nerve and the will? Can we carry through in an age where we will witness not only new breakthroughs in weapons of destruction—but also a race for mastery of the sky and the rain, the ocean and the tides, the far side of space and the inside of men's minds? Are we up to the task? Are we equal to the challenge? Are we willing to match the Russian sacrifice of the present for the future? Or must we sacrifice our future in order to enjoy the present?

From SENATOR JOHN F. KENNEDY's acceptance speech at the Democratic National Convention, July 15, 1960

THE UNITED STATES AND ITS GOOD NEIGHBORS

THE HISTORY OF THE UNITED STATES SINCE World War II shows that victory in a modern war places before the victors problems scarcely less complex than those faced by the vanquished. America was the only one among the major participants in the war to remain untouched by its devastation. And while in the past the economic boom caused by the needs of war had usually collapsed with the end of hostilities, this did not happen in America after World War II. On the contrary, consumer demands, left unfulfilled during the war, and the continued needs of national defense not only prevented a postwar depression but actually led to an unprecedented expansion of America's economy. The postwar problems that the United States faced, therefore, did not spring, as in the case of Europe, primarily from economic causes. America's problems came rather as a result of the sudden demands for world leadership made against a nation not sufficiently ready to exercise such leadership. Most Americans expected foreign and national affairs to go back to where they had been when the war started. But this hope was disappointed. The realization that a return to normalcy was impossible gave rise to the air of uncertainty and apprehension that characterized the first years of the Truman administration. The way in which Americans finally overcame their difficulties and shouldered their new responsibilities makes the years after 1945 seem less disheartening in retrospect than they appeared at the time.

THE SEARCH FOR A POSTWAR POLICY

The man who was to guide his country through one of its most crucial periods was a well-meaning politician who, upon suddenly becoming President when Franklin D. Roosevelt died on April 12, 1945, "felt like the moon, the stars, and all the planets had fallen on me." With an engaging modesty and a never-flagging energy, Harry S. Truman applied himself to his unenviable assignment. During the first months of his new office President Truman assumed the responsibility for decisions, such as the use of the atomic bomb, that would have staggered a more complex personality. But in doing so he still remained for some time to come the mere executor of the policies of his dynamic predecessor. It took a while before the new President began to show those signs not merely of leadership but also of statesmanship that the situation called for.

The most pressing task before the Truman administration was the conversion of the country from warlike to peaceful pursuits. This involved, first of all, the rapid demobilization of nearly nine million young men and women. Had it not been for the basic soundness of America's economy, such rapid demobilization might have brought on a major crisis. As it was, most of the veterans were either absorbed by industry or took advantage of the farsighted GI Bill of Rights, which aided millions of veterans in starting a business or in gaining a better education. The GI Bill was an important factor in that slow upgrading of American society that was one of the most striking results of the war. Defense industries, paying generously and attracting women as well as men, had also done their share in raising the economic and social level of lower-status groups and in making the majority of Americans decidedly middle class in outlook and aspirations.

While social reconversion was progressing smoothly, economic reconversion proved more difficult. Fundamentally, the issue was how to remove the maze of price and wage controls that had grown up during the war without further increasing the tendency toward inflation. The government tried to hold the line on price controls as long as there was a general shortage of such critical items as meat, automobiles, and new housing. But postwar price controls aroused the opposition of American business and incidentally helped to perpetuate the ugly practice of black marketeering that had sprung up during the war. At the same time labor, deprived of its income from overtime work, demanded the abolition of wage controls to meet the rising costs of living. When both government and industry stood firm against the lifting of wage controls, labor resorted to large-scale strikes. The effect of strikes was to aggravate shortages and to drive up living costs. There were two major strike waves in 1945 and 1946, and at one point the government was forced to take temporary control of railroads and coal mines. Although these strikes did bring some wage increases, the continued rise in prices soon wiped out the effects of such increases. These were bewildering times in which the world's richest nation, more prosperous than ever before, was hopelessly caught in the vicious spiral of an inflation for which there seemed no remedy.

There was a similar feeling of bewilderment in America's relations with the outside world. The very fact that foreign affairs did not take a back seat once the war was over but continued to hold the center of the stage was something discomfortingly new. Most Americans had firmly backed their country's war effort and her leading role in the founding of the United Nations. But once the fighting was over, these same people bombarded their congressmen with requests to get their men home as soon as possible. This rapid withdrawal of troops deprived the United States of its major source of influence abroad. It was only the growing threat of communism that gradually made Americans aware of their country's new responsibilities. Even the Republican opposition showed signs of this awareness. While the rank and file of the party, under the leadership of Senator Robert A. Taft, continued to be strongly isolationist, the leading Republican member of the Senate Foreign Relations Committee, Senator Arthur H. Vandenberg, came out in favor of a more active American foreign policy. But if America was to exert her power in world affairs, how and when and where was she to do so? Soviet expansionism was scoring a succession of triumphs, and Soviet obstructionism was crippling the effectiveness of the new United Nations. Yet the United States government seemed to stand by idly, hoping that the Russians might still prove amenable to a reasonable settlement of differences. President Truman, to be sure, had said as early as January, 1946, that he was "tired of babying the Soviets," and he had applauded Winston Churchill's "iron curtain" speech the following March. But the government's policy was still sufficiently aimless so that Secretary of Commerce Henry Wallace in September, 1946, could publicly advocate a more co-operative attitude toward the Soviet Union. And while the President's dismissal of Wallace seemed to indicate that the government intended to take a firmer line, specific signs of such firmness were still lacking from America's policy abroad.

In the light of the situation just described, it is not surprising that for the first time in sixteen years the congressional elections of 1946 returned a substantial Republican majority to both houses. Opposition to the Democratic New Deal, of course, had long been present in Republican circles. But with the unsettled conditions of the early postwar period, some of the former supporters and beneficiaries of the Democratic regime also now turned against the administration. The immediate effect of the 1946 elections was to jolt the government into taking a more decisive course. President Truman gave way on the issue of price and wage controls and removed virtually all checks except those on rent and some foods. The result was a gradual return of scarce goods and a steady rise in prices. Because the American consumer resisted the temptation of reckless spending, a runaway inflation was avoided. There was the threat of another coal strike, but the government used its emergency powers to prevent it. A new policy, initiated by General Motors and adopted by other industries, called for wage contracts that allowed for automatic increases corresponding to rising living costs. This practice went a long way toward pacifying labor unrest. In Congress, on the other hand, labor fared less well. The Taft-Hartley Act of 1947, passed over the President's veto, prohibited the use of union funds for political purposes, introduced a sixty-day notice before a strike or lockout, outlawed the closed shop, and gave the government the right to impose an eighty-day injunction against strikes that imperiled the nation's health and safety. The Labor-Management Act, its official name, at first was violently attacked by the large unions as a "slave-labor" bill. But their fears that the injunction would be used often and indiscriminately were not realized. In the spring and early summer of 1948 renewed strikes in the coal, steel, and railway industries were successfully resolved by government intervention. At the same time a further round of wage increases was granted to meet the continued rise in the cost of living.

While Congress and the administration failed to see eye to eye on most domestic issues, there was less disagreement in foreign affairs. We have already discussed the various measures, from Truman Doctrine to Marshall Plan, that marked America's initiative in meeting the Soviet threat. Much of the credit for this fresh approach to foreign policy belonged to Secretary of State George C. Marshall and to his deputy, Undersecretary of State Dean Acheson. During 1947 and 1948 the threat of a new war seemed terribly real. Congress already had approved the unification of the armed services under a new Secretary of Defense, and in June, 1948, it passed the first peacetime Selective Service Act in the nation's history. Still, the far-reaching commitments of the Marshall Plan were adopted only over the vehement opposition of the Taft Republicans. They objected to the plan's emphasis on Europe and predicted that it would leave the United States bankrupt. Largely due to the able support of Senator Vandenberg, the Foreign Assistance Act (Marshall Plan) was finally passed in March, 1948.

Because of the fumbling record of the Truman administration at home and its too-recent firmness abroad, the outcome of the 1948 presidential election seemed a foregone conclusion. As the South bolted from the Democratic Party, and Henry Wallace further split the Democrats by starting his own "Progressive Party," the Republican candidate, Thomas E. Dewey, seemed certain to win. But the seemingly impossible happened. Contrary to the "infallible" oracles of various public opinion polls, the underdog came out on top—Harry S. Truman was elected President in his own right and his party gained a majority in both houses. Many explanations were given for the Republican upset, but in the last analysis Truman was elected because he had the support of the substantial labor bloc, the Negro vote, and at least half the farmers. These were the groups that had profited from the New Deal in the past and that hoped to profit from the Fair Deal that the President announced for the future.

Their hopes were to be only partly fulfilled. The Eighty-first Congress in 1949 passed many of the measures its predecessor had turned down, from public housing and an increased minimum wage to farm supports, flood control, and soil conservation. Yet two of the major points of the President's program, the repeal of the Taft-Hartley Act and the enactment of federal civil-rights legislation, failed to win congressional support, largely because of the opposition of the southern Democrats. But the Fair Deal was more than just a domestic program, as President Truman had made clear in the famous Point Four of his inaugural address. In 1949 Congress authorized 5.4 billion dollars for the European Recovery Program, and an additional 3 billion dollars were granted in 1950. Support for these measures came from a coalition of Democrats and Republicans. A similar bipartisan policy insured the passage in July, 1949, of the North Atlantic Treaty. The treaty was passed despite the objections of Senator Taft and his supporters that the United States was thus committed to go to war in case of a Russian attack against western Europe. Thus by early 1949 the United States at long last had regained a measure of stability and was pursuing a policy that had the support of the majority of Americans. At this point a series of events at home and abroad combined to throw the country back into a crisis worse than the one it had just gone through.

THE GROWING FEAR OF COMMUNISM

One of the dominant characteristics of the postwar American climate of opinion was the growing fear of communism, not only abroad but at home. The strength of the American Communist Party, estimated at never more than seventy-five thousand members, was negligible compared to Communist strength in some European countries. But Americans felt that even a small number of Reds in key positions could seriously endanger the nation's security. Beginning in 1946, therefore, a series of congressional investigations were launched, hoping to ferret out possible Communists or their sympathizers from government positions. The careless methods used in these investigations and the lasting harm thus done to the reputation of innocent people caused deep concern among thoughtful Americans. But it became more and more common for an otherwise fair-minded people to condone such methods because of the end they claimed to serve. Several Communists were actually discovered and removed from sensitive positions, but this was done through the government's regular security agencies rather than through congressional investigations. In October, 1949, the eleven leading members of the American Communist Party, after a long and fair trial, were convicted of conspiracy to advocate the violent overthrow of the United States government. The case that caused the greatest stir, however, was that of Alger Hiss, formerly of the State Department, who was found guilty of having falsely denied under oath his former Communist affiliations and activities. There still remained people who refused to believe that Hiss was guilty. But to the majority of Americans, this well-born, well-educated, and well-connected young man symbolized the very treason they suspected in high places.

In this suspicion they were confirmed by Wisconsin's Senator Joseph McCarthy. This ambitious politician had long sought for an opportunity to gain nationwide publicity. Such an opportunity arose with the growing panic about communism in the government. The Senator's main target was the United States State Department and in particular Dean Acheson, Secretary of State since 1949. In a speech at Wheeling, West Virginia, in 1950, McCarthy asserted that he had a list of 205 Communist Party members or sympathizers still employed by the State Department. These claims were subsequently proved false. But this did not concern the Senator and the growing number of his supporters. In 1951 McCarthy directed his attacks against General Marshall, whom he accused of participating in a conspiracy "to the end that we shall be contained, frustrated and finally fall victim to Soviet intrigue from within and Russian military might from without." Instead of dissociating themselves from such indiscriminate mudslinging, more and more respectable Republicans, including Senator Taft, lined up with their colleague from Wisconsin, who so correctly seemed to gauge the temper of the nation. Congress had just passed the sweeping Internal Security Act of 1950, which required Communists and Communist-front organizations to register with the Justice Department. President Truman's unsuccessful attempt to veto this act was construed as further evidence of his softness toward communism.

THE WAR IN KOREA

The reality of the Communist threat, meanwhile, was brought home anew by events in Korea. We have already discussed the outbreak of the Korean War on June 24, 1950, and the intervention of the United States under the auspices of the United Nations. The firm stand taken by President Truman briefly united the country as it had not been united since the end of World War II. Even Senator Taft, while criticizing the administration's earlier Korean policy, supported the President. But as the Korean War bogged down into a bloody stalemate, the initial unity soon disappeared. Heavily outnumbered and inadequately equipped, the UN forces at first had to beat a hasty retreat. By early August, 1950, the UN army was confined to a small defensive perimeter around the port of Pusan in the southeastern corner of Korea. From there, beginning in September, General MacArthur in a brilliant counteroffensive cleared South Korea and drove the invaders across the thirty-eighth parallel toward the Yalu River, the border between North Korea and Communist China. At this point the war entered its crucial phase. Warnings from Red China and the presence of Chinese "volunteers" among North Korean forces had for some time raised the possibility of Chinese intervention. In October, 1950, President Truman traveled to Wake Island to discuss this vital matter with the UN commander-in-chief. But General MacArthur apparently did not believe that the Chinese would enter the war, or he was convinced that if they did, they could be beaten. In November, therefore, he launched a major drive toward the Yalu River, with the intention of ending the Korean War. Two days later massive Chinese forces intervened and within the next few weeks drove the UN armies back across the thirty-eighth parallel, inflicting terrible losses. By the spring of 1951 the UN forces had slugged their way back to the thirty-eighth parallel, and there they remained, locked in a seemingly hopeless stalemate with their far more numerous Korean and Chinese adversaries.

It was over the discussion of how to break this deadlock that the United States was thrown into its most violent domestic crisis since World War II. Disagreement over American Far Eastern policy had been of long standing. The government was aware of Asian sensibilities and wanted to avoid anything remotely smacking of colonialism. It had, therefore, repeatedly opposed the use of force on the Asiatic mainland and proposed instead to win native support and contain communism through economic and technical assistance. Yet such a policy, its critics charged, was not only slow and expensive, but, as China and Korea had shown, ineffective. Some opponents of the administration went still further and saw America's Asian policy as merely another manifestation of the pro-

Communist leanings of which they accused Truman and Acheson. Instead of diverting so much American money and manpower to Europe, these critics advocated all-out economic and military aid to those nations of Asia, and in particular Nationalist China, that were engaged in fighting communism. Specifically, they asked that the United States guarantee the integrity of Formosa and encourage a Nationalist attack against the Chinese mainland. This "Asia First" program appealed to many Americans as the best way of halting the creeping advance of communism. The program's popularity was further assured by the support it received from General Douglas MacArthur, a man long actively involved in Far Eastern affairs.

MacArthur at the start of the Korean War had advocated the use of Chinese Nationalist troops against North Korea. At that time he had been opposed by Dean Acheson for political reasons and by the Joint Chiefs of Staff on military grounds. Now that the war had frozen into a stalemate, MacArthur repeated his earlier proposal. He also emphasized the need for a blockade of the Chinese coast and the bombing of Communist bases beyond the Yalu to insure an early victory. President Truman, together with his political and military advisers, considered MacArthur's scheme dangerous, since it might lead to a major war in which America would not have the support of her allies. In the words of General Omar Bradley, chairman of the Joint Chiefs of Staff, this would have been "the wrong war, at the wrong place, at the wrong time and with the wrong enemy." Despite repeated warnings to desist, MacArthur nevertheless continued in his open criticism of the government's policy. Seeing no alternative, President Truman on April 11, 1951, relieved MacArthur of all his commands.

The news of MacArthur's dismissal hit like a bombshell. The uneasy suspicion that America's fate was in the hands of incompetents, if not traitors, suddenly seemed to be borne out. The issue appeared joined in the contest between a man whom his opponents still considered a small-time politician from Missouri and the nation's most glamorous military hero. The real issue of the military's subordination to civilian control was somehow overlooked. While MacArthur staged a triumphant return and the nation wept at his self-effacing promise to "just fade away," demands were heard for the impeachment of the President and his Secretary of State. But after a few weeks the furor gradually died down. The President's popularity, to be sure, never recovered from the blow it had suffered. But President Truman's loss did not become MacArthur's gain. The general, much to everyone's surprise, kept his promise and actually did fade away.

In the meantime the fighting in Korea continued, with Lieutenant General Matthew Ridgway serving as MacArthur's successor. In the summer of 1951 negotiations between United Nations and Chinese representatives for a cease-fire were begun at Panmunjom. Yet it took two more years of fighting and negotiations, with interminable haggling over the exchange of prisoners, before an agreement was finally signed on July 27, 1953. After thirty-seven months of fighting, costing more than 33,000 American lives and 22 billion dollars, the Korean War ended where it had begun, at the thirty-eighth parallel; and it ended not in victory, but in a truce. Since the achievement of the Korean War—halting the advance of communism—was not very spectacular, many Americans had already begun wondering during the war whether the fighting in Korea was really necessary and whether it was worth the high cost. When the war ended, there was very little rejoicing, only a feeling of infinite relief.

The Korean War, besides making enemies for the Democratic administration, also made itself felt in other ways. Economically, it brought to the United States the greatest wave of prosperity of all time. Employment set new records, and business profits soared. But with prosperity came further inflation, and those sections of the population with fixed incomes failed to share in the nation's new wealth. As is often the case in times of plenty, corruption became a common practice. These were the days of the "five percenters," when deep freezes and mink coats seemed to have become the accepted bribes in paying government employees for favors granted. A special committee under Senator Estes Kefauver, of Tennessee, uncovered mountains of evidence on the political influence of crime syndicates in various large communities, especially New York City. In addition, juvenile delinquency for the first time became a national problem.

A country thus agitated by scandals at home and an unsuccessful war abroad was in no mood for dealing judiciously with the barrage of falsehoods and half-truths issuing from those who, like Senator McCarthy, hoped to make political capital out of the nation's bewilderment. If there was one thing on which most Americans seemed to agree, it was the desire for a change in the government. The 1950 elections brought a first decline of Democratic strength in Congress. But the major change did not come until 1952. The elections of that year were unique in many respects. Rarely had there been a more important contest. Yet the candidates selected by each party were complete novices in the realm of high party and national politics. The Democratic nominee, Illinois Governor Adlai E. Stevenson, carrying the burden of an unpopular administration, conducted a distinguished campaign, marked by speeches of unusually high caliber. But it was the Republican candidate, Dwight D. Eisenhower, a great general but a political amateur, who won the election. The Eisenhower platform, with its slogan that it was "time for a change" and with its promise "to clean up the mess in Washington," seemed to express the feelings of the majority of Americans, even though some of them did not necessarily stand to profit from such a change. The Republican victory in the presidential contest was a landslide and a personal triumph for General Eisenhower, who carried thirty-nine states. On the congressional side the success of the Republicans was less spectacular, as they won only slim majorities in both houses. Yet there was a general feeling that after twenty years of Democratic rule a new era had started in American politics. The question was whether its tone would be set by the man who had won the election or by the party that had nominated him.

THE FIRST EISENHOWER ADMINISTRATION

President Eisenhower's most powerful contender for the Republican nomination had been "Mr. Republican" himself, Senator Robert A. Taft. And while the two had outwardly adjusted their differences for the sake of party unity, once the elections were over Taft's conservative influence made itself strongly felt in national affairs, even beyond his death in 1953. The Taft influence was shown in the composition of the new cabinet, in which businessmen and outspoken believers in free enterprise were given key positions. As a result, business rallied to support the government as it had not done in two decades. One of the Republican campaign promises had been to put the nation's finances on a sounder basis and, through rigorous economy, to reduce the high tax rate. Efforts were made to cut government spending and to balance the budget; but the continued drain of military spending at home and military as well as economic aid abroad made any radical tax relief impossible. In an effort to return to a free market in agricultural products, the government replaced the rigid price supports of the past with more flexible ones. The administration thus incurred the opposition of farm groups, who had been among the chief beneficiaries of past subsidies. An attempt to solve the farm problem by taking excess acreage out of production and setting up a "soil bank" was adopted in 1956. The trend toward greater freedom from federal control also came out in other measures. Some of these, such as the transfer to state jurisdiction of tidelands oil and the emphasis on private, rather than public, development of natural resources, were branded as "giveaways" by the Democratic opposition. In the elections of 1954 Democratic charges that the government was run for the benefit of the large corporations rather than the little man, be he farmer, laborer, or small businessman, resulted in a Democratic majority for both houses of Congress. There also was some fear at the time that America's economy had overexpanded and was headed for a depression. But such fears proved groundless. One of the major developments in American domestic affairs came in May, 1954, when the Supreme Court handed down a ruling outlawing segregation in the nation's public schools. While in some states school integration, beginning in 1955, proceeded smoothly, most of the southern states announced that they would use every peaceful means at their disposal to oppose what they considered an unwarranted interference with states' rights.

While the Eisenhower administration thus pursued an entirely new course in domestic affairs, its foreign policy generally continued along the lines of its predecessor. The new Secretary of State, John Foster Dulles, had served as Republican adviser on foreign affairs during the Truman era. As such he had supported America's far-flung military and economic involvements. Yet the growing cost of these commitments ran counter to the Republicans' emphasis on economy and increasingly came under attack from the followers of Senator Taft. On the other hand, the administration's efforts to trim its military budget by reducing the Army's ground forces and by using atomic weapons instead of men for "massive retaliation" were criticized by experts as weakening America's ability to halt the advance of communism in a limited war, as had been done in Korea. The termination of fighting in Korea shortly after President Eisenhower took office was claimed as a first success of his administration's firmness in dealing with the Chinese Communists. Yet the change in Russian policy, following the death of Stalin in March, 1953, may also have had something to do with ending the Korea impasse.

With a change in national leadership it might have been expected that the American people would lose their fear of Communist infiltration at home. But with a Republican majority in Congress between 1952 and 1954 Senator McCarthy at long last had a chance to do more than merely raise accusations. As chairman of the important Senate Committee on Government Operations and of its Permanent Subcommittee on Investigations, McCarthy now embarked on a series of investigations that became increasingly embarrassing to the Eisenhower administration. He first turned his spotlight on the State Department's overseas information service and in particular on its American libraries abroad. The result was a general purging of all works by "Communists, fellow-travelers, etc.," causing the removal, and in some instances the burning, of books by authors who were free from the slightest Communist taint. Such actions brought charges at home and abroad that America was trying to combat totalitarianism by totalitarian methods. At the beginning of 1954 McCarthy shifted his attentions to the Army, making the usual accusations of Communist infiltration. The nationally televised Army-McCarthy hearings showed the Wisconsin Senator at his most arrogant. The outcome of the hearings, while not entirely absolving the Army, still was sufficiently damaging to McCarthy for the Senate to pass a carefully worded move of censure against him. Soon afterward, the chairmanship of McCarthy's committees changed hands as a consequence of the 1954 elections, and the Senator suddenly found himself relegated to obscurity. The nightmare of "McCarthyism" was over, although its effects were felt for years to come.

The defeat of McCarthy completed the process by which President Eisenhower emancipated himself from the Republican old guard, many of whom had sided with the Wisconsin Senator. The President's popularity, which had helped win the election in 1952, continued to be one of the Republicans' major assets. There was never any doubt that the party wanted him to run again. A serious heart attack in 1955 and an intestinal operation in 1956 temporarily put President Eisenhower's candidacy in question, however. The Democratic nominee was again Adlai Stevenson, who carried on a vigorous campaign, attacking the administration's passive policy abroad and warning against the continued testing of hydrogen bombs. The Republicans, for their part, were content to stand on a record of "peace, prosperity, and progress." The outcome of the 1956 elections was a still greater landslide victory for Eisenhower than he had won four years earlier. But while the President carried forty-one states, the Democrats retained control of both houses of Congress. President Eisenhower's victory, therefore, was clearly a personal triumph. He himself, however, modestly interpreted it as a sign "that modern Republicanism has now proved itself, and America has approved of modern Republicanism."

THE SECOND EISENHOWER ADMINISTRATION

President Eisenhower's "modern Republicanism" has been described as "liberalism in terms of people's needs, conservatism in terms of their money." The President took a positive stand on moderate expansion of the government's social role, he favored federal aid to education, and he supported integration and civil rights. But he remained firm in his opposition to excessive spending and to subsidies that might lead to further inflation. Faced by a Democratic majority in Congress throughout his second term, Eisenhower's hands were tied on some partisan issues. But just as often as not, Democrats and Republicans were divided within their own ranks—conservatives against liberals—and collaboration between the liberal elements in both parties resulted in some constructive legislation. The government's foreign policy, at least until shortly before the end of the Eisenhower era, had the support of the majority of Americans.

President Eisenhower himself, in contrast to Roosevelt and Truman, remained remarkably free from personal attacks and criticism. His distinguished military career, his evident sincerity, and his friendly manner earned him the admiration and affection of most Americans. Only toward the end did his popularity begin to decline. Affection for "Ike" remained high, but admiration for his role as a national leader was wearing thin. Eisenhower's delicate health was partly responsible for this, since it narrowly circumscribed his activities. Still, he took upon himself the considerable burden of several extended goodwill tours abroad. Aggressive leadership at home, moreover, was foreign to Eisenhower's nature and contrary to his conception of the presidential office. And finally, the fact that he was the first president to have his tenure limited to two terms under the Twenty-second Amendment could not but weaken his power and effectiveness. Many of Eisenhower's responsibilities, especially during his several illnesses, were taken over by Vice-President Richard Nixon, who thus increased his own stature as well as that of his office. Nixon lacked the President's personal warmth and charm, but the initiative and ability shown in his work at home and on several difficult missions abroad earned him the respect of his party and made him the natural successor to Eisenhower as Republican nominee in 1960.

The record of any administration depends to a large extent upon the success of its economic policy. The United States continued to prosper under Eisenhower, as it had under Truman, until by early 1960 the nation's gross national product—the dollar value of goods and services—reached the magic mark of 500 billion dollars, or half a trillion. Despite continued production records, however, the nation's economy showed some weak spots. There had been a marked recession in 1958, and while the situation had steadily improved since then, the rate of growth had been slow. This was partly due to a major steel strike, which crippled that basic industry for almost six months in 1959 and caused widespread unemployment in related industries. But even after the strike had been settled at the turn of the year, the number of jobless continued to be about 5 per cent of the total labor force, a disquieting figure for a period of prosperity. The farm picture did not look much better. The administration's soil bank program, although it managed to withdraw millions of acres from production, did not solve the problem of surplus crops. With surpluses driving down prices, farm income continued to drop, while living costs and interest rates on short-term loans and mortgages were going up. With fewer farmers producing more crops on less land, due to improvement in agricultural techniques, the only real solution seemed to be for some farmers to seek a livelihood in something other than agriculture.

While America's economy thus had its weaknesses, it nevertheless continued to grow. By mid-1960 more persons were employed than at any time in American history. There also were, of course, more Americans than ever before. As the 1960 census showed, America's population had grown by 28 million in the previous decade and now stood at close to 180 million. As had happened in earlier periods of prosperity, public morality became lax and the Eisenhower administration was not spared its share of scandals. One of the more sensational involved the President's chief assistant, Sherman Adams, who resigned in 1958 after it had become known that he had accepted gifts from a close friend on whose behalf he had interceded with the government's regulatory agencies. A special House Subcommittee on Legislative Oversight, charged with looking into the operations of several of these agencies—the Federal Communications Commission, the Federal Power Commission, the Interstate Commerce Commission, the Civil Aeronautics Board, and the Federal Trade Commission—uncovered abundant evidence of unethical practices and forced the resignation of several commissioners who had accepted favors from the business interests they were supposed to regulate. The inquiry that caused the greatest stir dealt with "payola," that is, the payment of money or goods to broadcasters for "plugging" a certain product. The public was particularly shocked when it learned that many of its favorite quiz programs on radio and television had been "fixed." Here was an indication that corruption was not confined to the government but that it extended to other institutions of a semipublic nature such as the communications industry.

The labor unions fall into a somewhat similar category. With a total membership of close to eighteen million, the unions not only wield great political and economic power, but their huge funds make them a fruitful field for corruption. In 1957 the Select Senate Committee on Improper Activities in the Labor or Management Field (McClellan Committee) uncovered evidence of widespread fraud among labor officials. In one case at least, the International Brotherhood of Teamsters, the misuse of funds was so flagrant that this largest of all unions was expelled from the AFL-CIO. To impose stricter control upon organized labor and to curb some of its more arbitrary actions, Congress in 1959 passed a new labor law. Under its provisions unions must file regular financial reports, must disclose their administrative procedures, and must bar former convicts from holding office. Union members are protected against leadership abuses by a "bill of rights." The "secondary boycott"—that is, a union's effort to put pressure on one employer by striking against another with whom he has dealings—was made more difficult, and picketing was outlawed under certain circumstances. But while the new law does away with some of the worst practices of corrupt unionism, it does little to affect the power of the stronger unions. This was shown in January, 1960, when the steel workers emerged victorious from their long strike with increased wages and other benefits.

The most important domestic concern of the Eisenhower administration was over the related issues of desegregation and civil rights. We have already seen how the deep South had resisted from the start the Supreme Court's decision on school integration handed down in 1954. A subsequent ruling in 1955 gave the task of implementing the Court's decision to the lower federal courts and called for the admittance of students to public schools on a nondiscriminatory basis "with all deliberate speed." While border states like Maryland and Missouri complied with this order, the rest of the southern states used every possible means of resisting what they considered a violation of states' rights and "a clear abuse of judicial power." The most serious fight against integration happened in Little Rock, Arkansas, where federal troops had to be used in order to protect the handful of Negro students who insisted on their right to attend a hitherto all-white school. By 1960 little more than one-fourth of the South's 2,850 biracial school districts had been desegregated. In the remaining districts integration awaited the outcome of some fifty court cases in a dozen states. Meanwhile a campaign of passive resistance among Negroes was carrying the fight for integration beyond the field of education. A strike against segregated buses in Montgomery, Alabama, was won in 1958; and peaceful "sit-in" demonstrations in 1960 resulted in the opening of lunch counters to Negroes in many parts of the South.

Efforts to secure Negro rights by means of civil-rights legislation also were at least partly successful. The Civil Rights Act of 1957 reaffirmed the right of the Negro to vote, and the Civil Rights Act of 1960 provided the necessary safeguards to make sure that this right is enforced. Attempts to widen the scope of legislation to include school integration and equal job opportunities, however, ran into staunch opposition from southern Senators who fought even the slight concessions made in the first civil-rights measures passed since Reconstruction days. Nevertheless, the trend toward equal rights for Negroes was unmistakable, and even the most ardent believers in "white supremacy" were now aware of the fact that final integration was merely a matter of time.

We shall discuss America's foreign policy during the 1950's at greater length below (see Chapter 6). Its underlying theme and the subject of endless debates at home was the continued rivalry between the United States and Russia, especially in such important fields as military strength, scientific development, and economic growth. With more than half of its budget devoted to military spending, the United States has been concentrating its efforts upon closing the "missile gap" which still gives the Soviet Union a lead in long-range intercontinental ballistic missiles (ICBM's). In 1960 America scored a major success with the first successful firing of an intermediate-range fleet ballistic missile (FBM)—the Polaris—from a nuclear submarine. With some forty-five FBM submarines, each of them carrying sixteen missiles, scheduled for operation by 1965, the United States will have a deterrent force capable of surviving any sneak attack and of getting close enough to the Soviet Union to deliver their deadly cargo. "America," President Eisenhower asserted, "possesses an enormous defense power. It is my studied conclusion that no nation will ever risk general war against us." The President's critics, on the other hand, objected that the government's emphasis on nuclear retaliation left the country ill prepared to deal with "brush-fire" wars calling for traditional forces and weapons.

The military rivalry between the United States and Russia, as the above examples show, is in the final analysis a contest between the scientists of both countries. The most spectacular side of this contest has been the race for the exploration of outer space. Here, too, the Russians have held a commanding lead, not only by being the first to launch an earth satellite, but by putting far heavier satellites into orbit than the United States and by outdoing the United States in shots to the moon. If the Soviet Union should succeed in putting a man into space or on the moon ahead of the United States, such a feat would prove a major psychological victory, although from a military point of view its significance is not rated very high.

In the light of Russia's scientific achievements during the last few years, Premier Khrushchev's prediction that his country will some day surpass the United States economically cannot be dismissed as an empty boast. In 1960 American production was still unsurpassed, with a gross national product twice that of the U.S.S.R. But to keep this lead it is estimated that the United States economy will have to grow at the rate of at least 5 per cent each year. And there are those who doubt that this rate of growth will be maintained. Yet it is through her economic leadership that the United States ultimately hopes to win in the cold-war contest with communism for the allegiance of the underdeveloped and as yet uncommitted regions of the world.

Among the main charges leveled by the Democrats against the Eisenhower administration in the election campaigns of 1958 and 1960 was lack of leadership in foreign and domestic affairs. The congressional elections of 1958 brought a sweeping victory for the opposition, with Democratic majorities approaching two-thirds in both houses of Congress. Aware of how much was at stake in the presidential contest of 1960, both parties nominated unusually able contenders. Both the Republican candidate, Richard M. Nixon, and the Democratic nominee, John F. Kennedy, were cool-headed, tough-minded, and articulate young men. The platforms on which they ran were remarkable more for their similarities than for their differences. A strong defense and foreign policy, economic aid to Asia, Africa, and South America, stress on the need for continued economic growth, and a strong civil-rights program—these were the main points on which both parties saw almost eye to eye. Where they differed was on some details of domestic policy, such as what to do about aiding agriculture, the aged, education, and housing. Given the similarity of the Republican and Democratic programs, the campaign was less a contest of issues than of personalities. And here the question uppermost in everyone's mind seemed to be which of the two candidates would best be able to stand up to the Soviet Union in the critical years ahead.

The outcome of the presidential race was close. John F. Kennedy won a decisive majority of electoral votes, but the popular vote was very closely divided. The new president was the first Catholic and the youngest candidate ever to be elected to the White House. With Congress remaining under Democratic control, Kennedy now had an opportunity of carrying out his program of the "New Frontier." Those Americans who felt uneasy about the boldness of that program derived some comfort from the fact that Kennedy's running mate, Senator Lyndon B. Johnson, was a known conservative. Even so, the American people approached the Kennedy era with some apprehension as well as with expectancy.

THE UNITED STATES AND CANADA

The most important country in the Americas, next to the United States, is the Dominion of Canada. Larger in size than its southern neighbor, but with a population of only 17.5 million, this sovereign member of the (British) Commonwealth has made such amazing economic progress since World War II that she ranks today as one of the world's major industrial and commercial powers. The recent development of her vast resources of iron ore, oil, and especially uranium have opened unlimited vistas of future growth, from which not only Canada herself but also the United States can expect to profit. The United States has already invested more than 14 billion dollars in Canadian resources and industries. This figure represents more than one-third of total American investments abroad. Commercial relations between the United States and Canada exceed in volume those between any other two nations. A major step in United States–Canadian collaboration came with the opening in 1959 of the St. Lawrence Seaway and Power Project, which will prove a boon to transportation and industry in both countries. Aside from her economic importance, Canada is of the greatest strategic value to the United States as an ally in the cold war. As far back as 1940 the two nations initiated a united program of military planning through a Permanent Joint Defense Committee, which has been holding regular annual meetings in recent years. In 1950 Canada supported the United Nations in the Korean War with naval, air, and ground forces. As a member of NATO, Canada is also involved in the defense of Europe. She has collaborated with the United States in the construction of the Distant Early Warning (DEW) line of radar installations to provide protection against a polar attack upon the North American continent, and she has joined the United States in the creation of the North American Air Defense Command (NORAD).

Despite the close economic, military, and cultural ties between the two neighbors, Canada's feelings toward the United States in recent years have not always been too friendly. In the parliamentary elections of 1957 the middle-of-the-road Liberal Party was ousted from power after an unbroken reign of twenty-two years. Since then the Conservatives, led by Prime Minister John Diefenbaker, have been in control. The success of the Conservatives, especially in winning a landslide victory in 1958, has been due to their emphasis on Canadian nationalism, chiefly at the expense of the United States. Canadians have been worried for some time over the continued influx of American capital, fearful that their country may end up as an economic dependency of the United States. The fact that Canada suffers a yearly deficit of more than one billion dollars in its trade with the United States and the charge that the United States program for the disposal of surplus farm products cuts into Canada's wheat trade have made for added strain. It is not that Canadians have become violently anti-American so much as that they have become pro-Canadian. This new spirit of self-confidence and independence has shown itself not only in Canada's dealings with the United States but also in her relations with Great Britain. As the oldest among the Dominions, Canada is a loyal member of the Commonwealth. But this has not kept her from pursuing an independent course, as she did during the Suez crisis in 1956, when UN intervention in Egypt was due largely to Canadian initiative. Most Canadians are proud of the fact that Britain's Queen is also their Queen, but they refuse to recognize anything other than sentimental ties with the former mother country.

LATIN AMERICA IN TRANSITION

The history of Latin America since World War II has been a succession of political revolutions, economic crises, and social upheavals. The root of this unrest is poverty. Like the peoples of Asia and Africa, the masses of Latin America need to gain at least a minimum of economic security before they can hope to achieve political stability. To make use of their ample resources and thus escape their poverty, the twenty nations of Central and South America not only need outside aid, especially from the United States, but they also have to learn to co-operate with each other more closely than they have in the past. To bring about such harmony within the Western Hemisphere has been one of the aims of United States foreign policy. It has been made difficult in recent years because of a strong upsurge of Latin American nationalism, encouraged at times by Communist agitation.

Politically, Latin America has long been known for its instability. But while in the past one dictator usually followed another, most of the revolutions since World War II have resulted in victories of democracy. Beginning with Argentina's Juan Perón in 1955, one after another of the traditional strong men were overthrown—in Colombia, Peru, Venezuela, and Cuba—until by 1960 only the Dominican Republic, Paraguay, and to a lesser degree Nicaragua and Haiti were still ruled by dictators. Cuba remains in

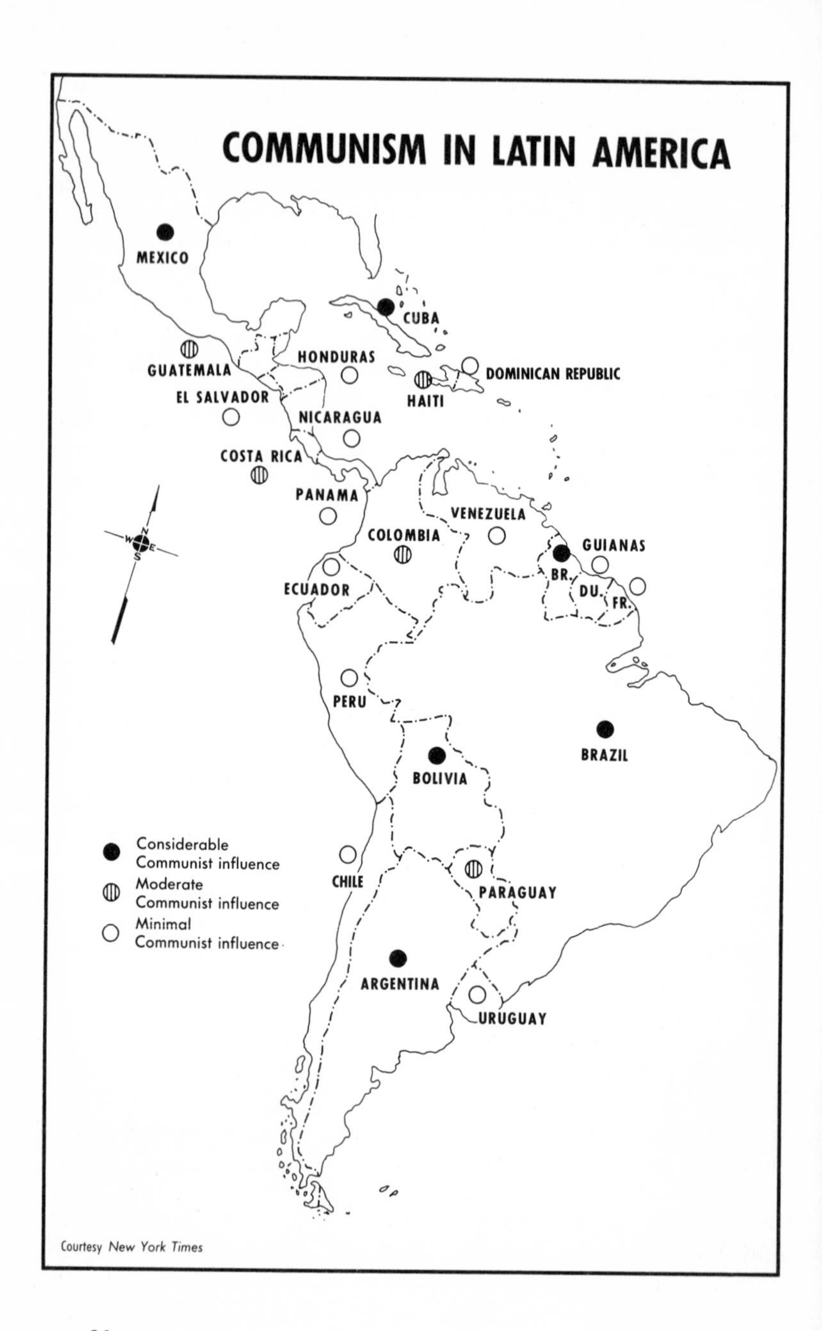
COMMUNISM IN LATIN AMERICA
MEXICO
CUBA
GUATEMALA
HONDURAS
DOMINICAN REPUBLIC
HAITI
EL SALVADOR
NICARAGUA
COSTA RICA
PANAMA
VENEZUELA
COLOMBIA
GUIANAS
BR.
DU.
FR.
ECUADOR
PERU
BRAZIL
BOLIVIA
CHILE
PARAGUAY
ARGENTINA
URUGUAY
N
E
S
W
Considerable Communist influence
Moderate Communist influence
Minimal Communist influence
Courtesy New York Times

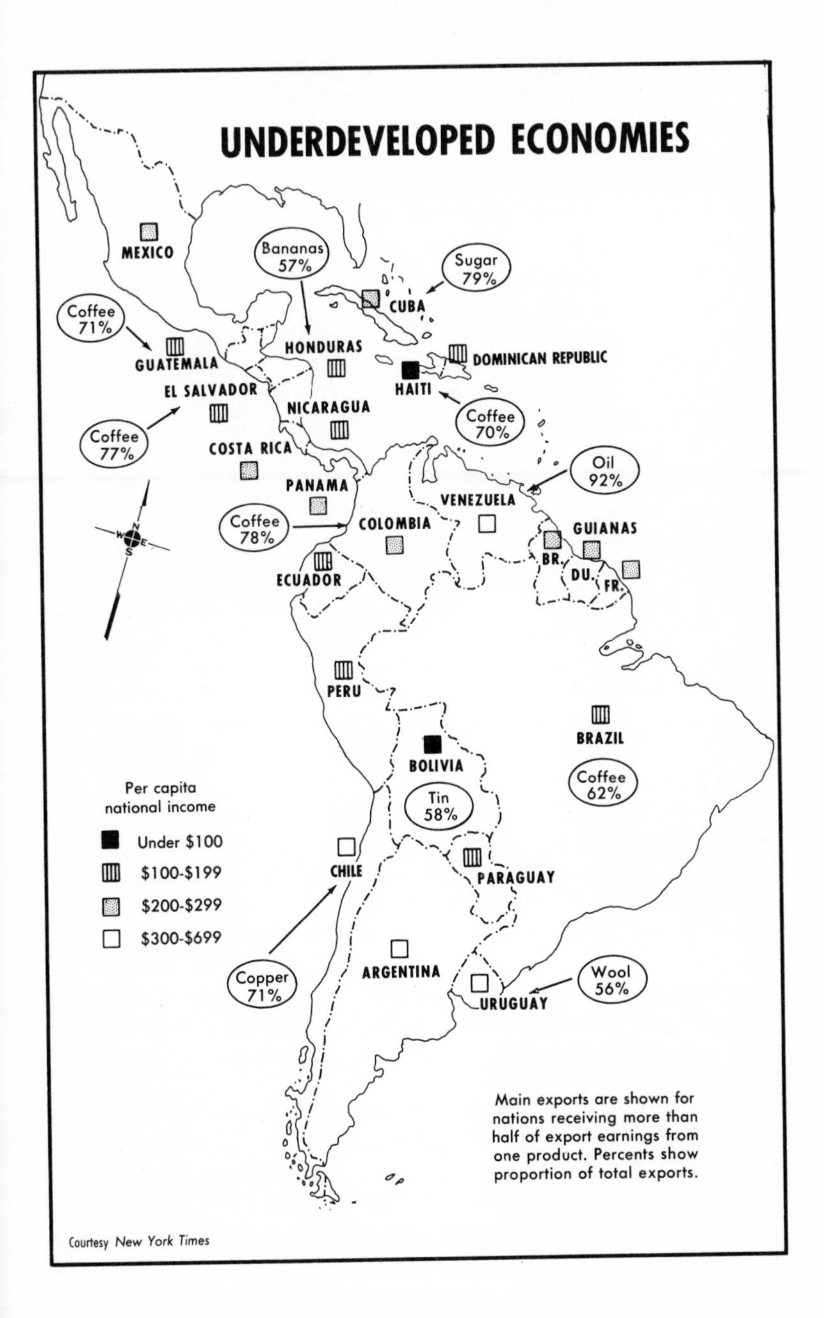
UNDERDEVELOPED ECONOMIES
MEXICO
Bananas 57%
Sugar 79%
CUBA
Coffee 71%
GUATEMALA
HONDURAS
DOMINICAN REPUBLIC
HAITI
EL SALVADOR
NICARAGUA
Coffee 70%
Coffee 77%
COSTA RICA
Oil 92%
PANAMA
VENEZUELA
Coffee 78%
COLOMBIA
GUIANAS
BR.
DU.
FR.
ECUADOR
N
W
E
S
PERU
BRAZIL
BOLIVIA
Coffee 62%
Per capita national income
Tin 58%
Under $100
$100-$199
$200-$299
$300-$699
CHILE
PARAGUAY
ARGENTINA
Copper 71%
Wool 56%
URUGUAY
Main exports are shown for nations receiving more than half of export earnings from one product. Percents show proportion of total exports.
Courtesy New York Times

a category by itself. Here the old-style dictatorship of Fulgencio Batista gave way in 1959 to the revolutionary dictatorship of Fidel Castro. Cuba's new leader has promised elections for some future time; but for the present he prefers to carry out his drastic reform program without consulting the Cuban people.

Even where representative institutions exist in Latin America, democracy is often tinged with authoritarianism. Lack of political experience, educational backwardness, and staggering economic problems make any Western-style parliamentary government, as we know it, impossible. In most countries the government is run by the growing middle class, industrial and commercial interests backed by the military and the Catholic Church. Under the leadership of men like Arturo Frondizi of Argentina, Juscelino Kubitchek of Brazil, Rómuló Betancourt of Venezuela, and Alberto Lleras Camargo of Colombia, these middle-of-the-road moderates are trying to solve their nations' problems by gradual, democratic means. But their rule is beginning to be challenged by the more radical masses, often left-wing and always ultranationalist. They look to the example of Cuba and Fidel Castro as a way out of their economic difficulties. Nationalism is nothing new in Latin America, and for some time past its favorite target has been the United States. But it is only recently that Latin American nationalism has taken such ugly forms as the demonstrations against Vice-President Nixon during his South American tour in 1958 and the many anti–United States riots in Bolivia, Panama, Cuba, and elsewhere. In some instances ultranationalism has led to the confiscation of foreign holdings, beginning as far back as 1938 with the seizure of American oil companies in Mexico and culminating in the recent wave of expropriations in Cuba. Latin American nationalism has proved a useful weapon in the hands of Communist agitators. The importance of communism in Latin America is far out of proportion to the small number of its actual followers. Even though the Communist Party has been outlawed in more than half the republics, its influence is felt throughout Central and South America. By infiltrating student and labor organizations, Latin America's Communists, under orders from Moscow, have been responsible for most of the anti-American demonstrations in recent years. There are Communists in the parliaments of at least six countries, and in Cuba Communists and their sympathizers have gained decisive influence upon the formulation of national policy.

The underlying cause of Latin American unrest, as was pointed out above, is poverty. It has become more dismal since World War II because of the alarming increase in population. Improvements in health and sanitation have been chiefly responsible for this unprecedented acceleration, which shows no sign of abating. The population of Latin America in 1960 is estimated at close to two hundred million, and if the present rate of growth continues, that number in another generation will be more than double. The result of this population explosion has been a steady lowering of per capita income. In 1960 the average annual income in more than half the Latin American republics was less than two hundred dollars, and in the cases of Bolivia and Haiti it was below one hundred dollars. Latin America has tremendous economic potentialities, due not only to such natural resources as oil, copper, tin, iron, nitrates, manganese, and gold, but also to the richness of its soil and its large reservoir of manpower. The development of these potentialities, however, is still only in its early stages. Natural resources, except oil, have hardly begun to be developed. Agriculture, to become more productive, requires the aid of large public projects for irrigation, storage, and improved transportation. Another need is for an adjustment of national products, providing for greater diversification and eliminating duplication. At present eleven of the Latin American countries receive more than half their export earnings from only one commodity. Any fluctuation in the world market price of that commodity, therefore, has the most serious repercussions. With many nations specializing in the same products, furthermore, competition is keen and trade within Latin America is negligible. Finally, economic reform, to be effective, calls for the education of the masses, millions of whom are still illiterate.

The governments of Latin America have made some efforts to solve their economic problems by self-help and mutual collaboration. Some of the countries have taken steps toward a common market, along the lines of the European Economic Community. But lack of transportation facilities, currency differences, and overlapping of national products make this a difficult task. Some progress has been made in regulating competition among the fifteen coffee-producing nations. In 1958 President Kubitschek of Brazil put forth a major development program, "Operation Pan-America." But such an ambitious scheme requires vast amounts of capital, and such funds Latin America does not have. Most of the countries suffer from chronic inflation and run yearly deficits, even without any major public works programs. The capital for economic development, therefore, has to come from the outside. And here Latin America is looking first and foremost to the United States.

THE UNITED STATES AND LATIN AMERICA

Ever since the early nineteenth century and the proclamation of the Monroe Doctrine, relations with her neighbors in Central and South America have been of major concern to the United States. In the years before World War II it became customary to refer to America's relations with Latin America as a "good neighbor policy." This policy demonstrated an enlightened self-interest that led to increasingly close inter-American co-operation, particularly in the economic field. Since World War II, however, with the growing involvement of the United States in world affairs, the relative significance of the Western Hemisphere countries in the general scheme of United States foreign policy could not help declining. As a result, the countries to the south have come to feel neglected by their powerful northern neighbor. Yet at the same time the threat of Communist aggression from within and without has made continued inter-American solidarity more important than ever.

To present a united front against this threat, the nations of the Western Hemisphere—all except Canada, Nicaragua, and Ecuador—signed the Inter-American Treaty of Reciprocal Assistance (Rio Treaty) at the Rio de Janeiro Conference in 1947. Its articles 3 and 6 provide that "an attack by any state against an American state shall be considered as an attack against all," and that the signatories shall consult on joint action "if the inviolability or the integrity of the territory or the sovereignty or political independence of any American state should be affected by an aggression which is not an armed attack." The latter provision was broad enough to cover a possible Communist attack from within. It was elaborated by the Caracas Declaration of 1954, which specifically stated that the spread of communism to the Western Hemisphere "would constitute a threat to the sovereignty and political independence of the American states, endangering the peace of America."

As a permanent body of inter-American consultation, the United States together with all the Latin American republics founded the Organization of American States (OAS) in 1948. The Charter of the OAS proclaims the equality of its twenty-one members and lays down the principle of nonintervention in their external and internal affairs. In addition, it calls for the pacific settlement of disputes and provides for consultation on all matters of common interest. The organs of the OAS are the Inter-American Conference, meeting every five years; the meeting of foreign ministers, to deal with emergencies; and the Council of the OAS, a permanent hemispheric parliament with headquarters in Washington. During its first twelve years, the OAS has successfully settled a number of feuds between some of its smaller members but has failed thus far to resolve a long-standing border dispute between Ecuador and Peru. A major test of OAS came in 1960, when it was asked to arbitrate the dispute between the United States and Cuba (see p. 98).

While the United States has been careful to respect the democratic character of the OAS, her preponderant power gives her a unique position among its members. This has been shown in the United Nations, where the countries of Latin America have usually followed the lead of their northern ally. In the all-important economic field, however, the United States, in the opinion of many Latin Americans, has not done as much as she should to justify her leadership. These critics point out that America has been giving far more aid to Europe, Asia, and even Africa, than to Latin America. Total United States aid to Latin America from 1946 to 1959 was 3.5 billion dollars, less than the aid given to Nationalist China. More than half of this, moreover, went for military assistance rather than for economic development. Other criticism has been leveled against United States tariff policy, which restricts the import of certain Latin American raw materials, especially ores. Finally, the fact that the United States did not withhold her support from the dictators while they were still in power caused added resentment among Latin American liberals. In reply to these criticisms, the United States has pointed to the almost 10 billion dollars of private funds invested in Latin America and to the yearly exchange of goods valued at more than 4 billion dollars. These figures show that America's interest in the economy of her southern neighbors is far from negligible. Any comparison with Europe, moreover, which is frequently made by Latin Americans, is considered meaningless, since the more highly developed European economy is able to absorb far greater sums.

Still, the mounting wave of anti-Americanism in Central and South America, climaxed in the attacks on Vice-President Nixon in 1958, has led the United States to reassess its Latin American policy. As a result, Washington has shown greater interest than before in some long-range development plans, such as "Operation Pan-America." In 1959 the United States made a dramatic gesture by contributing 45 per cent to a new billion-dollar Inter-American Development Bank, and in 1960 Congress authorized an additional 500 million dollars in development funds for Latin America. During his "mission of understanding" to South America in early 1960 President Eisenhower was received with a genuine warmth that was in marked contrast to the sullen hostility which Nixon had met two years before. This was interpreted as a sign that the latent good will in Latin America toward the United States is greater than it may have appeared in recent years, and that the future will see further evidence of collaboration between the North and South, to the benefit of both.

THE UNITED STATES AND CUBA

America's increased concern over Latin America coincided with and was influenced by important events in Cuba. On January 1, 1959, the rebel forces of Fidel Castro, after more than two years of guerrilla fighting, ousted the corrupt and repressive regime of Cuban dictator Fulgencio Batista. The victory of the "twenty-sixth of July Movement"—named after Castro's first abortive rising against Batista on July 26, 1953—ushered in a revolution aimed at bringing social justice and economic betterment to the island's 6.5 million people. The leaders of the revolution were all young men in their early thirties, foremost among them Fidel Castro, a dynamic leader of great popularity. His program called for agrarian reform, industrialization, and a far-reaching public works program. It had strong socialist overtones and to some observers smacked of communism. But Castro and his followers asserted that their revolution was "humanist and not Communist." By mid-1960 Cuba's entire agricultural economy and much of her industry had been nationalized, generally without compensation to the former owners.

Reaction in the United States toward the Cuban revolution at first was quite friendly. Economic relations between the two countries in the past had been close, with nearly a billion American dollars invested in Cuba and more than 500 million dollars worth of trade in either direction each year. In April, 1959, Prime Minister Castro paid an unofficial visit to the United States and was given a warm reception. There was hope at the time that Cuba would manage to stabilize her finances sufficiently to become eligible for United States aid. But the era of good feeling did not last long. There had already been disillusionment in the United States over the summary execution by the Castro regime of some five hundred of Batista's followers, accused of war crimes. Hopes for a democratic government were disappointed when Castro postponed elections indefinitely. And there was growing concern in the United States over the influence which men of known Communist leanings were gaining in Cuban affairs. The two most powerful officials after Castro were the Premier's brother, Raul Castro, Minister of the Armed Forces, and Ernesto ("Che") Guevara, president of the National Bank. The former has been designated by Fidel Castro as his possible successor, and the latter was placed in charge of Cuba's economy. Both men have strong Communist sympathies and have appointed a number of Communists and Communist sympathizers to important positions in the government.

Since the end of 1959 relations between Cuba and the United States have deteriorated rapidly. The responsibility for this has been almost entirely Cuba's. Whether from conviction or because he needed a scapegoat to stimulate revolutionary fervor, Prime Minister Castro has been accusing the United States of aiding the enemies of his regime in the hope of overthrowing it. To meet the imaginary threat of an American invasion, a large popular militia has been trained to supplement the regular army. Using the slogan "Cuba yes, Yankees no!" Castro and his associates are telling the Cuban people that all of their economic ills, past and present, are due to "American imperialism."

Washington in the beginning merely protested against these irresponsible attacks, hoping that in due time they would subside. America hesitated to take stronger action—such as cutting the sugar quota under which the United States paid a higher price for Cuban sugar than is paid on the world market—for fear that it might lead to retaliation against American interests in Cuba. But as Castro began confiscating more and more American property, these fears became meaningless. In February, 1960, developments in Cuba took a still more dangerous turn. At that time Castro's economic adviser, Ernesto Guevara, signed a commercial treaty with the Soviet Union under which the Russians promised to buy Cuban sugar and to give Cuba a hundred-million-dollar credit to buy Russian oil and machinery. This agreement was followed by trade pacts with several of Russia's satellites and with Communist China.

In the light of these overtures to the Soviet bloc and the continued expropriation of American investments in Cuba, the United States at long last decided to strike back. Upon authorization from Congress, President Eisenhower in July, 1960, halted American imports of Cuban sugar, thus causing Cuba to lose an estimated 150 million dollars per year. But this action merely increased Castro's defiance. His hands were strengthened when Premier Khrushchev threatened to launch intercontinental missiles against the United States if it intervened in Cuba. In a later speech Khrushchev attacked the Monroe Doctrine which, he said, had "outlived its time," had "died a natural death," and "should be buried." Communism thus apparently had no intention of relinquishing the foothold it had gained in the Western Hemisphere. The threat of a Soviet satellite on America's doorstep had suddenly become terribly real.

In August, 1960, the Organization of American States took up the Cuban question at a meeting in Costa Rica. Upon recommendation of United States Secretary of State Christian Herter, the OAS foreign ministers, with three abstentions, signed the Declaration of San Jose, which condemned "intervention . . . from an extracontinental power in the affairs of the American republics" and "the acceptance" of such intervention by any American power. While the United States interpreted the document as "a clear indictment of the Castro government," the other signatories under pressure of public opinion at home denied that the declaration constituted a condemnation of Cuba. Premier Castro, meanwhile, reaffirmed his ties with the Communist bloc and declared his readiness to accept the protection of Soviet rockets in case of "imperialist attack." With Cuba confiscating the last remaining American properties and threatening to move against the United States naval base at Guantanamo Bay, relations between the two countries appeared headed for an early showdown.

4

A SATELLITE SUBDUED

Citizens of Budapest pass bodies of Russian soldiers killed in the futile Hungarian uprising of 1956. WIDE WORLD PHOTO.

We Communists believe that the idea of Communism will ultimately be victorious throughout the world, just as it has been victorious in our country, in China and in many other states. . . . Just as in its time capitalism, as the more progressive system, took the place of feudalism, so will capitalism be inevitably superseded by Communism.

NIKITA S. KHRUSHCHEV, "On Peaceful Coexistence,"
Foreign Affairs, Vol. XXXVIII, October, 1959

THE SOVIET UNION AND ITS SATELLITES

THE MOST IMPORTANT SINGLE EVENT IN Russian history since World War II was the death of Premier Joseph Stalin on March 5, 1953. For a while it appeared as though the passing of the most powerful dictator marked the end of an era. But it soon became clear that Russia's supposedly "new look" was only a superficial change of mood and method, leaving the essence of communism and its aims unaffected. To make the Soviet Union the strongest nation on earth and to extend the influence of communism as far as possible are the supreme goals of Soviet leaders today as they were under Stalin. It was under Stalin that Russian communism made the most headway in pursuit of these aims. More than any other individual, this forbidding man was responsible for the divided and unhappy world in which we live.

RUSSIA UNDER STALIN

Joseph Stalin gave his name to a particularly rigid and orthodox type of communism. The term Stalinism covers many things. Politically, it brought to perfection the dictatorship of one party, and ultimately of one man, over a country of two hundred million people, using every means of control, from censorship to mass executions and slave labor, to reach its totalitarian goals. Economically Stalinism carried out nothing less than an industrial and agricultural revolution. Within one generation the Soviet Union was transformed into one of the world's leading industrial powers, at the same time increasing its agricultural efficiency and output through large-scale collective farming. In the field of foreign affairs, Stalin prior to World War II adhered to his policy of assuring first the victory of "socialism in one country," that is, Russia. He thus abstained, for the time being, from pursuing the fundamental aim of Soviet policy: the elimination of capitalism and the promotion of world revolution. During World War II the government's ambitious schemes of economic development were temporarily interrupted. But once the fighting was over, Stalinism continued where it had left off, becoming, if anything, more rigid at home and changing from a policy of isolationism in foreign affairs to one of territorial and ideological expansion.

In February, 1946, the first general elections since 1937 for the Supreme Soviet, the highest "legislative" authority in the U.S.S.R., produced the expected results. More than 99 per cent of the eligible voters participated, and, by more than 99 per cent, they endorsed the official list of Communist candidates. Membership in the Communist Party, which, under more liberal admission requirements during the war had almost reached the six million mark, was now again subjected to closer scrutiny, resulting in large-scale expulsions. The executive powers of the Soviet government continued to be vested in a Council of Ministers (prior to 1946 called Council of People's Commissars), with Stalin serving as Chairman, that is, Premier. But the real power, as in the past, rested with the Communist Party, its Central Committee, its eleven-member Politburo (since 1952 called Presidium), and its First Secretary, Joseph Stalin. The relationship between party and government has been compared to that existing between the board of directors and the managers of a large corporation, with most of the leading figures occupying corresponding positions of influence in both government and party. As for the relative standing of each individual within the Soviet hierarchy, the outside world depended for its information chiefly on whatever conclusions it wanted to draw from the lineup of Soviet dignitaries at official functions. Physical proximity to Stalin at such functions was usually interpreted as a sign of influence. Occasional changes were made in the Soviet hierarchy, such as the replacement in 1949 of Foreign Minister Vyacheslav Molotov by Andrei Vyshinsky, and of Defense Minister Nikolai Bulganin by Alexander Vasilevsky, and the appointment of Georgi Malenkov to succeed the party's leading ideologist, Andrei Zhdanov, who had died in 1948. Any such change usually led to speculation abroad as to the possible line of succession in case of Stalin's death. Yet the inner workings of the Soviet system continued to remain a deep mystery to outsiders.

There were other changes during the postwar era, mostly in the direction of greater orthodoxy, both in the Marxian and in the traditional Russian sense. In an effort to apply the teachings of Marx, as interpreted by Stalin, to all facets of Soviet life, the Central Committee of the Communist Party accused leading writers, artists, and scientists of losing touch with the masses by showing bourgeois influences in their work. The party forced the persons thus accused to confess and recant their "errors." The Russian people, who had always been kept fairly immune from contact with the West, now were isolated more than ever. They were indoctrinated with a nationalistic view of their country's past and present in which Russia emerged as the inventor and originator of all good things and Stalin as the greatest of national leaders and the father of his country. With this emphasis on Russian nationalism went a relaxation in the government's antireligious policy. Already during the war the Kremlin, recognizing the continued strength of religious feeling among the Russian people, had sanctioned the election of a new patriarch for the Orthodox Church. At the end of the war the government had restored half of the religious property that had been confiscated in the past. The Church repaid these concessions by abandoning its opposition to the Communist regime. Orthodox leaders welcomed the renewed recognition given to the institution of the family as the foundation of national life. Divorce was made more difficult and financial assistance encouraged large families. If some of these measures ran counter to the teachings of Marx, they may be explained as necessary concessions at a time when economic reconstruction and expansion called for continued sacrifices from a people already exhausted by war.

Stalin's great historic contribution lies in the fact that "he found Russia working with the wooden plough and left her equipped with atomic piles." No country ever experienced an industrial revolution as rapidly and against such terrific odds as did the Soviet Union. Today she ranks second among the world's industrial nations, and hopes to catch up with and ultimately surpass the United States. Russia's industrial revolution was carried on entirely through state planning rather than private initiative, and was pursued with a cold-blooded ruthlessness that has had no parallel, except perhaps in the recent history of Communist China. Partly as a result of purges but mostly from periodic famines, millions of Russians died so that "socialism in one country" could become a reality. Large-scale industrialization did not begin in earnest until the launching of the first Five-Year Plan in 1928. After ten years it had made sufficient strides so that the third Five-Year Plan, which was put into effect in 1938, for the first time permitted an increase in the production of consumer goods. Prior to this time, the emphasis had been on heavy industry, with production of everyday necessities, like clothing and household utensils, at a bare minimum. But just as the Russian people, after years of sacrifice, were about to taste some of the fruits of their labor, the war intervened.

It is difficult to get a clear picture of the economic effects of the war. Russia's losses, to be sure, were staggering, heavier than those of all the other Allied powers combined: more than seven million dead, more than twenty million homeless, and an estimated economic loss of nearly one-fourth of the country's prewar wealth. But the Russians had already begun reconstruction while the war was still in progress. They had shifted many of their major industries to regions beyond the reach of the German invaders, using the generous assistance of American Lend-Lease funds to make possible this shift. Soviet recovery after the war certainly would have been less rapid had the situation been as dismal as Soviet leaders, in their claims for large reparations, asserted. The task before the Soviet government in 1945 was twofold: to repair the damages of war and to continue the prewar process of industrialization. To achieve these aims, the fourth Five-Year Plan was launched in 1946.

It was completed in 1950, ahead of schedule, as usual, and with results that supposedly exceeded its original goals. Even if due allowance is made for the exaggeration of official Soviet statistics, the achievements of Russia's postwar economic development were remarkable. Production of coal, steel, electric power, and oil all showed substantial increases over prewar levels and the total output of the Soviet Union in the early 1950's was beginning to equal the combined productions of the three major nations of western Europe: Great Britain, France, and Germany. As in the case of the earlier Five-Year Plans, these gains were made possible only at the cost of great personal sacrifices on the part of the Russian people. Through a drastic currency devaluation in 1947 they lost most of their savings and had to work harder and longer to eke out a minimum existence. Consumer goods continued to be scarce, with even the most basic necessities available only at prohibitive prices, if at all. A fifth Five-Year Plan, to be completed by 1955, called for further increases in heavy industry, notably the production of steel, but it also held out some hope for more consumer goods.

Compared to the rapid growth of Russian industry under Stalin, parallel developments in agriculture were far less impressive. While industrial production between 1940 and 1952 almost doubled, agricultural output during the same period increased by only 10 per cent. The main features of Stalin's agrarian policy were collectivization (consolidation of individual holdings into large collective farms) and mechanization. Neither of these innovations appealed to the backward and conservative Russian peasant, who tried to resist the government's policy by every possible means. Resistance was met by reprisals, without markedly improving the situation. One of the main grievances of the peasantry was its inability to buy an equivalent in consumer goods for the foodstuffs it was asked to surrender. Just before World War II agrarian unrest had somewhat decreased, as peasants were permitted to cultivate small individual plots of an acre or less for their own use, free from state control. But once the war was over, the government again stepped up collectivization, not merely by extending it to regions recently annexed—such as the Baltic states—but also by merging the already existing collective farms into still larger supercollectives. By its very nature and tradition, agriculture was much more difficult to regulate than Russian industry, most of which had never known any system of individual ownership. The government was aided in its control over agriculture by a state-owned system of machine-tractor stations, which supplied the necessary mechanization for large-scale farming.

EASTERN EUROPE UNDER STALIN

The main events of Russia's foreign policy under Stalin are discussed elsewhere in this book (see Chapters 1 and 6). Whether proceeding by plan or pushed by events, Stalin after 1945 abandoned his earlier policy of isolationism. He took full advantage of the opportunities presented by the initial confusion of the postwar era to advance the fortunes of the Soviet Union and of world communism. These two aims have motivated Soviet policy from its beginnings. It is only in the methods used to realize these aims that we find the wide variety of attitudes, from aggressiveness to agreeableness, that characterize Russian policy at different times. With their belief in the inevitability of a Communist victory, Russia's leaders can afford to be patient; and with their strong hold over their own people and over Communists outside Russia, they can afford to be opportunistic, adjusting their policy to changing circumstances. Perseverance in long-range aims combined with expediency in short-range methods were the characteristics not only of Stalin and the men who ruled Russia before him but also of the men who succeeded him.

We have already noted the westward expansion of Soviet influence during the years immediately following World War II. Russia annexed outright some 185,000 square miles with nearly 25 million people, and she gained indirect control over another 560,000 square miles inhabited by almost 100 million. The Soviet Union was thus able to remake most of eastern Europe, with the exception of Finland, after its own image. This transformation was facilitated by a number of factors: the blindness of the Western Allies to Russia's ultimate aims, the actual occupation of the region by Russian troops, and the political and economic weaknesses of an area that already twice in our century had embroiled the world in a major war. In 1945 the nations of eastern Europe were exhausted by the heavy sacrifices of war and German occupation; they were divided by age-old nationalist rivalries; and they were disillusioned by the past failures of their governments, many of which had become Fascist dictatorships even before Hitler. Thus, the nations of eastern Europe presented the kind of political and spiritual vacuum that seems particularly favorable to the spread of communism.

A further factor aiding the communization of eastern Europe was the manner in which the transition from liberal regimes to "people's democracies" was brought about. With minor exceptions, developments in the eight states thus affected—Albania, Bulgaria, Czechoslovakia, East Germany, Hungary, Poland, Romania, and Yugoslavia—followed a common pattern. As a first step the Soviet occupation authorities sponsored the formation of coalition or "united front" governments made up of representatives from those groups that had opposed the Nazis during the war. The outward appearance of democracy was thus maintained, chiefly for the benefit of the West. Yet the Communist contingents of such coalitions, notably in Yugoslavia, Poland, and Albania, played a dominant role from the very start. By holding key positions, such as the ministries of interior and justice, and enjoying the support of the Russians, the Communists were able to consolidate their power. This power they used to suppress right-wing opposition groups and to initiate the first moves toward nationalization of industry and collectivization of agriculture. As soon as they felt sufficiently strong, the Communists proceeded to the second and more difficult step in their seizure of power. This was the gradual ousting, by threats or on trumped-up charges of treason, of their non-Communist coalition partners. The method and timing used differed with each country. In Yugoslavia and Albania the Communists had absolute authority from the very beginning. In Bulgaria and Romania the non-Communists gave way by the middle of 1945, in East Germany by early 1946, in Poland and Hungary during the first half of 1947, and in Czechoslovakia, as we have seen, not until early 1948.

In all these countries, with the exception of Czechoslovakia, the absence of a strong democratic tradition further facilitated communization. The only groups at all capable of putting up any opposition, and therefore the main targets of Communist attacks, were the agrarian socialist movements in the various countries. But despite the fact that they commanded a far greater following than their Communist partners, the agrarian socialists proved no match for the Communists and their skill at conquest by infiltration. Some agrarian leaders were allowed to go into exile. Others were able to escape. These fortunate ones became active abroad in organizations devoted to the future liberation of their homelands and helped to form in 1954 the Assembly of Captive European Nations (ACEN). As for the rest of the agrarian leaders, they were either jailed or executed on fabricated charges of espionage, treason, or sabotage. Another potential opposition force, the Catholic Church, strongly entrenched in such countries as Poland, Czechoslovakia, Hungary, and Yugoslavia, was similarly dealt with. Leading religious figures, like Cardinal Mindszenty of Hungary, Cardinal Wyszynski of Poland, and Archbishop (later Cardinal) Stepinac of Yugoslavia, were imprisoned on alleged charges of treason. Possessions of the churches were nationalized, and the minor clergy were deprived of all influence.

The victory of communism in eastern Europe was virtually complete by early 1948. Politically, one-party rule now prevailed in all the "people's democracies," despite the nominal existence of some of the former coalition parties. As in the Soviet Union, central committees of the Communist Party made all major political decisions and appointed all important officials, usually following instructions from Moscow. Like prerevolutionary Russia, most of eastern Europe, with the exception of Czechoslovakia, was predominantly agrarian. Again as in Russia, one of the major aims of the new regimes everywhere was to improve their backward agricultural economies through increased industrialization. There were various five- or six-year plans, and in Bulgaria industry actually began overtaking agriculture. Czechoslovakia, the only country already highly industrialized in the past, played a key role in aiding the industrialization of her neighbors and in supplying arms to the Eastern satellites. The Polish Six-Year Plan covering the years 1950–55 aimed at an increase of 154 per cent in heavy industry and only 111 per cent in consumer goods. This emphasis on heavy industry was also noticeable in most other countries of the Soviet bloc, resulting in the same low standard of living as in the Soviet Union. In the agricultural field, the emphasis again, as in Russia, was on forced collectivization, with widely differing results. There was considerable opposition among farmers and workers to the economic policy of their new Communist masters. Efforts at resistance were shown in absenteeism and slowdowns, but also in occasional riots, such as those in Czechoslovakia and East Germany in 1953. The harsh countermeasures taken by the various governments differed little from those used under Stalin in Russia. Albania, for example, with only 1.25 million people, lost more than 10,000 of its inhabitants through executions and an additional 30,000 persons were confined to slave labor camps.

Aside from introducing their own type of government and economy, the Russians were careful to maintain as close a hold as possible over their puppet states by means of ideological, military, and economic agreements. We have already discussed the formation of the Cominform, the signing of various mutual assistance pacts, and the inauguration of the so-called Molotov Plan via the Council for Mutual Economic Assistance (see Chapter 1). The general effect of these agreements was to integrate the satellite countries with each other and with the Soviet Union and to insure their maximum usefulness to the latter. To bolster Eastern military strength, the nations of the Soviet orbit were forced to maintain armed forces far beyond what their economies could support and exceeding the terms of the peace treaties signed in 1947.

Two countries in eastern Europe, East Germany and Yugoslavia, deserve special mention. The first is not really a nation at all, but only a part of one. We have already traced the gradual division of Germany in the early years of the cold war. The German Democratic Republic, as East Germany is called in the Communist world, was officially established in October, 1949. Its government, which thus far has not been recognized by either West Germany or the Western Allies, is dominated by the Socialist Unity Party (SED). Other more moderate parties continue a shadowy existence but wield no real influence. President of the republic until his death in 1960 was veteran Communist Wilhelm Pieck, and the post of Minister President is held by ex-Socialist Otto Grotewohl. The most powerful figure, however, is Walter Ulbricht, Communist leader of the SED. In September, 1960, Ulbricht became chairman of a new Council of State, which took over the functions of the presidency. In most essential respects the German Democratic Republic followed the course of the other "people's democracies." Most of its industries were nationalized and despite various handicaps and shortages, industrial production by 1954 had risen almost 80 per cent above the 1936 level. Agriculture fared less well, due to a haphazard land reform immediately after the war which divided the more efficiently run large estates among peasant proprietors. Attempts at collectivization were begun in 1948, but these have not proved very successful. Even though the region had always been among the most productive in Germany, it did not grow sufficient food, and large quantities had to be imported. The standard of living of the East Germans, consequently, remained far below that of their western brethren. Popular discontent with this state of affairs found release in a steady flow of refugees, mostly farmers, into the western Federal Republic. Nearly a million East Germans thus fled the East between 1950 and 1954. Matters were made worse by Russia's strict policy toward her occupation zone during the Stalin era. As a major source of reparations, the eastern republic was forced to pay far beyond the 10 billion dollars originally demanded by the Soviet Union. When reparations were officially discontinued in 1953, the drain on East Germany's economy continued as the Germans had to buy back those industrial enterprises that had been confiscated by the Soviets right after the war.

The case of Yugoslavia was quite different. While everywhere else in eastern Europe the Russians were tightening their hold, Yugoslavia alone was able to free herself from Soviet control. The Communist forces of Josip Broz, better known as Marshal Tito, having played a major role in liberating their country from the Axis, had from the beginning been far less dependent on Russian support than the Communist minorities elsewhere in eastern Europe. Yugoslavia thus remained relatively free from Russian interference. Still, in her internal developments, Yugoslavia at first followed closely the pattern found in the other satellites. Tito set up a "people's republic" in 1945, with a constitution closely resembling that of the U.S.S.R. Moderate opponents, such as General Mihailovich, were purged. The nation also embarked on a Five-Year Plan of industrial development and initiated a drive to collectivize agriculture. Outwardly, relations between Belgrade and Moscow appeared friendly, and until 1948 Yugoslavia was generally looked upon as firmly within the Russian orbit.

As we now know, differences between Tito and Stalin had begun to arise as early as 1945. The first disagreement came over the question of Trieste, where Tito felt he did not receive adequate Russian support. Discord ultimately extended to other fields, as the self-assured and able Yugoslav dictator made it plain that he intended to be master in his own house. The open break came in the spring of 1948, as the Russians first recalled their military and technical advisers, and then had Tito and his party expelled from the Cominform for doctrinal errors and hostility to the Soviet Union. This action was followed by a severing of all economic and military ties between the Russian bloc and its onetime member.

The break with Moscow, greeted in the West as a major

Russian setback, did not at first bring any change in Yugoslavia's domestic policy. Tito remained a Communist, although his ideology of national communism, or "Titoism," differed from the orthodox Stalinist line. In foreign affairs, on the other hand, the Yugoslav leader gradually moved closer to the West, not only economically, by concluding a series of agreements providing economic aid to Yugoslavia, but also politically. Tito opposed Chinese intervention in Korea, resumed diplomatic relations with Greece, and improved relations with Italy, which ultimately resulted in a settlement of the controversy over Trieste. Beginning in 1950 there also were signs of a certain liberalization in Yugoslavia's policy at home. Control over heavy industry and farming was decentralized. More than four-fifths of the collective farms were dissolved and participation in collectivization was made voluntary. A system of "workers' management" was adopted in industry, and production was put on a profit basis. The institution of political commissars was abolished, and the Communist Party henceforth was to rely on persuasion rather than compulsion. In addition, freedom of worship was granted, the secret ballot was introduced, and women were given the vote. In January, 1953, the Soviet-style constitution was revised in the direction of greater decentralization with a parliament of two chambers (a Federal Council and a Council of Producers) and a president (Marshal Tito). To strengthen her defenses, Yugoslavia in February, 1953, joined Turkey and Greece in a treaty of friendship (Treaty of Ankara), supplemented the following year by a military alliance (Bled Alliance). In addition, military funds and equipment from the Western powers, especially the United States, were extended to Yugoslavia beginning in 1951.

From all these changes it seemed quite clear that the break between Tito and Stalin was complete. Stalin feared that Yugoslavia's desertion and her pursuit of an independent, though still Communist, line might find imitators among the other satellites. He therefore used his influence over the Cominform to start a general purge of any Communist leaders who showed the slightest signs of independence. The resulting imprisonment or execution of a number of Communist stalwarts—Kostov of Bulgaria, Rajk of Hungary, Slansky of Czechoslovakia, Gomulka and Spychalski of Poland, and Ana Pauker of Romania—prevented any further defections and insured continued blind obedience among satellite Communists. At the same time Stalin laid plans for a major purge at home to consolidate his absolute power by ridding himself of any possible rivals among his lieutenants. It was at this critical point that the Russian leader died, leaving his country to the very men he had been about to destroy.

"COLLECTIVE LEADERSHIP"

Those foreign observers who had expected that the death of Stalin would unleash a struggle for his succession were disappointed. Outwardly, at least, the transfer of power went smoothly. Since there was no single individual strong enough to assume all of Stalin's vast powers, responsibility was divided among a group of his closest associates. Georgi M. Malenkov was appointed premier; Lavrenti P. Beria continued as chief of the all-powerful secret police; Vyacheslav M. Molotov, last of the "Old Bolsheviks," was again placed in charge of foreign affairs; and Marshal Nikolai A. Bulganin was made minister of defense, with Marshal Georgi K. Zhukov as his assistant. A little later another important appointment made Nikita S. Khrushchev First Secretary of the Communist Party's Central Committee. This was the post from which Stalin had risen almost thirty years ago to become dictator of the Soviet Union.

From all these changes it appeared as though one-man rule in Russia had been replaced by "collective leadership." Again there were Western observers who predicted that this state of affairs could not last and that Stalin's heirs would soon start quarrelling among themselves. These expectations seemed to come true when, less than four months after Stalin's death, Beria was expelled from the party for "criminal anti-party and anti-government activities," was arrested, and was executed. As far as could be determined, Beria's downfall was due to the other leaders' fear of the overriding influence that the political police and its chief had gained under Stalin. But the purge, in its violent form at least, stopped with Beria and some of his associates. The new regime now settled down to a policy at home and abroad that appeared to be a radical break with the Stalinist past.

The Soviet leaders began by decreeing a far-reaching amnesty of political prisoners. This was followed by promises of reform in the administration of justice, the methods of the secret police, and the running of the "corrective" (that is, slave) labor camps. Of still greater interest to the average Soviet citizen were the announcements made by Malenkov and by Anastas I. Mikoyan, the new minister of domestic trade, that a radical shift toward greater production of consumer goods was being contemplated, "to guarantee a new decisive expansion of the people's welfare." To appeal to the agrarian segment, government control of collective farming was relaxed, and renewed encouragement was given to the cultivation of small individual plots. In addition, agricultural taxation was lowered, some delivery quotas were reduced, and government payments for produce delivered by collective farms were raised.

Still more startling to the outside world than these signs of relaxation at home were the pronouncements on foreign policy made by Russia's new leaders. "There is not one disputed and undecided question," Premier Malenkov said in his inaugural address to the Supreme Soviet, "that cannot be decided by peaceful means on the basis of the mutual understanding of interested countries. This is our attitude toward all states, among them the United States of America." This certainly was a new kind of language for the Kremlin to use. And it was not long before words were followed by deeds. In the summer of 1953 the Soviet Union aided, or at least did not prevent, the signing of an armistice in Korea; a year later the fighting in Indochina was stopped; and in 1955 peace was at long last concluded with Austria.

The most obvious explanation for Russia's new policy of concessions at home and abroad was that it facilitated the transition from one regime to the next by easing tension and calming fears. It remained to be seen how long this "new course" would last. During 1954 there were already signs that the influence of Malenkov was declining, while Khrushchev was gradually emerging as the party's official spokesman. Late in 1954 an editorial in *Pravda* again favored Stalin's emphasis on heavy industry as the basis of Soviet economic and military might, thus reopening that basic issue in Russia's economy. A few months later the Central Committee of the Communist Party passed a resolution stating that "as before, the main task remains the expansion of heavy industry which represents the foundation of our whole national economy." The climax of what must have been a major internal struggle came on February 8, 1955, when Malenkov asked the Supreme Soviet to relieve him of his duties as premier on grounds of incompetence. In particular, he admitted responsibility for errors in agricultural policy, a field with which his rival Khrushchev had been equally, if not more, concerned. Whatever the real causes, the result of the crisis was that Defense Minister Bulganin, upon Khrushchev's recommendation, was appointed Malenkov's successor, with Marshal Zhukov assuming the post vacated by Bulganin. Malenkov, however, was neither exiled nor executed but was merely given a less important position, at the same time maintaining his membership in the Presidium of the Central Committee, the small clique that rules the Soviet Union. Apparently, even in its internal shakeups, the Soviet government had adopted a "new look."

The ouster of Malenkov was a major step forward in the steady rise to power of Nikita S. Khrushchev. Using his influence with the party's rank and file, this shrewd politician within the next three years managed to push aside one after another of his colleagues until in 1958 he emerged as the virtual successor to Stalin. The first to go after Malenkov was Molotov, who was removed as Foreign Minister in 1956. Shortly thereafter riots in Poland and a revolution in Hungary gave rise to dissatisfaction among the members of the Presidium with Khrushchev's policy. In June, 1957, a majority of the Presidium decided to challenge their powerful comrade. But it was already too late. Appealing to the Central Committee over the heads of the Presidium, Khrushchev succeeded in ousting the leaders of the opposition, among them Malenkov and Molotov, and in substituting a number of his own supporters. Khrushchev's maneuver was made possible because he had the support of the army, in the person of Defense Minister Zhukov, who now also became a member of the Presidium. But his political role was short-lived. Fearing Zhukov as a possible rival, Khrushchev in October, 1957, had him removed both from his post as minister and from the Presidium. The final victory of Khrushchev came in March, 1958, when he replaced Bulganin as premier, thus combining the two positions of party and government chiefs which Stalin had held before him.

This was the end of "collective leadership." Like Stalin, Khrushchev today is the acknowledged leader of the Soviet Union and as such the object of adulation at home and of admiration or hatred abroad. He is the public advocate of any major change in his government's policy, supreme arbiter in domestic disputes, and chief voice in Soviet foreign policy. But there are some important differences from the days of Stalin. Russia is no longer a police state run by terror and according to the whims of a paranoid individual. It is a complex bureaucratic dictatorship, administered as rationally and efficiently as its vast size and the character of its people permit. A single individual like Khrushchev can no more hope to manage this gigantic bureaucratic machine than the president of a large corporation can hope to run his enterprise without the assistance of top executives and trained subordinates. The executives and managers in the Soviet Union are supplied by the Communist Party. It is in the party, therefore, that final authority rests. Khrushchev, as head of the party, may have the decisive voice in selecting his lieutenants. But the fact remains that he needs a group of key men to help him run the Soviet Union. To that extent a measure of "collective leadership" still exists. Among the leading figures next to Khrushchev, the most influential are said to be Anastas I. Mikoyan, chief advocate of the "new course" since Stalin; Frol R. Kozlov, a leading member of the party's secretariat; Mikhail A. Suslov, expert on ideology and mouthpiece of what remains of Stalinist forces in Russia; Averki B. Aristov, active in the party's personnel division; and Nikolai G. Ignatov, influential in agrarian affairs. It is men like these who, individually or collectively, may determine the fate of Russia in case something should happen to Khrushchev.

THE KHRUSHCHEV ERA

The most striking feature of Soviet domestic policy since Stalin has been the abandonment of terror as an instrument of government. Ever since the execution of Beria the arbitrary use of force has been de-emphasized, police tribunals have been superseded by regular courts, and slave labor camps no longer are the symbol of Russian communism. The high point of this retreat from terror came in a blistering attack on Stalin by Khrushchev during the twentieth Congress of the Communist Party in Moscow in 1956. For four hours the First Secretary of the party, reportedly weeping at times, denounced the dead dictator, accusing Stalin of excessive self-glorification and abuse of power. Khrushchev charged that "many thousands of honest and innocent Communists" had died as a result of Stalin's "brutal acts of violation of Socialist legality," especially during the purges and forced collectivization of the thirties. Stalin, Khrushchev said, had been "a very distrustful man, sickly suspicious," and had become more so toward the end of his life. Even Stalin's conduct of the war, usually considered one of his great contributions, came under fire for the insufficient preparation of Soviet defenses and the unnecessary sacrifice of hundreds of thousands of Russian lives. Communist history, Khrushchev concluded, had been so deliberately twisted to satisfy Stalin's desire for praise, that it needed to be "thoroughly revised."

The world's reaction to this washing of Russia's dirty linen in public was one of extreme puzzlement. If Khrushchev's speech helped to dissociate the new Soviet regime from its predecessor, it did so at the price of causing confusion in Communist ranks and of giving invaluable ammunition to Russia's opponents abroad. Western critics were quick to point out that while Khrushchev had denounced Stalin for his personal crimes against loyal Communists, he had not renounced the principle of persecuting anti-Communists. Not long afterwards, moreover, the new Russian leader modified his stand, admitting that Stalin's errors had been justified at the time by the need "to safeguard the gains of the revolution." Still, the effect of the tirade against Stalin within Russia was such as to make any return to the repressive practices of the Stalin era difficult, if not impossible.

Not only did Khrushchev give the Russian people freedom from fear, at least as long as they remained loyal Communists, he also gave them many other things the majority of them had never known. "When you have a hungry stomach," he once said in the jovial manner he affects, "it is sometimes very difficult to understand the theory of Marxism-Leninism. But if you can have a nice apartment and good food as well as cultural achievements, then surely everyone must say: 'Certainly I'm for Communism.'" The Soviet Union today is still far removed from the Marxian ideal of a classless society. There is a wide gulf between the upper class—party secretaries, high-ranking bureaucrats, factory and farm managers, leading scientists, and the like—and the mass of workers and peasants. But Russia's leaders now seem to be aware of the benefits to be derived from giving their people some share in the nation's wealth. The result has been a series of measures aimed at mitigating the more glaring differences in income and privileges: a minimum wage has been set; social security benefits have been raised; secondary schooling has been extended; and production of consumer goods has been stepped up. In agriculture, emphasis has been on increased production of meat and dairy products, where Russia had been deficient in the past. Under the current Seven-Year Plan, which is to run until 1965, the Russian people have been promised not only necessities like new housing, but amenities like refrigerators and television sets. A start has even been made in reducing work hours, with the five-day week as the ultimate aim.

The liberalization of Russian life has also spread to the intellectual and cultural sphere. Where under Stalin criticism of government policy was synonymous with treason, such criticism is now permitted, as long as it does not attack basic Communist concepts. The fact that all information media are government-controlled, of course, keeps any unorthodox views from being spread. In the artistic field, "socialist realism" is still the official mode of expression; but "modernism," hitherto tabu, is now tolerated. Soviet writers in recent years have taken advantage of the new freedom to criticize or satirize the Soviet system. Some authors, like Ilya Ehrenburg and Vladimir Dudintsev, have been frowned upon for their outspokenness, and others, notably Boris Pasternak, were officially reprimanded and denied permission to publish some of their works in the Soviet Union. But none of them were given the punishment they would surely have received under Stalin.

The effects of the "thaw" in Soviet domestic affairs—and there have been other manifestations of it, such as the opportunity Russians now have of learning about Western culture—has been to awaken a spirit of loyalty and initiative among the Russian people that had been absent under the Stalinist system of strict obedience based on fear. The government under Khrushchev has made a conscious effort to encourage this initiative, especially in the economic sphere. In the past Russia's economic administration had been highly centralized, all decisions being made by various ministries in Moscow and handed down through a vast and cumbersome bureaucratic hierarchy. This practice has been abandoned by Khrushchev. Instead, regional Economic Councils now supervise most of the enterprises in a given area, except those requiring centralized administration. The managers of individual industries and collective farms have been given greater freedom and responsibility, in the hope that individual initiative, combined with state planning, will make for increased efficiency and insure the economic progress which is the overriding aim of Soviet policy.

Russia's economic goals are for the Communist bloc to outproduce the free world and for the Soviet Union to outproduce the United States. The first aim, according to Khrushchev, will be achieved by 1965, and the second some time between 1965 and 1970. In the opinion of some Western experts, the Russian premier's prediction is no empty boast. Russia has mineral resources far exceeding those of the United States; she has a labor force better disciplined than that of any country and better educated today than at any time in Russian history; and she has the technological "know-how"—as proved by her achievements in the space and missile fields—to make full use of automation and other revolutionary production methods. On the other hand, there are also certain obstacles to Russian progress. Her labor supply has been seriously affected by the reduced birth rate due to World War II, and most workers are still living in European Russia, rather than in the mineral-rich Urals. Russia's capital resources, furthermore, while huge, are not considered sufficient for the vast expansion program contemplated, especially as large funds are needed for defense, space exploration, housing, and other non-productive projects. And finally, the perennial issue of consumer goods versus heavy industry has by no means been resolved. For the time being the Russian government adheres to its slogan "heavy industry first." But it remains to be seen how long this can be maintained in a country whose masses, for the first time, have begun to enjoy some of the rewards of their long and hard work.

These problems, however, do not seem to worry Khrushchev. "Whether you like it or not," he told the West in 1958, "history is on our side. We will bury you." At the end of the Seven-Year Plan in 1965, according to the Russian premier, the Russian people will have produced more of everything—steel, machine tools, homes, shoes, television sets, food—than they have ever produced before. By 1970, he promises, the Russians will enjoy the highest standard of living in the world. The Seven-Year Plan predicts a yearly rate of growth of more than 7 per cent, and results of the last few years bear out this prediction.

The weakest segment of Russia's economy has always been agriculture. Despite the fact that her arable land exceeds that of the United States, the Soviet Union has never yet been faced with the problem of surpluses, which are such a constant headache in the United States. Farming has been the special concern of Premier Khrushchev. Beginning in 1954 he sponsored a program to open up vast areas of virgin soil in Kazakhstan, second largest of the fifteen Soviet republics, and in other parts of Central Asia and Siberia. Thousands of young people were sent out to cultivate these new lands, and despite some reversals in 1957 and 1959, the experiment has proved successful. Another one of Khrushchev's innovations has been increased emphasis on feed grain production, especially corn, to boost the output of meat. In these and other respects he has drawn freely on the advice and example of American farm experts. The basic solution to the farm problem in Russia continues to be sought through collectivization on an ever larger scale, granting at the same time greater independence to individual collectives. In 1958 the machine-tractor stations were discontinued and their equipment sold to the collective farms. To provide greater incentives, the compulsory delivery system has been abolished, capital investment in agriculture has been stepped up, taxes have been lowered, and farm prices have been raised. Russia's farm problem has by no means been solved. But where in the past there used to be periodic crises, there has been a slow yet steady advance in recent years.

Another sphere in which the Soviet Union has made considerable headway under Khrushchev is foreign trade. Under Stalin domestic difficulties and red tape interfered with commercial expansion abroad. Since then things have changed. Russia's exports and imports today still lag far behind those of the United States and western Europe. Nevertheless, sufficient progress has been made to cause America some concern. Most Soviet trade continues to be within the Communist orbit. But concerted efforts are also being made to increase exchange with the free world, particularly with the underdeveloped countries. Extending easy credit on long terms, the Russians and their satellites have signed trade pacts with India, Indonesia, Afghanistan, Egypt, and Cuba. Soviet exports to underdeveloped regions in 1960 were estimated at three billion dollars. Special attention has also been given to boosting Soviet trade with the United States. Khrushchev has offered to buy large quantities of American capital goods—machines and machine tools—if the United States will take raw materials in return or extend credit to the U.S.S.R. There are several obstacles to such a scheme, however, foremost among them the Kremlin's refusal, thus far, to settle its World War II Lend-Lease debt with the United States. Trade between the two superpowers has improved lately, but it is doubtful that it will ever reach the several-billion-dollar mark which Khrushchev has set as his goal.

SOVIET FOREIGN POLICY UNDER KHRUSHCHEV

Russia's motives for expanding her commercial contacts with the free world were not only economic, but also political. We shall discuss below the details of East-West relations during the last few years (see Chapter 6). The keynote of these relations was the search for some form of "coexistence" between the free and Communist worlds. Khrushchev sounded the coexistence note at the opening session of the same Party Congress in 1956 at which he launched his attack against Stalin. In his Secretary's report he asserted that Communist strength made a future war between communism and "capitalist imperialism" no longer inevitable. The working people of the world, he said, would "sooner or later" recognize "the advantages that communism holds out" and would effect a peaceful change from capitalism to socialism, that is, communism. Until then the First Secretary advocated "peaceful coexistence." "Indeed," he said, "there are only two ways: either peaceful coexistence or the most devastating war in history. There is no third alternative." Later on during the Congress he claimed that the Russians "want to be friends with the United States and to co-operate with it in peace and international security and also in the economic and cultural fields. We propose this with good intentions, without holding a knife behind our backs."

Such statements certainly were a far cry from Stalin's anti-Western and anticapitalist tirades. But since they were soon afterwards followed by renewed acts of communist agitation in the Middle East and by the ruthless intervention of Soviet troops in Hungary, the United States could hardly be blamed for not taking Khrushchev's honeyed words at face value. Instead, Washington preferred to adhere to its cold-war strategy of containment. Russia's growing economic might, moreover, soon posed a new challenge to the West. "We say to the leaders of the capitalist states," Khrushchev said in 1959, "let us try out in practice whose system is better, let us compete without war. This is much better than competing in who will produce more arms and who will smash whom. We stand and always will stand for such competition as will help to raise the well-being of the people to a higher level."

Here a new front had been opened in the cold war, a front, moreover, on which the capitalist West had always thought itself superior to the Communist East. At times, as in early 1960, Russia seemed on the verge of abandoning her economic challenge in favor of more drastic means to force a showdown. But she soon again returned to competitive economic coexistence as the major theme of her foreign policy. By proving that communism is superior to capitalism in assuring the good life for all, Russia hopes to win to her side, and to the side of communism, the as yet uncommitted peoples of the world, whose ultimate allegiance may decide the outcome of the cold war.

REVOLT AMONG THE SATELLITES

One of the best ways of testing the sincerity of Russia's peaceful pronouncements on foreign policy is to see what changes, if any, her relations with the satellite nations of eastern Europe have undergone during the Khrushchev era. The same Western observers who expected Russia to become embroiled in civil war once Stalin's iron grip had been removed, also speculated on possible uprisings among the enslaved nationalities behind the iron curtain. But such expectations proved premature. The "new course" adopted by Stalin's successors in Russia was soon imitated in the satellites. "Collective leadership" became the order of the day; political prisoners were released; there was a shift in emphasis from heavy industry to consumer goods; and collectivization in agriculture was modified or abandoned. A second wave of anti-Stalinism occurred in 1956, following Khrushchev's blast against the architect of the satellite system. Reaction differed from country to country. Almost everywhere Communist leaders suddenly realized that, like Stalin, they might be accused of "one-man rule." To forestall such charges, they began to rehabilitate the dead, those former comrades they had only recently helped to liquidate on suspicion of Titoism. In Bulgaria Stalinist leaders were replaced by more moderate Communists. In Czechoslovakia some second-string leaders were purged. In Poland an amnesty was proclaimed for some eighty thousand persons and notorious Stalinists were dismissed. And while workers' riots at Poznan in June, 1956, were put down with the usual harshness, the trial of the surviving rioters, by Communist standards, was fair and the verdict moderate.

None of the actions just described had in any way weakened Moscow's domination over eastern Europe. On the contrary, the Soviet Union in 1955 had strengthened its hold by sponsoring the Warsaw Pact of mutual assistance (usually considered the Eastern counterpart of NATO), which united the armed forces of the Soviet bloc under the command of Soviet Marshal Ivan Konev, and permitted Russia to station troops within the satellite countries. Furthermore, the admission to the United Nations in December, 1955, of those satellites not yet members (Albania, Bulgaria, Hungary, and Romania) was seen as an indication that the *status quo* in eastern Europe was recognized by the rest of the world. Still, there were some signs of a growing desire among the satellite regimes, if not for complete independence from Soviet control, at least for greater freedom from constant Russian interference. Such freedom Tito had won for Yugoslavia in 1948, although at the price of being expelled from the Communist family. What if a *modus vivendi* could be found between Tito and communism? This, it seemed, was the aim of the new men in the Kremlin. Their dealings with Yugoslavia, therefore, were observed with intense interest by all satellites.

Relations between Moscow and Belgrade, chiefly due to Soviet initiative, had improved rapidly since 1953. The climax came in 1955 and 1956 as first the Cominform (which had expelled Yugoslavia in 1948) was dissolved, then Foreign Minister Molotov (who had led the fight against Tito) was dismissed, and finally Tito visited Moscow to repay an earlier visit by Khrushchev and Bulganin. At the end of his stay Tito and Bulganin signed an agreement officially renewing relations between their two countries and charting a common course on many important issues of foreign policy. Still more important was a simultaneous declaration by Tito and Khrushchev, in their roles as Secretaries of their respective Communist parties, defining the principles that were to govern relations between the Communist parties of sovereign states. Its key sentence declared that "the roads of Socialist development are different in different countries." Here was a belated recognition by the Kremlin of one of the main principles of Titoism: that not all Communist countries need follow blindly the Russian lead and example. The implications of this Moscow Declaration were not lost upon the satellites who, already restive, now became even more so. In the course of 1956 it became clear that the Soviets were getting worried over the desire for emancipation from Russian rule among their subject peoples. In the fall of the year Khrushchev, in long talks with Tito, tried to find ways of reconciling the spread of Titoism with continued Soviet domination over eastern Europe. At this point, in late October, 1956, events in Poland and Hungary took the initiative out of Russian hands.

Both these countries had been known in the past for their fervent nationalism; both were devoutly Catholic; both harbored a deep-seated hatred of Russia that went back long before the advent of communism; and both, under the provisions of the Warsaw Pact, still had to endure the presence of large Soviet garrisons on their soil. The roots of the upheavals that occurred within these two satellites, therefore, were quite similar. Both revolts were motivated by strong nationalist sentiments against the domination of a hated foreign power. In the revolts themselves, however, there were significant differences between Poland and Hungary. These differences were mainly responsible for the success of rebellion in the one and its failure in the other.

Events in Poland grew largely out of the general relaxation of Communist rule that had taken place there in the early months of 1956. One of the country's leading Communists, Wladyslaw Gomulka, who had been purged on charges of Titoism in 1948, had been rehabilitated in the spring of 1956. But Gomulka refused to rejoin the government as long as Soviet Marshal Konstantin Rokossovsky remained Polish defense minister and a member of Poland's Politburo. In October, 1956, despite the intervention of Khrushchev and Molotov, Gomulka had his way: the Politburo elected him party secretary and ousted Rokossovsky. For a tense moment it looked as though the Russians might use force to counteract this nationalist revolt of Poland's Communists. But as there were threats of large-scale popular unrest, Gomulka succeeded not only in getting the Soviet leaders to withdraw their forces to the frontiers, but also in calming down his compatriots. He told his people that future relations with Russia would follow the pattern laid down by Tito and that the nation's political life would become more democratic. National elections were scheduled for 1957; persons guilty of participating in the Poznan riots were pardoned; Soviet officers who held high posts in the Polish armed forces were removed; and Cardinal Wyszynski was freed after three years' detention. Here, then, was an example of how to engineer a successful rebellion and to achieve at least partial freedom from Soviet interference. It was this example of Poland that inspired the Hungarians to try for similar concessions.

The situation in Hungary was much more complicated. Here, too, a great deal of resentment had built up, not only against Russian domination, but against communism in general. The peasants hated collectivization, the workers suffered from a low standard of living, and the whole population opposed the antireligious policy of the Communist regime. Control of the Hungarian Communist movement had long been contested between

Matyas Rakosi, a dedicated Stalinist, and Imre Nagy, a loyal Communist, but with strong nationalist leanings. After Stalin's death Nagy had become premier of Hungary, but in 1955 Rakosi had taken over. In 1956 Rakosi, too, was forced to give way, but his replacement, Erno Gerö, while an anti-Stalinist, was still a loyal follower of Moscow. When the news of Poland's successful rebellion reached Budapest in late October, therefore, thousands of Hungarians, especially students and workers, demanded the reinstatement of Nagy. The Gerö government immediately invited Soviet troops to help restore order. To satisfy the rioters, however, the Communist Central Committee also made Nagy premier. Nagy thereupon promised "democratization and improved living standards" and urged the crowds to disperse. But the rioters refused to go home. When they were fired upon by Soviet tanks, they fought back with arms supplied by the Hungarian army. From Budapest the rebellion spread to the provinces, and from an initial fight against the Russians, the revolt now turned against communism as such, especially the hated political police who had been responsible for most of the repressive measures of the Communist regime. Premier Nagy continued his efforts to restore calm. He invited two non-Communists into his government, abolished collectivization, declared a general amnesty for the rebels, and promised free elections and the establishment of a multiparty system. Still more important, he succeeded in getting the Russians to withdraw their tanks from Budapest.

Up to this point, the Hungarian revolution, in its general outlines, had fairly well followed the Polish example. Moscow, moreover, now announced far-reaching concessions for all its subject peoples. In a sweeping statement, comparable only to Khrushchev's indictment of Stalin eight months earlier, the Soviet Union admitted that in its dealings with the satellites it had committed "violations and mistakes which belittled the principle of equality." Instead, Russia's leaders now proposed to regulate their economic relations with eastern Europe in such a way as to recognize "national sovereignty, mutual advantage, and equality." They declared their readiness to revise the Warsaw Pact so as to eliminate the further stationing of Soviet troops on satellite soil. The aim of the Soviet Union, this hopeful pronouncement concluded, was to create a "Commonwealth of Socialist States," bound together by ties of ideology and common interests rather than force and terror.

But no sooner had this astounding confession of guilt and promise of reform been made, than the Russians again reversed their course. Hungarian insurgents had continued their fight against the withdrawing Soviet forces, and in their ransacking of Communist headquarters, the revolutionaries had made plain their anticommunism. It was this anti-Communist, as well as anti-Russian, nature of the Hungarian revolt that prompted Russia's renewed reprisals. On November 1 the Russians turned their tanks around and proceeded to put down the revolution. Premier Nagy thereupon repudiated the Warsaw Pact, declared Hungary a neutral country, and addressed an appeal to the United Nations to help defend Hungarian neutrality. But the Western powers at the time were preoccupied with events in the Middle East, where the Suez crisis was reaching its climax (see p. 153). On November 4 the Russians launched a full-scale offensive against Budapest, unleashing a reign of terror not only against the insurgents, but also against those Communists who had strayed too far from the pro-Moscow course. A new Communist dictatorship headed by Janos Kadar was set up, with a program that embodied some of the promises that Nagy had made earlier. The new program, however, did not include free elections, a multiparty system, and the proclamation of Hungarian neutrality. In the bloody aftermath of Hungary's heroic struggle for independence, some 35,000 persons were imprisoned, hundreds were put to death, and 186,000 of the freedom fighters fled abroad. The final chapter in the Hungarian tragedy was not written until 1958, when Imre Nagy and his closest associates were executed upon orders from Moscow.

THE SATELLITES UNDER KHRUSHCHEV

There have been no major outbreaks of resistance to communism in eastern Europe since 1956. Yet even though the satellite system withstood its gravest crisis and Russia continued to rule supreme, the liberalization that we have seen at work in Soviet domestic affairs continued also to be felt in the satellite countries. The basic Communist aim of economic development through heavy industry and collectivization remains the same today as under Stalin. But a good many concessions have been made in recent years to counteract the discontent that had first flared up in East Germany and Czechoslovakia in 1953 and had culminated in the risings in Poland and Hungary three years later. Terrorist methods and purges, so common under Stalin, have been abandoned; efforts are being made to improve living standards by raising wages, increasing social security benefits, and making available more consumer goods and better housing; and there has been at least some relaxation of cultural orthodoxy. The Soviet Union is counting on the nations of the Communist bloc to play their part in the drive to challenge the economic lead of the West. While under Stalin the satellites were exploited as tributaries, they have since become beneficiaries of Soviet aid; and where in the past they were mere puppets of Moscow, they are now junior partners in a joint enterprise.

The hold which Russia and communism have over the satellites, of course, differs in each country. It is least strong in Poland. For a while after 1956 it even seemed as though Wladyslaw Gomulka might become another Tito. Just as in Yugoslavia, collectivization in Poland was abandoned, industrial management was decentralized, economic aid from the West was welcomed, and a measure of cultural freedom was granted. More recently, however, this trend has been reversed. Under the Polish Seven-Year Plan (1959–65), the state has again tightened its grip on the economy in an attempt to double or even triple production in certain key industries. Some efforts are now being made at collectivization; and "anti-Socialist influences" in the cultural sphere are being discouraged. Still, Poland continues to occupy a unique position halfway between a satellite and a true ally of the Soviet Union. Gomulka and his Polish United Workers' (Communist) Party are trying to steer a careful course between keeping their people quiet and satisfying the Russians. The latter have shown considerable understanding for this delicate task and have permitted Poland a degree of autonomy not enjoyed by any other satellite.

East Germany and Czechoslovakia are in a different category. Here, too, popular unrest had led to riots in 1953, but they had been quickly subdued, and the fate of Hungary discouraged any further opposition. As the most highly industrialized among the satellites, these countries are of greatest importance to the Soviet development scheme. East Germany, firmly controlled by Communist boss Walter Ulbricht, has only recently emerged from long years of austerity. The government has promised the East Germans that they will catch up to the West German standard of living by 1965. But even so, the exodus of thousands of refugees to the

West each month continues. Similar promises of economic gains made by the Communist rulers in Prague are more likely to be fulfilled. Czechoslovakia is the most prosperous of all the satellites and the government of Antonin Novotny, while hardly more popular than Communist regimes elsewhere, is tolerated for that reason. Both East Germany and Czechoslovakia are still having trouble with their farmers, many of whom have resisted collectivization. Czechoslovakia intends to solve this problem under her third Five-Year Plan (1961–65) through complete socialization and amalgamation of existing collectives into larger and more efficient units.

Like East Germany and Czechoslovakia, the remaining four satellites in southeastern Europe—Hungary, Romania, Bulgaria, and Albania—are following a neo-Stalinist line of heavy industry and collectivization, which recognizes the leadership of the Soviet Union while allowing for certain national differences. Such policy has been aptly described as "neo-Stalinism in one country." In Hungary the outward signs of the 1956 uprisings have been carefully erased, although the human scars of the tragedy remain. Russia and some of the other Communist states have bolstered the government of Janos Kadar with massive economic aid and the Hungarian people on the whole are living better today than they have for some years past. Industrialization has been fostered and collectivization has made rapid progress since 1958. Romania is efficiently run by Gheorghe Gheorghiu-Dej and his associates. Like most Communist rulers, they have made ambitious plans for doubling their nation's industrial output by 1965. Bulgaria is one of the most docile of satellites, tied to Russia by a friendship that goes back to the nineteenth century. Her agriculture is almost wholly collectivized and her industrial progress has been most remarkable. Albania, finally, is more primitive and isolated than any other Communist state, deeply dependent on Soviet aid and a faithful follower of the Kremlin's line.

The one discordant note in the Communist concert of eastern Europe continues to be Yugoslavia. We have seen how she had again drawn closer to Moscow during the days immediately after Stalin's death. But this rapprochement did not last long. In an attempt to assert his continued independence, Tito in 1958 issued a program for the Yugoslav Communist Party which denied the Soviet Union's claim to leadership in the Communist world, accused the Soviet state of violating some basic concepts of

Marxist-Leninist theory, and blamed the East as much as the West for the international tension of the cold war. Moscow's reaction to this criticism "spearheaded against the socialist countries" was to turn its back once again on Tito. The Yugoslav leader, for his part, has not reciprocated by cutting his ties with the Communist states. He has recognized East Germany, even though it cost him the good will of the West German Federal Republic. He has dissociated himself from the military commitments to Greece and Turkey. And he has renounced military aid from the United States, while welcoming continued economic aid. In the eyes of the world, this makes him a "neutralist," a category which, Tito claims, does not exist. "There can be no neutral nations," he has said. "That does not mean one must belong to a power bloc. . . . Yet one can co-operate with everyone."

It is difficult to make any final evaluation of the changes that have taken place in Russia's relations with her satellites during the Khrushchev era. The main difference has been summed up this way: While until 1956 it was expected that every eastern European Communist regime imitate and follow the lead of the Soviet Union as closely as possible, today such conformity is expected only in what the Russians consider essential. Western observers have wondered whether the admission of the satellites to limited partnership was a sign of strength or weakness. Most of them seem to agree that it was the former, that Russia's position in eastern Europe at present is stronger than ever. The only uncertain factor in the Communist world today is Red China, which may some day challenge Russia's leadership (see Chapter 5). The question, finally, that has been asked most frequently in the West since Stalin's death is whether the changes that have taken place in the Communist world will work for or against peace. The answer to this will lie in the way in which the free world will rise to the challenge of "competitive coexistence" that has emerged as the major issue in the East-West struggle (see Chapter 6).

5

UNDERDEVELOPED COUNTRIES

This street scene in Lagos, Nigeria, is typical of the way in which many of the world's former colonial peoples still live at the present time. WIDE WORLD PHOTO.

Hundreds of millions of people throughout the world have learned that it is not ordained that they must live in perpetual poverty and illness, on the ragged edge of starvation. Their political leaders press the point home. In a variety of ways this drive is moving forward by fits and starts, often uncertain of its direction. It is sometimes involved in the free world struggle against communism, sometimes not. It is clearly in the interests of the United States that we assist this movement so that these countries may take their places as free, independent, progressing and stable members of the community of nations.

PRESIDENT DWIGHT D. EISENHOWER,
in an address to Congress, February 17, 1960

THE END OF COLONIALISM

SOME OF THE MOST IMPORTANT CHANGES since World War II have happened in Asia and Africa. Colonialism, that is, the domination of whites over nonwhites, has been on the defensive at least since World War I. But it was only after 1945 that it suffered its decisive defeat. One after another, peoples that had never known political independence or had lost such independence long ago, have won their freedom. As a result, the number of the world's sovereign states has grown by more than forty, and colonialism is today very much a thing of the past. There are many reasons for the recent success of these native revolts: the weakening of the Western colonial powers as a result of the war; the spread of communism and its appeal to backward peoples; the rise of a Western-educated native intelligentsia providing the necessary leadership in the struggle for independence; and most important, the growth of nationalism among the peoples of Asia and

Africa. This colonial nationalism, in the opinion of its adherents at least, is quite different from the chauvinistic nationalism that we have known in the Western world. It is, in the words of President Sukarno of Indonesia, "a young and progressive creed, . . . a struggle for the simple human demands which the rest of the world has long taken for granted."

The actual events of the various native revolts have differed widely and will be treated separately. Yet almost all the new nations that have thus sprung into existence have been equally concerned with three major issues: (1) opposition to any form of colonialism; (2) demand for full racial equality; and (3) need for economic and technical aid. In their relations with the rest of the world, on the other hand, these nations have followed quite different courses. Some of them have aligned themselves with one or the other side in the cold war. But the majority of them have come to realize the advantages of maintaining an independent, neutral position. This enables them to bargain for help from both East and West and to play the role of an important "third force" in the global balance of power.

THE INDEPENDENCE OF INDIA AND PAKISTAN

The first major additions to the community of free nations after World War II came in 1947 with the transformation of India, Britain's most valuable colony, into the two sovereign dominions of India and Pakistan. India's struggle for independence has a long history, dating back before World War I. It was led by India's largest political party, the Indian National Congress, under British-educated Mohandas K. Gandhi and Jawaharlal Nehru. The problem of independence was complicated by the extreme diversity of the vast subcontinent, inhabited by some four hundred million people speaking at least thirty different languages. Aside from the regions directly administered by the British, there were more than five hundred native states under indirect British rule. In addition, the French and Portuguese held some small bases along the Indian coast. As for the population of India, it was divided by a rigid caste system, by wide extremes of wealth and poverty, and by religious differences between a Hindu majority and a large Moslem minority. The latter, organized in the Moslem League under Mohammed

Ali Jinnah, feared suppression by the Hindus and demanded an independent Moslem state of Pakistan.

The struggle for independence reached its culmination during World War II. The British, recognizing the inevitable, were perfectly willing to set India free, but to prevent internal chaos insisted that a workable government be set up first. As a transition measure the British at the end of the war sponsored the election of a constituent assembly in which both Hindus and Moslems were represented. Hindu-Moslem differences over the future of India, combined with serious food shortages, caused frequent riots and thousands of deaths. In early 1947 the British government announced its intention of transferring governmental power into Indian hands not later than the middle of 1948. It was largely due to the good offices of Britain's last viceroy, Lord Louis Mountbatten, that the Indian problem was finally solved. In many communities religious fanaticism flared into savage riots, of which Gandhi himself became a victim. But by August 15, 1947, the process of partition was completed, and on that day both India and Pakistan were made into dominions, that is, fully sovereign states. They were to remain members of the Commonwealth for one year, after which they were free to withdraw. India in 1949 became a federal republic, the Union of India, but decided to stay within the Commonwealth. Pakistan in 1956 followed India's example and likewise became a republic. The large number of native states were given the choice of setting up a third independent state or joining either India or Pakistan. They adopted the second alternative, with most of them joining India.

The island of Ceylon off the southeast coast of India, in the past administered separately from British India, was granted self-government in 1946 and was admitted to full dominion status in 1948. In its foreign policy, the government of Ceylon at first leaned to the West. Since 1956, however, it has taken a neutralist stand and drawn closer to the Communist powers. There has also been agitation for changing Ceylon from a dominion into a republic. As for the smaller French and Portuguese holdings on the Indian mainland, France relinquished her foothold in 1954, but Portugal, despite Indian nationalist agitation, has held on to the region around Goa on the west coast. Another disputed area that has caused considerable tension is the former native state of Kashmir in the extreme north. Its people are predominantly Moslem. When the Hindu Maharajah of Kashmir sought to join the region to India, Moslem tribesmen from Pakistan invaded Kashmir where they became involved in war with Hindu forces from India. The United Nations finally intervened and in 1948–49 was able to negotiate a cease-fire. India and Pakistan agreed on a plebiscite to determine the status of Kashmir, but sporadic border clashes have continued and the plebiscite has never been held. India, meanwhile, is holding the richest two-thirds of Kashmir, while Pakistan controls the rest.

There have been other difficulties between India and Pakistan, caused chiefly by the hurried withdrawal of the British and the almost impossible task of dividing India's assets between the two new republics. Additional problems arose over the exchange of nearly twelve million Moslems and Hindus, which led to a murderous civil war, especially in the Punjab region. The resulting ill feeling has made any peaceful collaboration between India and Pakistan extremely difficult. Yet at the same time the two are closely interdependent. Pakistan holds much of the strategic northern frontier and most of the best agricultural lands. India has the more valuable natural and industrial resources and the manpower to defend the subcontinent against possible invasion. It was only when Communist China began encroaching upon India's frontiers in 1959 that relations between India and Pakistan improved and some progress was made in settling their many disputes.

The Union of India, with an area one-third the size of the United States and a population of four hundred million, is by far the more important of the two states. Because of Britain's longstanding practice of using Indians at all lower administrative levels, the change of regimes, except for the consequences of partition, went smoothly. Politically, the Congress Party of Prime Minister Nehru has been able to maintain a parliamentary majority. It has lost some of its popular following in recent years and a multiparty system is now in the making. Communism, considering the country's poverty, has not been a serious threat, although Communist influence in some states, such as Kerala, has been strong. India's main problems have been economic. Its large population, growing at the rate of six million each year, and still mostly illiterate, is desperately poor and undernourished. The government is doing its best through measures ranging from birth control to land reform and industrialization. But since India refrains scrupulously from limiting individual freedom, progress has been slow. An added difficulty has been the persistence of social customs and practices officially outlawed, such as the caste system and the subjection of women.

In its efforts to improve the country's economy, the Indian government has followed the Communist practice of state planning through five-year plans. Its major reforms have been concentrated on agriculture. Policies have varied between the very effective community projects (improving farming methods, largely with American aid) and the less effective movement of land distribution advocated by Shri Vinoba Bhave, a disciple of Gandhi. In industry the main emphasis has been on basic industries and long-range public projects. The effect of such projects will take time to be felt. India has abundant natural resources that have hardly begun to be developed. What she needs more than anything is foreign capital. The United States has contributed more than 2 billion dollars to India's economic development and in recent years the Soviet Union, too, has supplied large funds. Even with such outside help, however, India still has a long, hard road. If she succeeds in her efforts, India will have proved to the other underdeveloped countries that progress can be had through economic planning without paying the heavy price of communism.

In her foreign relations India has followed a course of nonalignment with either side in the cold war. The architect of this policy is Prime Minister Nehru. His basic aims are laid down in the famous "five principles" formulated in 1954: "Respect for other countries' territorial integrity and sovereignty; nonaggression; noninterference in other nations' internal affairs; equality and mutual benefit; and peaceful coexistence." Despite this declaration of neutrality, India in the past has leaned more toward the East than toward the West. Her leaders have professed admiration for the Soviet Union, have supported Russia's stand on such crucial issues as disarmament and opposition to regional military alliances, and have consistently favored the admission of Red China to the United Nations. To understand India's position, we must remember her traditional policy of nonviolence, inherited from the days of Gandhi; her long and bitter first-hand experience with Western colonialism; and the fact that India is situated much closer to China and Russia than to the West. Still, in the last few years Indians have come to take a somewhat less favorable view of communism. The first disillusionment came with Russia's ruthless in-

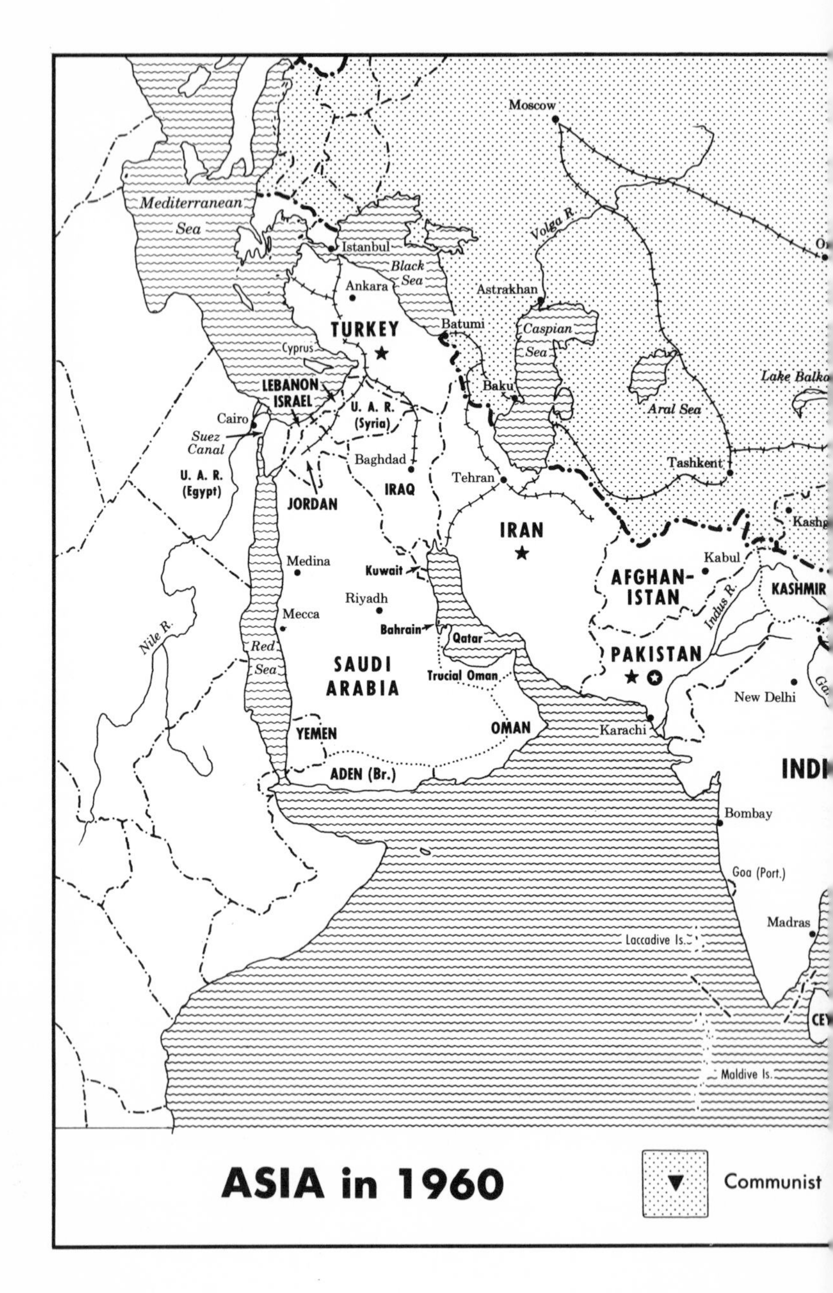
Moscow
Mediterranean Sea
Istanbul
Black Sea
Ankara
Astrakhan
Volga R.
TURKEY
Batumi
Caspian Sea
Cyprus
Baku
Aral Sea
Lake Balka
LEBANON
ISRAEL
U. A. R. (Syria)
Cairo
Suez Canal
U. A. R. (Egypt)
Baghdad
IRAQ
Tehran
Tashkent
JORDAN
IRAN
Kashg
Kabul
Medina
Kuwait
AFGHAN-ISTAN
KASHMIR
Riyadh
Mecca
Indus R.
Nile R.
Bahrain
Qatar
PAKISTAN
Red Sea
SAUDI ARABIA
Trucial Oman
New Delhi
YEMEN
OMAN
Karachi
ADEN (Br.)
INDI
Bombay
Goa (Port.)
Madras
Laccadive Is.
CE
Maldive Is.
ASIA in 1960
Communist

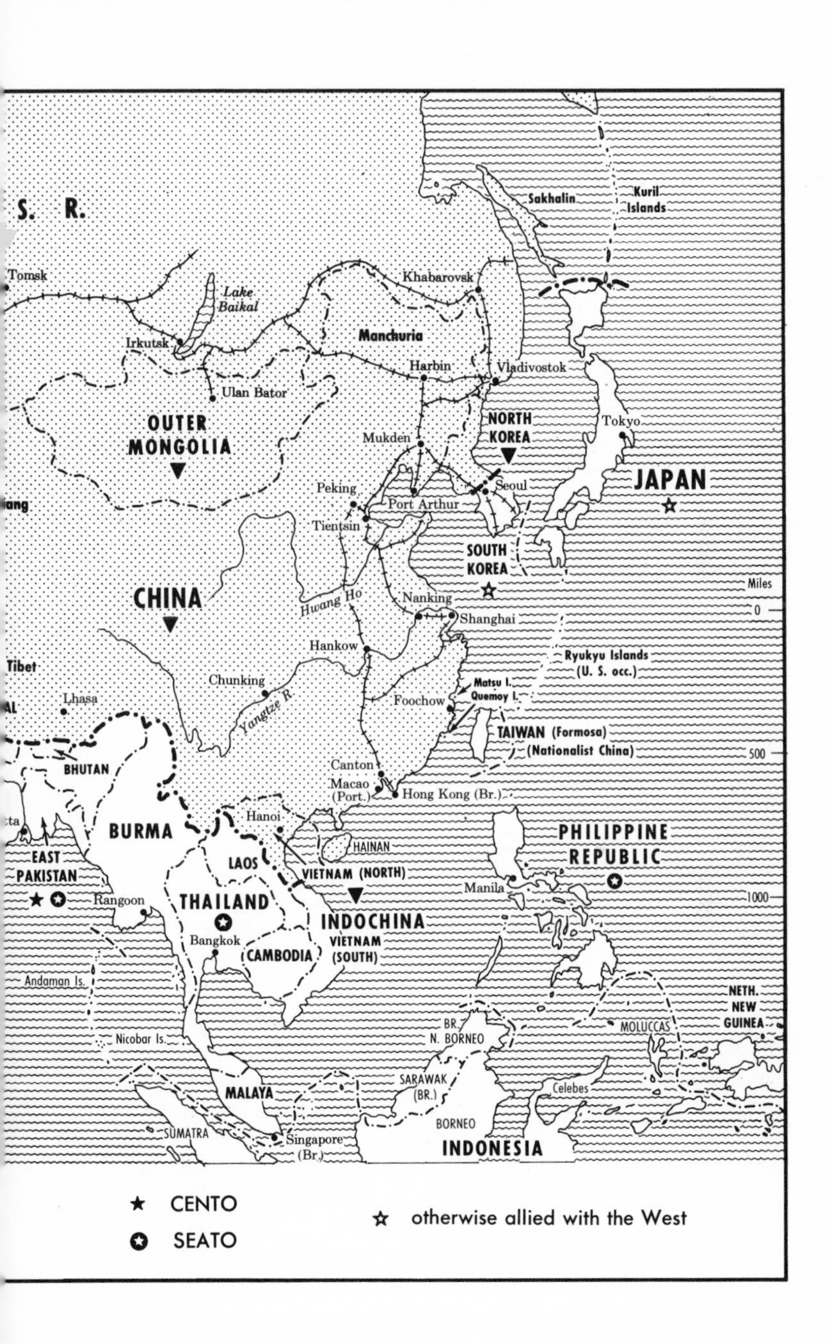
S. R.
Tomsk
Lake Baikal
Irkutsk
Ulan Bator
OUTER MONGOLIA
Manchuria
Khabarovsk
Sakhalin
Kuril Islands
Harbin
Vladivostok
Mukden
NORTH KOREA
Tokyo
JAPAN
Peking
Port Arthur
Seoul
Tientsin
SOUTH KOREA
CHINA
Hwang Ho
Nanking
Shanghai
Miles
0
500
1000
Hankow
Ryukyu Islands
(U. S. occ.)
Tibet
Chunking
Yangtze R.
Lhasa
Foochow
Matsu I.
Quemoy I.
TAIWAN (Formosa)
(Nationalist China)
BHUTAN
Canton
Macao
(Port.)
Hong Kong (Br.)
Hanoi
BURMA
HAINAN
PHILIPPINE REPUBLIC
EAST PAKISTAN
LAOS
VIETNAM (NORTH)
Manila
Rangoon
THAILAND
INDOCHINA
Bangkok
CAMBODIA
VIETNAM (SOUTH)
Andaman Is.
NETH. NEW GUINEA
BR. N. BORNEO
MOLUCCAS
Nicobar Is.
SARAWAK (BR.)
Celebes
MALAYA
BORNEO
SUMATRA
Singapore (Br.)
INDONESIA
★ CENTO
✪ SEATO
☆ otherwise allied with the West

tervention in Hungary. This was followed by China's similar action in Tibet. Finally, India herself felt the direct threat of Communist aggression when in 1959 Red China laid claim to certain border regions in Kashmir and in the area of India's Northeast Frontier Agency. Attempts to settle these differences by negotiation failed, as Indian nationalism stood firm against foreign encroachment. Nevertheless, India's relations with China remain correct and she continues to profess friendship for the Soviet Union. The genuine affection of the Indian people for the United States, on the other hand, was shown in the warm reception they gave President Eisenhower during his visit in 1959.

While India thus tries to steer a middle course in world affairs, her sister-nation, Pakistan, as a member of both the Southeast Asia and the Central Treaty Organizations, has squarely thrown in her lot with the West. Pakistan has banned the Communist Party, although she maintains relations with Communist China. In her domestic affairs, Pakistan, during the first decade of her independence, went through troubled times. With the death of Mohammed Ali Jinnah in 1948 the country lost its most capable political leader. Representative government existed in name only, as professional politicians ruled an illiterate population to suit their own personal ambitions. In 1958 the army finally stepped in, dissolved Parliament and proclaimed martial law. Since then Pakistan has been under the military dictatorship of British-trained General Mohammed Ayub Khan. Pakistan's political instability has interfered with her economic development. The country, only one-third as large as India, is divided into two areas separated by a thousand miles of Indian territory. Pakistan's population of ninety million is split among several nationalities that have little in common except their Moslem religion. Literacy in 1947 was only 14 per cent, the average life span was little more than twenty years, and per capita income was fifty dollars per year. About 80 per cent of Pakistanis are farmers, with wheat, rice, cotton, and especially jute the major crops. Pakistan has few natural resources and industrialization is still only in its beginnings. Some economic progress has been made under Ayub Khan, and some of the popular enthusiasm that prevailed during the early years of the new nation has been rekindled. The United States has given Pakistan more than 1 billion dollars in economic and technical aid, but a large military budget is a constant financial drain. While a gradual approach to representative government is being made on the local level, the establishment of democracy at the top is still remote.

COMMUNIST CHINA

Of still greater importance than the emancipation of India from three centuries of British rule has been the emergence of Communist China as a major factor in world affairs. We have already discussed the Chinese Civil War and the establishment of the People's Republic of China in 1949 (see Chapter 1). Despite Red China's exhaustion from fighting against both Chiang Kai-shek and Japan, the new regime almost immediately became involved in another conflict in Korea. The Korean War cost China an estimated 840,000 casualties and 2.4 billion dollars and put China under a partial economic embargo at a most critical time. Despite these initial difficulties, the Communists were able to complete their subjugation of some six hundred million Chinese. This achievement testifies to the inherent strength of Chinese communism.

The communization of China was a gradual process, involving not only a complete political and economic change, but also a social and psychological transformation. The first years of the new regime, aside from economic reconstruction and the Korean War, were devoted mainly to "purifying" the ranks of China's Communists, reducing the power of the middle class, and "remolding" the minds of Chinese intellectuals along Marxist lines. Communist functionaries guilty of "commandism," that is, lording it over the people, were purged from the ranks, and the Communist Party, heretofore strongest among the peasants, was gradually given a larger component of industrial workers. Such age-old Chinese vices as "corruption, waste, and bureaucratism" were attacked and bribery, tax evasion, and stealing of state property were eradicated. Combining terror with persuasion, this policy of "criticism and self-criticism" succeeded in converting the majority of Chinese into obedient and, in some cases, enthusiastic followers of the new regime.

When it came to organizing the government, China's Communists closely followed the Russian model. Under the constitution of 1954 "supreme state power" is vested in a "National People's Congress" of 1,200 elected members. The influence of this body, however, is as insignificant as that of Russia's Supreme Soviet. Executive power is in the hands of the chairman of the republic (president)—a post held until 1959 by Mao Tse-tung and since then by Liu Shao-chi—and of a State Council (cabinet) under Premier Chou En-lai. As in Russia, the real power rests with the Communist Party. It is dominated by its Central Committee and its chairman, Mao Tse-tung. This former peasant's son—at once poet and politician, classical scholar and warlord, Marxist theoretician and ruthless dictator—is thus the most powerful man in Communist China. Next to Mao there are a handful of other key figures. Besides Liu Shao-chi and Chou En-lai, these include Chu Teh, for years leader of the Chinese Red Army, Chen Yun, the party's chief spokesman on economic policy, and Teng Hsiao-ping, secretary general of the party. These men, together with Mao, form the standing committee of the party's twenty-man Politburo and exercise a kind of collective leadership.

According to the constitution, the main task of the Chinese state is "to bring about, step by step, the socialist industrialization of the country." This goal was to be achieved in three five-year plans. The first of these, covering the years 1953 through 1957, went under the slogan "production and austerity," which well describes all of Communist China's economic policy. China's economy in the past had been predominantly agrarian. To win the support of the peasants, one of the first acts of the Communists had been to divide the large holdings of the former landlords. Since this interfered with efficient production, however, the first Five-Year Plan called for a change from individual cultivation toward large-scale collectivization. By the end of 1957 agricultural output still lagged, but industry had made great strides, increasing its yearly production by 25 per cent. Even so, Western observers remained sceptical about China's future, predicting that it would take at least another generation before she would become a first-class industrial power.

This estimate had to be drastically revised after 1958. Beginning that year the Communists launched their second Five-Year Plan, the aim of which was to catch up with and surpass Great Britain in the output of steel, coal, and other major products. Adopting measures far more radical than any employed by Stalin during the 1930's, China by the end of 1960 claimed to be producing seven times as much coal, ten times as much electric power, and eighteen times as much steel as she had in the best years before the Communists took over. Railway and highway mileage were said to be more than twice what they were before 1949 and vast new regions in Central Asia, rich in oil, minerals, and fertile soil, had been opened up by millions of new settlers. Even discounting some of these claims as propaganda, such achievements are impressive. The dramatic promise made in 1958 of a "great leap forward" is certainly being fulfilled. "Truly heaven-shaking changes have taken place in China," Premier Chou En-lai exulted in 1959, "the Chinese people have turned from slaves in a hell on earth into fearless masters of their own destiny."

The second half of this statement is far from true. Communist China's economic gains have been made at the price of unheard-of sacrifices on the part of the Chinese. The most novel feature of the second Five-Year Plan was the formation of the so-called people's communes. These were large mergers of collective farms, including several thousand peasant households and covering many square miles. The purpose of these new social units was first and foremost to make for greater efficiency and output in agriculture. The ultimate aim of the communes, it seems, is more than merely economic. Through strict regimentation and collective living, China's traditional family system is to be eradicated. Members of a commune work and live together; their children are raised in communal nurseries; work is supplemented by drill in a communal militia; and with all basic needs supplied, wages are cut to a minimum. Here is a wholly new form of Communist society, more revolutionary than anything ever seen in Russia. The commune system, which is now also being introduced in the cities, is the ultimate in Communist control. The individual becomes a mere cog in a monstrous machine, geared toward greater and greater production. His fate is to work and obey, to live and endure.

The "great leap forward," which started out on a wave of semihysteria in 1958, has been somewhat modified since. Life in the rural communes has lost part of its drabness as peasant families have been given back some land and a few domestic animals for their own use, and as a limited amount of individual income has again been permitted. But this may be a tactical rather than strategic retreat, made necessary by agriculture's failure to keep up with production goals. There can be no doubt that the Communist regime is strong enough to enforce any policy it feels necessary, no matter how harsh. Mao Tse-tung has admitted that his regime has liquidated more than 800,000 persons. Western sources put the number of victims at between 10 and 20 million. No wonder there have been few reports of open resistance from China. A population ruled by terror, however, can hardly be expected to achieve the optimistic goals which the "great leap" calls for. The Communists, therefore, have perfected more subtle ways of "socialist re-education" through indoctrination and brainwashing. In 1957 Mao Tse-tung startled the world by conceding that not all was harmonious even in a Communist society. There may be "contradictions," he said, "between the masses of the people and their leaders." To resolve these contradictions they must be brought into the open. "Let a hundred flowers bloom," the Chinese leader said, "let a hundred schools of thought contend." The people must be encouraged to speak their minds so that their grievances can be known and corrected. This invitation to let off steam actually brought some outspoken criticism of the regime; but when this criticism became too violent, Mao turned against the crops of "poisonous weeds" that crowded out the flowers and the campaign of self-criticism was abandoned.

One of the most effective means of quieting discontent at home is to turn it against real or imaginary enemies abroad. The basic tenets of Red China's foreign policy have been its ardent anti-Americanism and its professions of friendship for the Soviet Union. United States–Chinese tension has several causes in addition to the fact that Americans and Chinese have fought each other in Korea. America has steadfastly refused to recognize Red China and has supported the Nationalist Chinese regime of Chiang Kai-shek on Taiwan; she has stood firm against admission of Communist China to the United Nations; and she has imposed an embargo on trade with the Chinese mainland. The Communists, on their side, have made the usual charges of American "imperialism," have accused the United States of using germ warfare in Korea, and have arrested a number of Americans, including missionaries, as alleged spies. There have been several occasions since Korea when the United States and China seemed on the verge of war. The main trouble was over the offshore islands between Taiwan and the mainland, especially Quemoy and Matsu. Since 1954 the Communists have intermittently bombarded these Nationalist outposts and in 1958–59 a Communist invasion of the islands seemed imminent. The presence of the United States Seventh Fleet to protect shipments of supplies to the islands discouraged such action, however. Since then, Communist propaganda attacks upon the United States have served to keep alive that air of tension which the Reds need in order to justify the many sacrifices they are demanding of their people.

Relations between Red China and the Soviet Union, to all appearances, have been most friendly. The two countries are not only neighbors but allies, bound together by close military, political, and economic ties. Under a thirty-year treaty of "friendship, alliance and mutual assistance" signed in 1950, Russia has helped China to build up a huge modern army and to carry out her sweeping program of industrialization. More than half of China's exports go to the U.S.S.R. and in return she receives capital goods, technical aid, and military supplies. While the two powers are thus collaborating closely, there are nevertheless certain areas in which they disagree. Russia has been critical of China's commune system which, the Chinese claim, will hasten the transition to a Communist utopia. China has opposed the Soviet Union's professed aim of peaceful coexistence with the United States. And both powers have been rivals in Outer Mongolia which, although a Russian satellite, is still considered part of China. There is always the possibility that Communist China, as she becomes less dependent upon Russia's aid, may challenge the latter's position of leadership within the Communist world. For the time being, however, the two present a united front on most issues.

In her relations with the other nations of Asia, Red China has tried to capitalize on the widespread opposition to colonialism by harping on a policy of "Asia for the Asians." In recent years she has given small amounts of economic aid to some of her neighbors, notably North Korea and North Vietnam. Her simultaneous claims for border regions in India, Burma, and Nepal, however, have shown that China's primary aim is to extend her sphere of power. The true nature of Chinese Communist rule became obvious during the revolt in Tibet in 1959. That remote and mountainous country had enjoyed a special status within the Chinese People's Republic under an agreement signed in 1951. When the Chinese proceeded to violate this agreement and to communize Tibet's Buddhist society, sporadic violence flared into general rebellion. The Dalai Lama, Tibet's temporal head, fled to India, and the uprising was suppressed with utmost savagery. Since then China has been charged with aiming to exterminate the Tibetan people altogether. There certainly can no longer be any doubt that the Chinese are every bit as ruthless in their aims and methods as the

Russians. Hungary and Tibet are merely two sides of the same coin. Still, if communism should prove economically successful in China, it would have great appeal in the eyes of Asia's poverty-stricken millions, especially in the critical area of Southeast Asia.

NATIONALISM IN SOUTHEAST ASIA

Because of its strategic position and natural wealth, Southeast Asia, the area east of India and south of China, is one of the chief targets of Communist expansion. With the exception of Thailand, there have been Communist revolts in all of its countries. In the case of North Vietnam, Communist conquest has been successful. Prior to 1945 only Thailand was independent. Since then the Philippines, Burma, Indonesia, Vietnam, Laos, Cambodia, and Malaya have gained sovereignty. Southeast Asia is a wealthy region, inhabited by two hundred million people. It produces five-sixths of the world's natural rubber, more than half of its tin, two-thirds of its coconut products, and most important, 60 per cent of the world's exportable rice. A look at the map, furthermore, testifies to Southeast Asia's important strategic location across the main lines of communication between Europe and the Far East.

Like all underdeveloped regions, Southeast Asia is predominantly agricultural. Except for Indonesia, it does not as yet suffer from overpopulation. Its standard of living, while higher than in other parts of Asia, is still very low, and health conditions are extremely poor. What Southeast Asia needs most is to develop better-balanced national economies, with greater diversification (away from the limited number of staple commodities like rice, tin, or rubber) and increased industrialization. But such improvements are impeded by the general backwardness of the area (widespread illiteracy, lack of communications, and so forth), its racial and linguistic diversity, and its general political instability. Nationalism has been a major force in Southeast Asia for several decades. But its victory, by removing the strong hand of the former colonial powers, has had a disruptive effect and has increased the danger of Communist expansion. At the same time opposition to colonialism makes most of the new nations of Southeast Asia reluctant to align themselves with their former masters. Instead, these countries prefer a policy of neutralism, which further tends to weaken their power to resist communism.

In looking at the individual nations of Southeast Asia, we find a wide variety of political and economic problems that defy any further generalization. Some, like Thailand and the Philippines, have followed a relatively stable course. Thailand, never subject to colonial rule, is a constitutional monarchy with a king who is revered but has little power. In the last twenty-five years the country has seen a succession of more or less corrupt military regimes. The latest of these, headed by Field Marshal Sarit Thanarat, took over in 1958. Sarit differs from his predecessors in his sincere efforts to clean up the government and to draft a new constitution. Thailand is a fertile and underpopulated land. The vast majority of its twenty-three million people are farmers, and most of them grow rice, which is Thailand's chief commodity of export. Thailand has trouble with its Chinese minority, some 15 per cent of the population (including many Communists), but compared to the rest of Southeast Asia, the politically passive Siamese lead contented lives.

The same cannot be said of the close to twenty-four million Filipinos. The Philippine Republic was born on July 4, 1946, when the United States lived up to a promise made twelve years earlier of setting free its former possession. The government of the Philippines is closely modeled after that of the former mother country. There have been Communist disturbances, led by the Hukbalahap rebels ("Huks"), but with the arrest of their leaders in 1954 these have subsided. The most pressing problems of the young republic are economic. Due chiefly to the damages in World War II and the separation from the United States, Philippine recovery has been slow, and widespread poverty still prevails. The government of President Ramón Magsaysay started on an ambitious reform program in 1953, which was cut short by the president's death in 1957. Under his successor, President Carlos Garcia, the islands have fared less well. Still, because of their potential wealth, greater degree of modernization, and sound democratic system, the Philippines are better off than most other Southeast Asian countries.

While Thailand and the Philippines have openly aligned themselves with the West, the rest of the nations, with the exception of Communist North Vietnam and pro-Western South Vietnam, are officially neutral. Burma's break away from the British Empire in 1948 came as the result of amicable negotiations; and while she refused to join the Commonwealth, her relations with Great Britain have remained cordial. The Union of Burma is a federal republic with a parliamentary government. Except for two brief intervals, it has been headed by Prime Minister U Nu, one of the outstanding leaders of postwar Asian nationalism. The government's economic program is moderately socialist. Like Thailand, Burma is underpopulated and one of the world's leading producers of rice. The standard of living of the twenty-one million Burmese is low, and the government has few funds for economic development. United States government aid was terminated at Burma's request in 1953, because American-made arms were finding their way into the hands of Nationalist Chinese refugees. American aid was resumed in 1957. Burma also has serious political problems. The national unity that helped the Burmese gain independence in 1948 went to pieces shortly afterwards. After a decade of domestic strife and vain efforts to deal with communism, U Nu resigned his premiership in 1958 and General Ne Win formed an emergency government. The general suppressed the Communists, instituted a number of urgent reforms, and, after free and democratic elections in 1960, returned his power to U Nu. In her foreign policy Burma has been neutral. As a result of events in Tibet and of border conflicts with Red China, however, the government of U Nu has recently become more pro-Western.

The biggest Southeast Asian nation is Indonesia, with some 18,000 islands and close to 90 million people. It is also the most disorganized. The Republic of Indonesia proclaimed its independence in 1945, after more than three centuries of Dutch rule. The Dutch did not easily let go of their prized possession. It took four years and a costly war before they recognized Indonesia's freedom; and even then the new republic remained part of the Dutch-Indonesian Union until 1954. Since then relations between the Netherlands and Indonesia have become increasingly hostile. In 1957 Indonesia seized more than a billion dollars worth of Dutch assets, and in 1960 she severed diplomatic relations with The Hague. These acts were in retaliation against Dutch refusal to yield Netherlands New Guinea, or West Irian, which the Indonesians claim as theirs.

As in so many former colonial countries, political inexperience and general backwardness have kept democracy from taking hold in Indonesia. The island nation has been ruled more or less dictatorially by President Achmed Sukarno, another of Asia's leading nationalists. Under Sukarno's "guided democracy," opposition parties have been banned and parliament has been replaced by a Provisional People's Congress in which Nationalist, Moslem, and

Communist forces are represented. Indonesia's well-organized Communist Party claims a membership of more than a million. President Sukarno, who has been accused of Communist leanings, has defined his ideology as belief in God, democracy, nationalism, social justice, and humanitarianism. There have been several revolts against his policy of "guided democracy," the most serious in Sumatra and Celebes in 1958.

Indonesia's political instability has increased her economic difficulties. Her output of rubber and rice has actually declined in recent years, and only petroleum production has gained. With more than half of her population living on Java, industrial development of the island is imperative. To make any headway substantial foreign capital is needed. Private investment has been scared away by the socialist tendencies of the Sukarno regime and by a stifling system of economic control. Indonesia has used her neutralist position in the cold war to attract government aid from both East and West. This has brought such heavy indebtedness that more than half of the country's gross national product is needed to repay foreign credits. The extreme poverty of the rapidly growing population, meanwhile, is a boon to the Communists and their promises of land and better living conditions.

The most restless and unstable region of Southeast Asia has not been Indonesia but Indochina. A former French possession, intensively colonized during the past century, Indochina includes three nations: Vietnam, Laos, and Cambodia. Resistance against French rule after World War II was led by the League for the Independence of Vietnam. The Vietminh, as the League was called, consisted of many factions, but its most effective components were the Communists. In 1945 the Communist Vietminh leader, Ho Chi-minh, proclaimed a provisional Republic of Vietnam. French refusal to recognize the new regime was the signal for war. While French forces had little difficulty in restoring control over Laos and Cambodia, Vietnam became the scene of a drawn-out conflict. The French did most of the fighting, and the United States bore a substantial share of the expense. By 1954 most of northern Vietnam was in the hands of the Vietminh, and the same year the French suffered a major defeat at Dien Bien Phu. At this point an armistice was concluded under which Vietnam was left divided. A plebiscite to decide the future of the whole country, scheduled for 1956, has never been held.

The free nations of Indochina—Laos, Cambodia, and South

Vietnam—were given autonomy within the French Union in 1949 and became fully sovereign states in 1955. All three have similar problems. Economically, they are trying to make their agrarian societies more productive so as to give their people higher standards of living. Cambodia is the most successful in this respect, accepting economic aid from both the East and West. South Vietnam has difficulty building a viable economy without raw materials for industrialization. And Laos remains the most backward of all the Southeast Asian nations. Politically, the three countries are officially neutral. Cambodia, however, has been on good terms with Communist China; and Laos in 1960 also began making its peace with the Communists. The authoritarian regime of Ngo Dinh Diem in South Vietnam, on the other hand, leans strongly toward the West. Both Laos and South Vietnam have suffered from guerrilla campaigns of Communist partisans, supported by North Vietnam. Because of Indochina's strategic location as a buffer between the Communist world and anti-Communist Thailand, it is one of the most important battlefronts in the cold war.

The only country in Southeast Asia where a former colonial power succeeded in restoring its control after World War II was Malaya. Its three races, Malays, Chinese, and Indians, had fared well in the past, and there was no objection when British rule was resumed in 1945. But the war, in Malaya as everywhere else, had aroused a desire for autonomy. This the British granted in 1946 with the establishment of the Federation of Malaya. The country gained complete independence in 1957, when the Federation became a sovereign member of the Commonwealth. Differences among the three races and intermittent Communist insurrections are among Malaya's main political problems. To support its fast-growing population, Malaya relies chiefly on exports of rubber and tin. The government has embarked on a program of diversification and industrialization to make its economy more flexible.

Most of Southeast Asia, as this brief survey shows, suffers from political instability and economic backwardness. Racial, religious, and political differences, moreover, make any co-operation among its several nations difficult; and the similarity of their economies prevents the creation of a mutually complementary and internally balanced regional economy. To achieve some degree of unity against the threat of communism is of the utmost importance. A start in this direction was made with the initiation in 1950 of the Colombo Plan for Co-operative Economic Development in South and Southeast Asia. Its members, besides the Asian nations directly concerned, include the United States, Britain, Australia, Canada, New Zealand, and Japan. The Colombo Plan tries to improve the economies of the Asian states through co-operative effort and with the help of member countries outside the region. In its first decade the plan has chiefly provided technical assistance but also some economic aid.

In the military field, too, efforts have been made to protect free Asia from communism. In 1954 the United States, Great Britain, France, Australia, New Zealand, Pakistan, Thailand, and the Philippines formed the Southeast Asia Treaty Organization (SEATO). Its parties agreed to co-ordinate their efforts for mutual defense against aggression and subversion. SEATO, however, does not obligate members to take military action, nor does it have permanently allocated forces or a supreme commander. Some of the most important non-Communist countries of Asia, moreover, are not members. SEATO, therefore, is not comparable in strength or significance to NATO, its European counterpart. To make sure that SEATO was not misconstrued as an attempt to suppress colonial nationalism, its members signed a separate declaration, the "Pacific Charter," which promised "to promote the self-government and to secure the independence of all countries whose people desire it and are able to undertake its responsibilities." Still more important was the assurance of the Charter that its signatories would help "to promote higher living standards, economic progress and social well-being" for Southeast Asia. Here lies the real answer to Southeast Asia's manifold troubles.

NATIONALISM IN THE MIDDLE EAST

One of the most turbulent scenes of rebellion against Western influence since World War II has been the Arab world and the Middle East, the area bridging the continents of Africa and Asia, from Morocco in the west to Iran in the east. It consists of three political sections: the Arab states, the non-Arab Moslem states, and Israel. We are here primarily concerned with the Arab states. Israel is really a Western community surrounded by a hostile and backward region. The young nation, through hard work and large amounts of foreign aid, has made tremendous strides in the first twelve years of its independence. The non-Arab Moslem states—

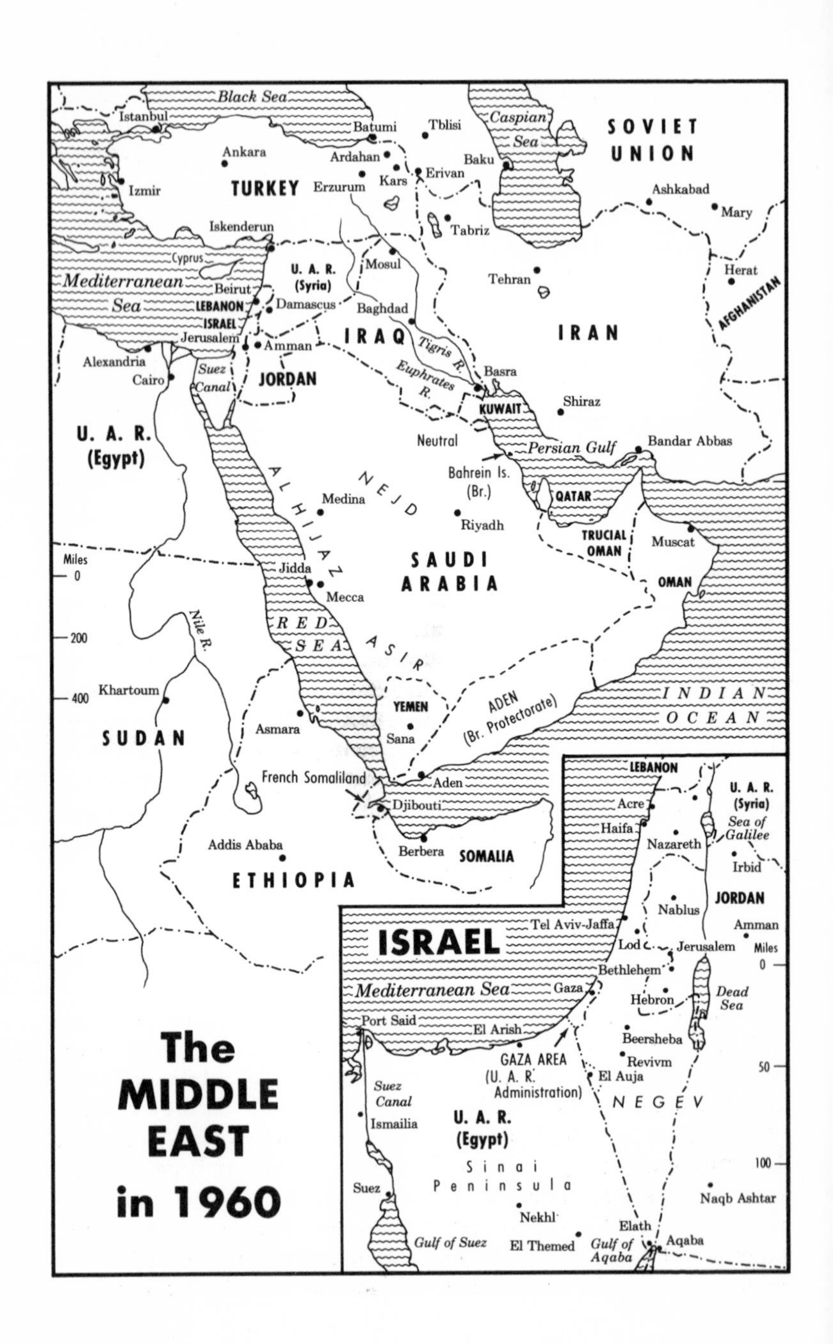

Black Sea
Istanbul
Batumi
Tblisi
Caspian Sea
SOVIET UNION
Ankara
Ardahan
Baku
Izmir
TURKEY
Erzurum
Kars
Erivan
Ashkabad
Mary
Iskenderun
Tabriz
Cyprus
U. A. R. (Syria)
Mosul
Tehran
Herat
Mediterranean Sea
Beirut
LEBANON
Damascus
Baghdad
AFGHANISTAN
ISRAEL
Jerusalem
Amman
IRAQ
Tigris R.
IRAN
Alexandria
Euphrates R.
Basra
Cairo
Suez Canal
JORDAN
KUWAIT
Shiraz
U. A. R. (Egypt)
Neutral
Persian Gulf
Bandar Abbas
Bahrein Is. (Br.)
QATAR
AL HIJAZ
NEJD
Medina
Riyadh
TRUCIAL OMAN
Muscat
Miles
0
200
400
SAUDI ARABIA
Jidda
Mecca
OMAN
Nile R.
RED SEA
ASIR
Khartoum
YEMEN
ADEN (Br. Protectorate)
INDIAN OCEAN
SUDAN
Asmara
Sana
French Somaliland
Aden
Djibouti
Addis Ababa
Berbera
SOMALIA
ETHIOPIA
LEBANON
U. A. R. (Syria)
Acre
Haifa
Nazareth
Sea of Galilee
Irbid
JORDAN
Nablus
ISRAEL
Tel Aviv-Jaffa
Amman
Lod
Jerusalem
Miles
0
Bethlehem
Mediterranean Sea
Gaza
Hebron
Dead Sea
Port Said
El Arish
Beersheba
Revivm
50
GAZA AREA (U. A. R. Administration)
El Auja
Suez Canal
NEGEV
Ismailia
U. A. R. (Egypt)
100
Sinai Peninsula
Suez
Naqb Ashtar
Nekhl
Elath
Gulf of Suez
El Themed
Gulf of Aqaba
Aqaba
The MIDDLE EAST in 1960

Turkey and Iran—are both old nations. Turkey underwent a thoroughgoing social and political revolution after World War I under the benevolent dictatorship of Mustafa Kemal Ataturk, who died in 1938. The first free elections in 1950 brought to power Premier Adnan Menderes, leader of the conservative Democratic Party. His increasingly repressive policy threatened to undo many of the gains which democracy had made in Turkey. In 1960, therefore, an army junta, headed by General Cemal Gursel, ousted the Menderes regime and promised "to organize free and fair elections for the formation of constitutional and democratic government." Turkey's new rulers also reaffirmed their adherence to the Western alliance system of which Turkey is a key member.

Iran, like Turkey, has been firmly in the Western camp. Both nations have long been exposed to Soviet pressure. There were some signs of anticolonialism in Iran after World War II. The most serious crisis occurred during the premiership of Mohammed Mossadegh in 1952–53, when the Iranian parliament nationalized Britain's oil industry along the Persian Gulf. The matter was settled by a compromise in 1954, under which Iran receives a large share of the oil royalties. The leading political figure of Iran is Shah Mohammed Riza Pahlevi. Although a constitutional monarch, his influence is all but absolute. In an effort to counteract Soviet propaganda the "reform shah" has done much to improve his country's economy. A Seven-Year Plan, begun in 1957, calls for industrial development and agrarian reform. Iran's mainstay continues to be aid from the United States. Communism, except during the time of Mossadegh, has not been a serious threat. Still, the poverty of the masses provides a fertile breeding ground for unrest and possibly revolution.

The Arab world of the Middle East is a harsh terrain of desert wilderness, broken by occasional fertile valleys and oases. It is inhabited by some seventy million Arab Moslems, most of them desperately poor tenant farmers. Despite its economic backwardness, however, the Arab Middle East is of greatest importance. Geographically, it lies astride the shortest route between Europe and Asia; economically, it contains about 50 per cent of the world's known oil resources; and spiritually, it serves as the religious focus of more than three hundred million non-Arab Moslems living as far away as Southeast Asia. Outwardly, the Arab world presents a certain unity, based on community of language, culture, and religion. But below the surface there are many divisive forces, chiefly due to rivalries among Arab leaders. The one sentiment that more than anything unites the Arab masses is their nationalism. And the strongest ingredient in this nationalism is hatred of any kind of foreign domination.

Before World War II only four of the Arab nations were independent, at least nominally: Egypt, Iraq, Saudi Arabia, and Yemen. Since then all but Algeria have won their freedom. Liberation from foreign control, however, did not solve the many problems of these countries. Arab society is still sharply divided into a tiny minority of extremely wealthy merchants and landowners and a huge mass of destitute peasants. Between these two extremes is a small, progressive middle class, mostly professional people educated in the West. Most of the Arab countries have excellent liberal constitutions, but these cannot conceal the basically authoritarian nature of their governments. Only after the dismally low standard of living of the Arab peoples has been raised can there be any hope for political changes in the direction of greater democracy. Economic development, however, can be achieved only with the aid of those very same foreigners whom Arab nationalism has been so eager to oust. To find a *modus vivendi* between Arabs and outsiders in the Middle East has been one of the concerns of international politics since World War II.

There is one issue on which the whole Arab world has seen eye to eye, and that is opposition to Israel. The outward manifestation of Arab unity has been the Arab League. Organized in 1945, it includes all the Arab states, although Tunisia and Morocco are more loosely affiliated with the League. We have already discussed the Arab-Israeli war in 1948–49 (see Chapter 1). Subsequent border clashes led to a resumption of war between Israel and Egypt in 1956. Fighting was stopped once more by UN intervention, and for the next few years the Israeli-Arab borders remained relatively quiet. Tension continued, however, as the Arabs boycotted Israel and Israeli ships were refused passage through the Suez Canal. Arab refugees in countries adjacent to Israel, meanwhile, have grown to over a million. They are leading a marginal existence on charity dispensed through the United Nations. Attempts to integrate them into their new surroundings have been resisted both by the refugees and by their fellow-Arabs. A solution of the refugee problem is the prerequisite for any improved relations between the Arabs and Israel.

When it comes to issues outside the Arab world, such as which side to take in the cold war, the Arabs have been far from united.

Among the many divisions within the Arab world, the most important is that between Egypt and Iraq. Egypt, because of her large population and strategic location, is the most important among the Arab nations and from the beginning has tried to assert her leadership over the rest. Iraq, on the other hand, has sought to draw together the northern Arab states in the "fertile crescent" between the eastern Mediterranean and the Persian Gulf. In their foreign policy, Egypt since 1952 has followed an anti-Western or at best neutralist course, while Iraq until 1958 was pro-Western and only since has turned neutral. As for some of the other Arab powers, Jordan has traditionally been close to Iraq; Syria in 1958 united with Egypt to form the United Arab Republic; Saudi Arabia has vacillated between the two camps; and Lebanon has tried to remain on the fence. The differences between Egypt and Iraq came out into the open when Iraq in 1955 joined Great Britain, Turkey, Iran, and Pakistan in the Middle East Treaty Organization (METO), or Baghdad Pact. Its purpose was to meet the threat of Communist aggression. Its immediate effect was to widen the rift within the Arab world. As a countermove, Egypt and Syria signed a mutual defense treaty, the Damascus Pact. But the division manifest in these pacts did not interfere with Arab unity on the issue of Israel. This was brought home during the crisis touched off by Egypt's seizure of the Suez Canal in 1956.

Egypt had undergone a major change in 1952, when the Egyptian army overthrew the corrupt regime of King Farouk I. The leader of the new Egypt is Colonel Gamal Abdel Nasser, who wields almost absolute power as president, with the right to name his own parliament. Egypt's most pressing problems are economic. To raise the living standard of her twenty-four million people, Nasser's program calls for agrarian reform, development of natural resources, and increased industrialization. Outstanding among his projects is the plan for a gigantic dam and power station near Aswan on the Nile. Such a dam requires enormous funds. The United States and Great Britain at first agreed to help finance the project. But when it became clear that President Nasser was also asking for aid from the Communist bloc, which was already supplying him with arms, and when the Egyptian leader sought to arouse Arab nationalism by reviling the West, the United States and Britain in the summer of 1956 withdrew their offer. Nasser thereupon retaliated by nationalizing the Suez Canal, claiming that its income was needed to pay for the Aswan Dam.

Nasser's act of defiance almost plunged the world into a major war. While the West, under United States leadership, was still trying to negotiate a compromise, another perennial source of trouble, sporadic fighting along the Israel-Egypt border, flared up again. On October 29, 1956, the world was startled by the news that Israeli forces had invaded Egypt's Sinai Peninsula and were moving toward the Suez Canal. Britain and France immediately demanded withdrawal of both Israeli and Egyptian troops from the canal and acceptance of Anglo-French occupation of the canal zone. When Nasser rejected this ultimatum, British bombers began raiding Egyptian airfields, and a few days later British and French troops landed on Egyptian soil. The Israeli and Franco-British moves came as a complete surprise to the United States. At a dramatic session of the UN General Assembly, an American resolution for a cease-fire and withdrawal of all attacking forces was passed by an overwhelming majority. The verdict of the United Nations, at first rejected by Britain, France, and Israel, was finally carried out and a UN Emergency Force was sent to the Sinai Peninsula to keep peace between Israel and Egypt.

The outcome of the Suez crisis was a major defeat for the West. Relations between the United States and her European allies were seriously weakened, while Communist propaganda branded the intervention in Egypt as a blatant example of Western imperialism. The winner was President Nasser. In the spring of 1957 the Suez Canal reopened under Egyptian control. The Russians loaned Egypt the necessary funds to start the Aswan Dam and in time the West, too, came forth with funds, mainly for the improvement of the Suez Canal. The fact that Nasser succeeded in getting aid from both sides placed him among the more successful neutralists. At the same time he enforced rigid measures against communism in Egypt. Within the Arab world Nasser emerged as the acknowledged leader of Arab nationalism. In 1958 a big step toward Arab unity was taken when Egypt and Syria joined forces in the United Arab Republic under the presidency of Nasser. Attempts to take over the smaller nations of Lebanon and Jordan, however, failed, chiefly because the United States, since the Suez crisis, has taken a more active hand in Middle Eastern affairs.

In January 1957 President Eisenhower promised armed assistance against Communist aggression to any nation in the Middle East that requested it. This new "Eisenhower Doctrine" was first applied in Lebanon in 1958. A call for help from the Lebanese government against an Egyptian-inspired uprising resulted in the temporary occupation of the country by United States marines. The situation seemed especially critical because of simultaneous events in Iraq. In July 1958 nationalist forces in that country, in a bloody revolt, overthrew the pro-Western regime of King Faisal II. The new government of Abdul Karim Kassem recognized the United Arab Republic and left the Middle East Treaty Organization. For a while it looked as though the victory of the nationalists in Iraq would be to Egypt's advantage. But as Premier Kassem refused to recognize Nasser's claim to leadership in the Arab world, their two countries again became bitter rivals. The situation in Iraq, meanwhile, is far from stable. Despite valiant efforts at economic reform, conditions for the majority of Iraqis have become worse rather than better since 1958. Like Egypt and Syria, Iraq is high on the list of recipients of Soviet aid; but while Nasser has suppressed communism in the United Arab Republic, Kassem has tolerated it, hoping that he can control and use Iraq's strong Communist faction. The United States, in an attempt to save the Baghdad Pact, joined the remaining members in 1959 in forming the Central Treaty Organization (CENTO) which, like its predecessor, aims to contain the spread of communism.

The Arab states of North Africa other than Egypt, while not really part of the Middle East, nevertheless are more deeply involved in the events of that critical area than in the affairs of Africa. With the exception of Algeria, they all have won their freedom since World War II: Libya was released from UN trusteeship in 1951; Sudan became a republic in 1956; and the same year both Morocco and Tunisia were granted full sovereignty by France. Economically, all these nations depend heavily on foreign aid. In the past such aid has come chiefly from the United States. More recently, the Communist bloc also has begun to do its part. Tunisia, under President Habib Bourguiba, is the most pro-Western nation of the region. Morocco's King Mohammed V leans somewhat to the East. Both Libya and Sudan are officially neutral, but their people are attracted by Nasser's appeal to Arab nationalism. The main source of tension in North Africa has been the Algerian war, in which Arabs everywhere have sided with the rebels and against the French.

The last and smallest country of the Middle East to become independent was the island of Cyprus. After four years of violence between Greek and Turkish Cypriotes, in which the British mother country was caught in the middle, the Republic of Cyprus finally

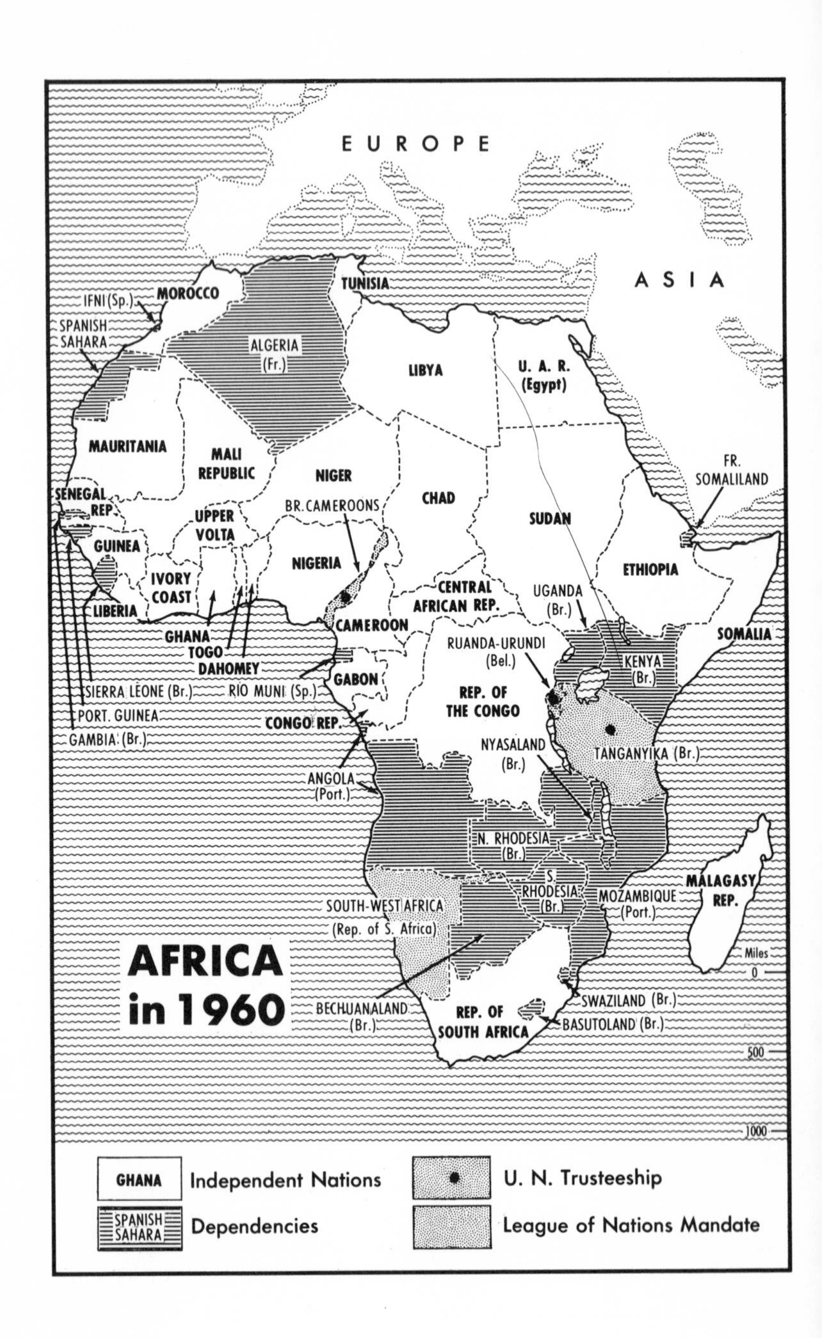
EUROPE
ASIA
MOROCCO
IFNI (Sp.)
SPANISH SAHARA
ALGERIA (Fr.)
TUNISIA
LIBYA
U. A. R. (Egypt)
MAURITANIA
MALI REPUBLIC
NIGER
CHAD
SUDAN
FR. SOMALILAND
SENEGAL REP.
UPPER VOLTA
BR. CAMEROONS
GUINEA
IVORY COAST
NIGERIA
ETHIOPIA
LIBERIA
CENTRAL AFRICAN REP.
UGANDA (Br.)
GHANA
TOGO
DAHOMEY
CAMEROON
SOMALIA
RUANDA-URUNDI (Bel.)
KENYA (Br.)
SIERRA LEONE (Br.)
RIO MUNI (Sp.)
GABON
REP. OF THE CONGO
PORT. GUINEA
GAMBIA (Br.)
CONGO REP.
NYASALAND (Br.)
TANGANYIKA (Br.)
ANGOLA (Port.)
N. RHODESIA (Br.)
S. RHODESIA (Br.)
MOZAMBIQUE (Port.)
MALAGASY REP.
SOUTH-WEST AFRICA (Rep. of S. Africa)
AFRICA in 1960
Miles
0
500
1000
BECHUANALAND (Br.)
REP. OF SOUTH AFRICA
SWAZILAND (Br.)
BASUTOLAND (Br.)
GHANA Independent Nations
SPANISH SAHARA Dependencies
U. N. Trusteeship
League of Nations Mandate

celebrated its independence in 1960. Archbishop Makarios, who had led the fight for independence, was elected president. The new nation remained within the Commonwealth, and Britain retained her military bases on Cyprus.

With the exception of Turkey, Iran, Tunisia, and Cyprus, the countries of the Middle East and the Arab world today are following a neutralist course. National pride and the hope for economic aid from both East and West are responsible for this nonalignment. If, nevertheless, some of the Arab nations seem more friendly toward the East, this may be explained by their past experiences with Western imperialism. Communism as such has been a problem only in Iraq. As a revolutionary force its importance has been overshadowed by nationalism. This does not mean that a closer affiliation between the Arab world and the Communist bloc would not seriously weaken the Western position in the cold war. To maintain what remains of Western influence in the Middle East, without further arousing Arab nationalism, is the difficult task of the Western powers at the present time.

TURBULENT AFRICA

The tide of colonial nationalism, after sweeping through Asia and the Middle East, has finally also reached Africa. In 1950 there were still only four sovereign states on that vast continent. Ten years later their number had grown to twenty-six, seventeen of which had won their independence in 1960. With the remaining British colonies in Central and South Africa approaching independence or at least self-government, the only examples of traditional colonialism in Africa today are the Spanish Sahara and the large Portuguese holdings in Angola and Mozambique. And even here, change will be merely a matter of time.

Most of the recent victories of African nationalism have been won in the hitherto least developed part of the continent south of the Sahara Desert. This region, abounding in natural resources, is inhabited by some 165 million Africans and about 4 million whites. Most of the latter live in the Union of South Africa. The native peoples are still extremely backward, illiterate, and poor. Tropical diseases, thanks to the efforts of the former colonial powers, have been virtually stamped out, at least in the more densely populated areas. But the resultant population growth has far outrun the food supply, so that much of Africa is chronically undernourished. There is nowhere any tradition of political unity, the tribe having always been the largest unit of native life. And with some seven hundred different dialects there is no common language other than French or English. Diversity and complexity are the outstanding characteristics of the Dark Continent.

The only unifying force throughout Africa is nationalism. In its deep-seated distrust of the white man, African nationalism is not content with half measures. It demands complete and immediate independence, despite the fact that most Africans are hardly ready for it. This headlong rush into freedom has caused many difficulties. The way in which these are being solved depends not only on the natives but on the former colonial powers. Because even though most of Africa today is nominally independent, the West still has a great deal of influence. There is no uniformity in the relationships between whites and natives, but a few general patterns can be distinguished.

Only in one African country today is a white minority trying to hold on tenaciously to a predominating European culture. The Union of South Africa is ruled by its three million whites, who constitute less than one-fourth of the total population. The nonwhite majority (Africans, Indians, and "colored," that is, mulattoes) has been granted a few concessions; but these fall far short of the growing demand for full equality. In 1948 the South African government adopted a program of strict racial segregation, or *apartheid*. It aims at the complete separation of races, restriction of franchise for nonwhites, forced resettlement of Africans in rural areas, school segregation, and a lower educational standard for African children. The inferior status of the native is thus to be perpetuated by every possible means. The result has been mounting unrest, riots, and bloodshed. How much longer this repressive policy will succeed is impossible to say. Meanwhile the attempt to reverse by force the inevitable trend toward racial equality has earned South Africa the censure of most of the civilized world, including the other members of the Commonwealth.

A better solution of dealing with native demands for equal rights has been adopted in such British territories as Kenya, Uganda, the Federation of the Rhodesias and Nyasaland, and Tanganyika. Here, too, white minorities have tried to perpetuate their exclusive control. But Britain has been able to restrain the resident whites and to enforce native participation in government with a view toward ultimate independence.

A similarly enlightened policy has been followed by France. We have already seen how the former French colonies that had comprised French West Africa and French Equatorial Africa were given autonomy in 1958 and complete freedom in 1960 (see pp. 47, 50). Only one of them, Guinea, decided to leave the French Community and to accept economic aid and technical assistance from the Communist bloc. The other fourteen republics are still associated with the Community, although their ties are economic, military, and cultural rather than political.

The most successful African nation to become independent in recent years has been the former British colony of the Gold Coast. Under the able leadership of Prime Minister Kwame Nkrumah, the state of Ghana, as it is now called, has made remarkable progress since it became a free and sovereign member of the Commonwealth in 1957. Such progress has been possible only because of continued help from the former mother country. This fruitful co-operation between whites and blacks holds the best promise for orderly evolution in Africa. It has been evident in most British and French possessions. It is the absence of such collaboration which largely accounts for the chaos that has ruled in the Congo, since its independence in mid-1960.

The Republic of the Congo, one-third the size of the United States and with some fourteen million natives, is one of the richest countries of Africa. The Belgians, during their seventy-five-year rule, did much to develop the region's economy, but did nothing to train the Congolese for self-government. When the French in 1959 began liberating their neighboring Congo Republic, riots in the Belgian Congo called for similar concessions. To put an end to disorders that interfered with their business interests, the Belgians gave in far too quickly and on June 30, 1960, the Congolese government of Premier Patrice Lumumba took office.

Events since then have demonstrated the error of Belgium's precipitant action. Within hours after independence the Congolese army mutinied and the Congolese people rioted. As the whites began fleeing the country, order broke down completely. Premier Lumumba, a high-strung and erratic young man, blamed everything on the Belgians and asked the United Nations to intervene and force the complete withdrawal of Belgian troops. The efforts of Secretary General Dag Hammarskjold and a UN Emergency Force finally succeeded in getting the Belgians out. But this did not solve the Congo problem. In the interim there had arisen strong opposition to Lumumba's high-handed policy among some of the Congo's six provinces, notably Kasai and Katanga. In September, 1960, the Congo's President Joseph Kasavubu, with the aid of the army under Colonel Joseph Mobutu, removed Lumumba as premier, charging him with creating chaos and showing pro-Communist leanings. With the government thus split among rival factions, the situation in the Congo remained explosive.

The bitter lesson of the Congo shows what can happen if a primitive people is given independence too early. There is still hope that some way may be found by which Belgians can continue their civilizing work in the Congo for the benefit of both the Africans and themselves. Much depends on the kind of leadership which the Congolese people will have on their difficult road to self-government. The importance of good leadership has been shown by Kwame Nkrumah of Ghana, Tom Mboya of Kenya, and Julius Nyerere of Tanganyika. There is always the danger that native disorders may aid the rise of communism. Thus far Communist influence in Africa has been surprisingly small. Only in the Union of South Africa has there been a vigorous Communist underground. One of the most effective antidotes to communism is seen in a healthy trade-union movement. The beginnings of such a movement in Africa exist and deserve Western support. Still more important as a protection against communism is economic aid. More and more of it is given to Africa each year. But such aid must be without any political or military strings, because if there is one thing on which all the new nations of Africa agree, it is their desire to be rid of foreign influence. Neutralism is a potent force throughout the whole continent.

THE AFRO-ASIAN BLOC

The road to independence in the former colonial regions of Asia and Africa differed from country to country, depending on the attitudes of the colonial powers and on the degree of maturity of the native peoples concerned. Yet there were also certain similarities of problems and experiences to suggest some kind of collaboration among the many nations that so recently had won their freedom. Most of them, moreover, felt that by working together, their influence on questions affecting them all might be stronger. It was these considerations that led to several conferences, both among the nations of Asia and Africa and among the African nations alone.

The first Asian-African Congress met at Bandung, Indonesia, in 1955. It was a truly historic occasion. Twenty-nine countries participated, representing about half the world's population. As was to be expected from so large and diverse a gathering, the specific achievements of the conference were few. But as far as establishing a common attitude on basic issues was concerned, the meeting was a success. The members agreed overwhelmingly in their condemnation of colonialism, advocacy of universal membership in the United Nations, and censure of racial discrimination. They also advocated general disarmament and economic co-operation with each other and with the rest of the world. Discussion throughout the conference was on a high level and free from any bitterness against the white powers.

The same could not be said for the next meeting, the Afro-Asian People's Solidarity Conference, which convened at Cairo in 1957. It was an unofficial assemblage of peoples rather than governments and was attended by representatives from forty countries, including the Asian members of the Communist bloc. Under the subtle instigation of the Soviet Union, its deliberations and resolutions followed a clearly Communist line. The Russians used the occasion to make vague but impressive promises of "stringless" aid to African and Asian countries. Not only imperialism and racialism, but the Baghdad Pact and the Eisenhower Doctrine were condemned as threats to world peace.

In 1958 the nations of Africa founded their own Conference of Independent African States. At its first meeting in Accra, Ghana, eight members attended. In 1960, when a second meeting was held in Addis Ababa, Ethiopia, delegates from some twenty states, either independent or hoping to be soon, were present. The Union of South Africa was excluded from both meetings and its racial policy was condemned in the strongest terms. France was also censured for her refusal to grant independence to Algeria and for exploding nuclear devices in the Sahara. When it came to taking more positive action, however, such as implementing various proposals for African unity, agreement was less evident. Kwame Nkrumah of Ghana advocated a strong union of African states. This proposal was rejected by the rest of the participants who suspected Nkrumah of seeking to extend his authoritarian rule beyond the borders of Ghana. There were other differences, especially border disputes, among the new African nations. And while the Arab members of the Conference advocated a firm stand against Israel, the states south of the Sahara welcomed the economic and technical assistance they were receiving from Israel.

If the African states thus found it difficult to see eye to eye among themselves, it has been harder still for the whole Afro-Asian bloc to chart a common course. This was evident in the United Nations. With more than forty new countries joining the United Nations since 1945, their potential influence is great. But there has not yet been a major issue on which these countries have presented a united front. Most of the Asian states have been independent for a decade or more and take a far less radical view of colonialism than some of the younger states of Africa. "The rising tide of color," feared by many in the West, is very much a reality today. This does not mean, however, that it must lead to racial violence, as in the Congo and in South Africa. The more responsible leaders in Asia and Africa are aware of the danger and futility of racial intolerance. They realize that just as their countries could not have reached their present state of development without colonialism, so they will not be able to solve their remaining problems without continued aid from the former colonial powers. The problem of the underdeveloped countries is a joint responsibility of the whole civilized world and the greatest challenge of our era of competitive coexistence.

6

THE "BIG TWO" IN 1959

NEW YORK TIMES PHOTO.

Yes, we are living in a world of fear. The life of man today is corroded and made bitter by fear, fear of the future, fear of the hydrogen bomb, fear of ideologies. Perhaps this fear is a greater danger than the danger itself, because it is fear which drives men to act foolishly, to act thoughtlessly, to act dangerously.

PRESIDENT SUKARNO of Indonesia,
at the opening of the Bandung Conference in 1955

COMPETITIVE COEXISTENCE

THE COLD WAR, AS WE HAVE SEEN, DID not break out overnight. It came as the result of a gradually mounting crisis between the East and West, in which action by one side usually brought on an equally strong reaction by the other (see Chapter 1). The years immediately after 1950 saw the climax of the international tension that had been building up since 1945. If a major showdown involving the atomic strength of Russia and the United States was avoided at that critical time, the reason was that the suicidal folly of a nuclear war had already become all too obvious. It was the realization that war as a means of settling international disputes was ruled out which made leaders on both sides explore the possibility of finding a peaceful solution to their differences. This search for peaceful coexistence began shortly after Stalin's death in 1953 and lasted until 1956. The events of the latter year showed that compromise between the free and Communist worlds was impossible. Coexistence continued to prevail after 1956, but it did so as an alternative to mutual annihilation rather than as a step toward lasting peace. Competitive coexistence, as East-West relations have been described, is but a euphemism for cold war.

THE CLIMAX OF THE COLD WAR

Our discussion has already touched on most of the important international events since 1950. On the Communist side, the attack against the West continued at first to be concentrated on Korea. After the Korean War bogged down into a stalemate, Communist pressure shifted to Indochina. There were other scenes of more "peaceful" Communist expansion. In 1951 Tibet was subjected to the domination of Communist China; Southeast Asia experienced a continuous series of Communist disturbances; and elsewhere in the world any former colonial people rebelling against the West could count on Communist support. Russia's relations with Communist China continued to be close, and the Soviet hold over the satellite countries of eastern Europe appeared unshakable.

The West, meanwhile, was busily building its network of alliances to halt the spread of communism. These countermoves had started in 1947 and had reached their first peak in the North Atlantic Treaty Organization in 1949 (see p. 29). The strengthening of Western defenses went into high gear during the Korean War. In the military sphere, armed forces were increased until the gross imbalance between East and West was substantially reduced. America's military budget was increased from an average of 14 billion dollars per year before 1950 to 21 billion dollars in 1951. In diplomacy, political and economic matters were more and more overshadowed by questions of military security. American foreign aid was increasingly directed into military channels. NATO was perfected into a closely co-ordinated defense mechanism. Regional alliances were extended to other parts of the world with the Tripartite Security Treaty (ANZUS Treaty) of 1951, the Southeast Asia Treaty of 1954, and the Middle East Treaty of 1955. The latter two treaties, although signed during the period of coexistence after 1953, nevertheless were repercussions from the shock caused by the invasion of South Korea in 1950. Not only did the West consolidate its existing forces, it also cast about for new allies. With the conclusion of a Japanese Peace Treaty in 1951 and the subsequent United States–Japanese defense agreement, an American foothold was gained in the Far East. In Europe the integration of West Germany into NATO (1955) similarly strengthened the Western position. Further Western gains were derived from the rapprochement between Yugoslavia and the West after 1950, and from the treaty between the United States and Spain in 1953.

ALLIANCES OF THE UNITED STATES

Regional Treaties

Organization of American States (OAS)—1947

Argentina	Dominican Republic	Nicaragua
Bolivia	Ecuador	Panama
Brazil	El Salvador	Paraguay
Chile	Guatemala	Peru
Colombia	Haiti	United States
Costa Rica	Honduras	Uruguay
Cuba	Mexico	Venezuela

North Atlantic Treaty Organization (NATO)—1949

Belgium	Greece (1951)	Portugal
Canada	Iceland	Turkey (1951)
Denmark	Italy	United Kingdom
France	Luxembourg	United States
German Federal	Netherlands	
Republic (1955)	Norway	

Tripartite Security Treaty (ANZUS)—1951

Australia	New Zealand	United States

Southeast Asia Treaty Organization (SEATO)—1954

Australia	Pakistan	United Kingdom
France	Philippines	United States
New Zealand	Thailand	

Central Treaty Organization (CENTO),
formerly Middle East Treaty Organization (METO)–1955

Iran	Pakistan	United Kingdom
Iraq (until 1959)	Turkey	United States (1959)

Bilateral Treaties

United States—Philippines 1951
United States—Japan 1951, 1960
United States—Republic of Korea 1953
United States—Republic of China 1954

While both East and West were thus avidly working for a military balance of power, developments in the atomic field gave added significance to what otherwise would have been merely a traditional race for armaments and alliances. Until 1949 the United States had a monopoly of atomic weapons. With the explosion of an atomic bomb in the Soviet Union in September of that year, competition invaded the atomic field as well. In 1952 America tipped the atomic balance by testing the first hydrogen weapon; but the next year the Soviet Union again caught up with the United States by producing its own H-bomb. A stage had now been reached where opponents in a future war might totally destroy each other. "Safety," in Winston Churchill's words, "will be the sturdy child of terror, and survival the twin brother of annihilation." To find means of avoiding another war, therefore, became one of the major tasks of diplomacy. And the surest way to prevent war was seen in limiting conventional weapons and outlawing atomic ones.

Efforts in this direction had already been made under UN auspices immediately after 1945 (see p. 31). But the mounting tensions of the cold war had prevented any arms reduction. The main differences between the East and West on disarmament were on matters of procedure. The Soviet Union insisted from the start that as a first move all atomic weapons should be prohibited and existing stockpiles should be destroyed. As a next stage, conventional arms should be reduced. The final step, the Russians proposed, should be some system of limited international inspection to assure compliance with these disarmament provisions. The Western nations, on the other hand, suggested exactly the reverse: first, the establishment of an effective system of inspection; then, reduction of conventional armaments; and finally, prohibition of atomic weapons and continued international inspection. Here the matter more or less rested until late 1953, when President Eisenhower's "atoms for peace" plan touched off a new round of high-level discussions on atomic matters. The Eisenhower proposal was one of several indications that a new phase in East-West relations was at hand.

THE SEARCH FOR COEXISTENCE

The hope that two such diametrically opposed systems as the free, democratic West and the authoritarian, Communist East might exist peacefully side by side was nothing new. Such hope had guided American policy at the end of World War II and had led to most of the concessions that were made to the Russians at that time. Once Americans had awakened to the continued threat of world communism, however, they had drastically changed their attitude. Instead of idealizing the Soviet Union as a wartime ally, they now saw communism in its true light as the free world's greatest enemy. The majority of America's allies at first approved of and shared this changed attitude. Only when the terrible consequences of a possible atomic war were realized by western Europeans did they become restive under United States leadership and begin to criticize American foreign policy.

Such criticism was part of a general decline in American popularity abroad. After his famous goodwill flight around the world in 1942, Wendell Willkie, Republican candidate for the presidency two years earlier, had commented upon the "genuine affection" he had met wherever he went. "I came home certain of one clear and significant fact," he concluded, "that there exists in the world today a gigantic reservoir of good will toward us, the American people." Had Willkie lived to repeat his trip ten years later, he would have returned with a far different story. Some of the countries he had visited earlier would now have been closed to him, and in others he would have found the slogan "Ami go home!" chalked on walls. The story of how America's "reservoir of good will" came to be drained is complicated. Much of it was due to circumstances beyond American control, such as the emergence of new regimes capitalizing on Communist-inspired anti-Americanism, or the resentment of peoples growing tired of seeing American soldiers in their midst, be they occupation troops or allies. Yet there were also certain American policies which caused uneasiness abroad. Many Europeans feared that the United States might once more turn isolationist and concentrate on the military defense and economic development of the Western Hemisphere. Measures like the McCarran-Walter Act, which restricted immigration into the United States, or the proposed Bricker amendment to the American Constitution, which, had it been adopted, would have given Congress the power to pass on executive agreements with foreign countries, were interpreted as signs of a new American nationalism. America's refusals to ease its trade relations by lowering tariff barriers, removing quotas, and putting its reciprocal trade policy on a more permanent basis were seen in a similar light. Finally, there was always "McCarthyism," which antagonized many of America's best friends.

Nobody could deny, of course, that the United States showed

an increasing awareness of its new responsibilities as a world power. The manner in which America executed this leadership, however, left much to be desired in the opinion of foreign critics. The most common criticism was that America during the cold war emphasized military aid at the expense of economic assistance. In her search for allies, furthermore, America was accused of a lack of discrimination by favoring such former or present Fascist nations as Germany, Japan, and Spain. Occasional threats that the United States might withdraw its military forces or its economic aid from Europe if its allies failed to do as they were told were seen as signs of isolationism or of unwarranted interference in the domestic affairs of other nations. The particular target of much of this foreign criticism was America's Secretary of State John Foster Dulles. Dulles had stressed the need for an "agonizing reappraisal" of his country's foreign policy in the light of American self-interest; he had threatened "utilizing the deterrence of massive retaliation" by atomic weapons at times and places of America's choosing; and he had spoken of "rolling back" the iron curtain by encouraging rebellion among the Soviet satellites. Such blunt utterances were felt to be careless and irresponsible, since they might involve everyone in what Arnold Toynbee called "annihilation without representation."

America's intransigence toward the Russians was deplored particularly at a time when, following the death of Stalin in March, 1953, the leaders in the Kremlin proclaimed a "new course" in Soviet domestic and foreign affairs. How could the world be certain, people abroad asked, that Russia was not sincere in its new policy, if the United States persisted in rejecting all Soviet overtures? In December, 1953, President Eisenhower met his French and British colleagues—Premier Joseph Laniel and Prime Minister Winston Churchill—in Bermuda to discuss the recent changes in Russia and to map out a common policy. As usual, the United States was far more reluctant than its allies to accept the Soviet Union's peaceful declarations at face value. To strike a positive note, however, President Eisenhower, immediately after the Bermuda Conference, put before the United Nations his "atoms for peace" plan. In this proposal he urged the powers to co-operate in developing peacetime uses of atomic energy, and he suggested the donation of fissionable materials to an international pool in order to aid peaceful atomic development. The calming effect of this generous scheme, however, was obliterated shortly afterwards by Secretary Dulles' statement on "massive retaliation."

The search for a basis of possible coexistence was thus a slow process. The fact that the Big Four foreign ministers, after an interlude of several years, resumed their talks at a conference in Berlin in early 1954 was a hopeful sign. Another important meeting, this one devoted to Far Eastern affairs, took place in the spring of 1954 at Geneva. With nineteen nations attending, the novel feature of the Geneva Conference was the presence, for the first time at such a meeting, of Communist China. The main objectives of the talks were to reunite Korea (where an armistice had been reached the year before) and to end the fighting in Indochina. Although the efforts with respect to Korea failed, the powers did restore peace to Indochina (see p. 147). It was while the Geneva Conference was still in session that the Western leaders made their first open declarations that echoed Russia's proposals for peaceful coexistence. In June, 1954, Winston Churchill, whose "iron curtain" speech in 1946 had sounded the start of the cold war, publicly reversed his earlier stand and came out for a more moderate attitude toward Russia. "I am of the opinion," he said, "that we ought to have a try for peaceful coexistence—a real good try for it"; and he added, "I am very much in favor of patient, cool, friendly examination of what the Russian intentions are." Two days later President Eisenhower gave qualified approval to Churchill's views when he agreed that the East and West must "find ways of living together."

There were other indications during the remainder of 1954 that the United States was ready to follow a more conciliatory policy. On several occasions President Eisenhower came out against the strong Far Eastern measures advocated by some "old-guard" Republicans. In the course of the year some American troops were withdrawn from South Korea, and the economic embargo against Communist China was eased somewhat. The United States did sign a treaty with Chiang Kai-shek in December, 1954, guaranteeing Taiwan and the Pescadores; but the United States was careful to commit Nationalist China not to attack the Chinese mainland without American consent.

THE FIRST "MEETING AT THE SUMMIT"

The high point of optimism that a new phase in East-West relations had arrived was reached during the summer of 1955. The year got off to a bad start when the Chinese Communists seized some of the smaller Nationalist-held islands between Formosa and the

Chinese mainland. For several weeks it appeared as though war between the United States (supporting Chiang Kai-shek) and Red China was inevitable, especially as the latter began threatening the key islands of Matsu and Quemoy. But by late April the Communists suddenly became more moderate and agreed to solve the problems of the Formosa straits by negotiation. There was a similar relaxation of tension in Europe. In May, 1955, the Soviet Union suddenly declared its readiness to sign an Austrian peace treaty, largely on terms which the West had advocated all along (see p. 60). In view of these and other indications of Communist moderation, the moment seemed auspicious to hold a top-level conference between Eastern and Western leaders. The "meeting at the summit," as the talks between President Eisenhower, Premier Bulganin, Prime Minister Eden, and Premier Faure were called, took place in Geneva in July, 1955.

This was the first meeting of the Big Four since the Potsdam Conference ten years earlier. The atmosphere of the discussions was cordial, and the "spirit of Geneva" tended to obscure, for the moment at least, the continued differences between the two camps. The conference dealt with four main subjects: German reunification, European security, disarmament, and the improvement of East-West relations. On none of these topics except the last did the powers reach any agreement. The first two points were closely related, since Soviet opposition to German reunification was allegedly based on the fear that a reunified and rearmed Germany would pose a threat to European security. The three Western leaders placed the German issue first, calling for immediate free elections to bring about reunification. To meet Russian fears of possible German aggression, they were willing to consider some general European security plan, a partial limitation of armaments, and a demilitarized area between the East and West. The Russians, on the other hand, were afraid that free German elections would result in a Communist defeat and insisted that European security should take precedence over German reunification. The Soviet negotiators, among them Khrushchev, proposed the dissolution of NATO and of its Eastern counterpart, the Warsaw Pact, and the substitution of an all-European security system that would include the United States. This last concession became meaningless, however, when the Russians also called for the ultimate withdrawal of all non-European forces.

Similar divergence of views existed on the issue of disarmament. President Eisenhower, in one of the conference's most dramatic speeches, again stressed the need for effective control as the first step in any disarmament plan. The President suggested that the U.S.S.R. and the United States exchange complete blueprints of their military establishments and permit unlimited aerial inspection to check on hidden concentrations of arms. The Russians refused to accept this "open skies" proposal. Instead they insisted that a ban on all nuclear weapons precede any system of inspection. The only subject on which agreement, at least in principle, was reached concerned the desirability of improving economic and cultural relations between the East and West. No specific measures were discussed, however, on how to bring about such improvement.

Despite a spirit of genuine friendliness, the accomplishments of the Geneva Conference were small indeed. It had been understood from the start that these top-level deliberations were to be exploratory and that more detailed discussions would take place at a later meeting of the Big Four foreign ministers. In the interim it appeared as though the summit meeting actually had improved the international climate. In August, 1955, an International Conference on the Peaceful Uses of Atomic Energy at Geneva brought together scientists from the Communist and free worlds to exchange information for the first time in twenty years. In September the Russians caused a pleasant surprise when they announced their readiness to withdraw from Finland's Porkkala Peninsula (see p. 18). Exchange visits by Russian and Western teams of experts and an increased flow of tourists across the iron curtain were seen as further signs that East-West relations had really changed.

But there were also indications that the change did not go very deep. When Chancellor Adenauer visited Moscow in September, 1955, to discuss the establishment of diplomatic relations between the Soviet Union and the German Federal Republic, he was told that West Germany's membership in NATO was the main obstacle to German reunification. Shortly thereafter the Soviet government reaffirmed the legitimacy of the East German Communist regime and the permanence of Germany's eastern frontiers, as established at Potsdam (see p. 14). About this same time the West was troubled by the news of an arms deal between Czechoslovakia and Egypt, which showed Communist intention of trying to meddle in the affairs of the Middle East. At the tenth session of the UN General Assembly in September, Secretary of State Dulles once again crossed verbal swords with Foreign Minister Molotov.

Such signs of continued East-West tension did not augur well for the Geneva Conference of the Big Four's foreign ministers that took place in October and November, 1955

The foreign ministers, taking up once again the issues discussed three months earlier by their heads of state, did not come any closer to agreement. On the tangled issue of German reunification, the Russians now asserted that there were two German governments and that reunification should be brought about through agreement between them. To the West this attitude indicated that Russia feared defeat in a free election and preferred to maintain the division of Germany. The disarmament discussions again foundered on Russia's refusal to agree to any effective plan of mutual inspection, and the matter was referred for further discussion to the UN Disarmament Commission. As for improving economic and cultural relations between the East and West, the Russians rejected Western requests to permit Russian citizens to travel freely outside Russia, to abolish censorship within the Soviet Union, and to reduce trade barriers. All in all, then, the efforts of the foreign ministers came to nothing. As the conference proceeded, it lost all traces of the cordiality that had prevailed at the summit meeting and again displayed the spirit of bitter recrimination that had prevailed at all earlier conferences.

THE COLD WAR CONTINUES

The search for peaceful coexistence by way of a settlement of East-West differences had thus failed. For a while the lull in the cold war continued. In January, 1956, Soviet Premier Bulganin, in a letter to President Eisenhower, offered the United States a twenty-year treaty of friendship and co-operation. The President turned the offer down, however, objecting that such a treaty might "work against the cause of peace by creating the illusion that a stroke of the pen had achieved a result which, in fact, can be obtained only by a change of spirit." Such a change of spirit, it seemed, was actually under way. Khrushchev's denouncement of Stalin at the Twentieth Party Congress, the announcement of a drastic cut in Soviet armed forces, and the Khrushchev-Tito declaration endorsing "different roads to socialism" in different countries, all were seen as hopeful signs that Russia's leaders were sincere in their advocacy of a "new course" at home and abroad.

At this point events in Hungary and the Middle East dashed all such hopes. Russia's role during the Suez crisis was mainly one of fanning the flames of Arab nationalism. By supporting Egypt throughout, Moscow not only won Nasser's gratitude, but was able to pose as a champion of anticolonialism in the eyes of Asians and Africans. Russia's gain in the Middle East, however, was offset by the loss of face she suffered because of her intervention in Hungary. The UN General Assembly condemned the Soviet Union for depriving the Hungarians of their freedom, and in this action even some of the neutralist nations concurred. While Russia's prestige was shaken, the influence and popularity of the United States remained high. With the proclamation of the Eisenhower Doctrine in early 1957, America served notice that she was ready to challenge the spread of Soviet influence in the Middle East. The Russians continued to sound the coexistence note. "There have been many cases of marriages without love where people get along," Khrushchev said in 1957. "Let us do it—without love, but getting on together." After what had happened in 1956, Americans could hardly be blamed for being suspicious of any such "marriage of convenience."

There were no major international crises in 1957. Nevertheless it was a crucial year in the cold war. The most important developments occurred within the Soviet Union. In July, 1957, Khrushchev won his victory over the "anti-party" group in the Presidium, emerging as the supreme voice of communism. A month later Russia announced the successful test of an intercontinental ballistic missile. While the West remained sceptical of Soviet claims to leadership in the missile field, the Russians on October 4, 1957, launched their first earth satellite, Sputnik I. The successful launching of a second satellite, weighing half a ton and carrying a dog, proved beyond any doubt that the Soviet Union possessed rockets powerful enough to deliver a nuclear warhead over an intercontinental distance. The failure of America's effort to launch her own test satellite in December, 1957, merely underlined the fact that the Russians held a substantial lead in a field in which the United States had always been thought superior. The balance of power in the cold war had suddenly and dramatically shifted to Russia's advantage.

The result of this shift was confusion in the West and a stiffening of attitude in the East. The NATO heads of government, meeting in Paris in December, 1957, agreed that the United States should give intermediate-range missiles to any NATO partner willing to accept them. At the same time America's allies urged that ways be found to check the arms race by negotiating with the Russians. The disarmament plan most widely discussed at the time was one of "disengagement." Its main advocate was Poland's Foreign Minister Adam Rapacki. What he proposed was a ban on the production of nuclear weapons and their elimination from central Europe (East and West Germany, Poland, and Czechoslovakia), followed by a reduction and separation of military forces in that critical area. The Russians advanced several versions of such "disengagement" schemes, and similar proposals were made in the West. But the United States suspected that Russia's motives were not so much to lessen tension and to facilitate a political solution as to weaken NATO. America launched her first satellite, Explorer I, in January, 1958. The Russians maintained their lead by putting their far bigger one-and-one-half-ton Sputnik III into orbit. Premier Bulganin, meanwhile, wrote a series of letters to President Eisenhower, asking for another summit conference. In these and other statements the Russians made free with vague but high-sounding proposals intended to make them appear as champions of peace. When asked to come to grips with specific issues of the cold war, however, they refused to commit themselves.

Besides waging a diplomatic offensive against the West, the Communists were also responsible for several serious international crises in 1958. In the Middle East they supported President Nasser in his drive to unify the Arab world. When the United States and Great Britain sent troops to Lebanon and Jordan, respectively, to protect these nations against Nasser, the move was denounced by Soviet Foreign Minister Andrei Gromyko as "unprovoked intervention" stemming from greed for "oil, oil and again oil." Next came the crisis in the Far East, where Chinese Communist attacks on Quemoy and Matsu brought on a war scare which was resolved only by America's firmness in protecting Nationalist Chinese convoys to the offshore islands.

The most irresponsible act of throwing the world into a state of fear was Premier Khrushchev's announcement in November, 1958, that the Soviet Union no longer recognized the occupation rights of the Western powers in West Berlin. France, Britain, and the United States flatly rejected this latest Communist challenge, but the Soviet leader remained firm, setting a six-month deadline after which West Berlin would become a "free city." The future of Berlin, of course, was part of a larger question, the future of

Germany, which had been a key issue in the cold war from the very beginning. Both East and West had repeatedly gone on record as favoring German reunification. The West proposed free all-German elections leading to an integrated state with an independent foreign policy. The East, on the other hand, insisted that unification be brought about in direct negotiations between the governments of East and West Germany and that the resulting federation withdraw from both NATO and the Warsaw Pact. This solution would insure a permanent foothold for communism in Germany, while at the same time removing the threat of a strong West German army equipped with nuclear weapons. It was for these reasons that the West had rejected all Soviet proposals for German unification. By challenging the Western position in Berlin, Khrushchev hoped to reopen the German question.

When the Communists discovered, however, that their policy of threats, far from weakening, actually strengthened and united the free world, they decided once again on a more conciliatory approach. Ever since Stalin's death Soviet leaders had relied heavily on personal diplomacy, traveling widely abroad and inviting important foreigners to visit the Soviet Union. This exchange program reached its high point in 1959. In January Khrushchev's right-hand man, First Deputy Premier Anastas I. Mikoyan, during a tour of the United States urged an early summit meeting to settle major East-West differences. In July President Eisenhower's right-hand man, Vice-President Nixon, on a visit to Russia called for "increasing the contacts between the leaders and peoples of our two countries." Meanwhile attempts of a foreign ministers' meeting to reach preliminary agreement on important issues, especially Berlin and Germany, ended in a deadlock. But this failure was overshadowed by the announcement in August, 1959, of plans for an exchange of visits between President Eisenhower and Premier Khrushchev.

The Russian leader came to the United States in September, 1959, and stayed for ten days. During that time he traveled widely, talked freely, and showed himself an indefatigable advocate of the Communist cause. The high point of the visit came during the last two days, which Khrushchev spent as President Eisenhower's guest at the latter's retreat in Camp David. The major topics discussed by the two men and their advisers were Berlin and disarmament. On neither of them did they reach any agreement. Negotiations on Berlin were to be reopened later, but without the time limit on which Khrushchev had insisted earlier. As for disarmament, the two leaders agreed to "make every effort to achieve a constructive solution." The chief gain from the Camp David discussions was the personal contact they permitted between the world's two most powerful men. President Eisenhower afterwards described Khrushchev as "an extraordinary personality"; and Khrushchev praised the President's "wise statesmanship," adding, "I got the impression that he sincerely wanted to liquidate the cold war." The "spirit of Camp David," like the "spirit of Geneva" four years earlier, became the byword for what was expected to be a new phase in East-West relations.

THE SUMMIT MEETING THAT FAILED

One of the results of the Eisenhower-Khrushchev talks was to ease the way toward another summit meeting. Prime Minister Macmillan of Great Britain had long favored such a meeting, feeling that as long as the East and West "kept talking" the danger of war would be minimized. The United States, now that Premier Khrushchev had lifted the time limit on the Berlin issue, also was ready to give the summit a try. The only resistance came from President de Gaulle of France, who wanted a conference on issues much wider than Berlin and disarmament, and who insisted that a summit meeting needed careful long-range preparation. It was De Gaulle's approach that prevailed. The second "meeting at the summit" was not held until the spring of 1960. The interim was taken up with prolonged negotiations within the Western camp, culminating in a meeting of Western leaders at Paris in December, 1959. Most of these preliminary talks dealt with the agenda for the summit conference. While no formal list was prepared, it was generally understood that the summit would deal with the problems of Germany and Berlin, disarmament, and the relaxation of East-West tensions. These points, it will be noted, were similar to the ones that had been discussed at the first summit meeting in 1955 and at almost every East-West meeting before and since.

While the Western Allies were getting ready to present a united front at the summit, President Eisenhower and Premier Khrushchev went on extended goodwill tours to proclaim the peaceful intentions of their countries and to win the sympathy of the neutral and uncommitted nations for their respective causes. The President in December, 1959, traveled some twenty-two thousand miles visiting eleven countries. Wherever he went, he was given a warm reception and his message of "peace and friendship in freedom" was generally applauded. The climax of Eisenhower's trip came in India, where unprecedented crowds cheered him as a trusted friend. "We have honored you, Sir," Prime Minister Nehru told the President, "because you have found an echo in the hearts of our millions."

Not to be outdone, Premier Khrushchev went on the road in February, 1960. He traveled only twelve thousand miles, but he had already covered twice that distance during the previous six months. His reception, while friendly, was not as warm as on an earlier tour he had made in 1955 and did not compare with the welcome given President Eisenhower. Khrushchev's suggestion that Asians turn their backs on Western aid was embarrassing to countries that heavily depended on such aid, and his attacks against Western colonialism found little echo among the neutralist nations. On the positive side, Khrushchev promised "to help the peoples of the former colonial countries in every way possible to attain economic independence and sharply raise their standard of living." He followed up his promise by a large Soviet credit to Indonesia.

From various Soviet statements during the spring of 1960, it seemed unlikely that the Russians were ready to make any major concessions on the issues separating the East and West. Still, there was always the hope that once Khrushchev met the Western leaders face to face, he might turn off his propaganda barrage and that in a friendlier atmosphere some limited progress toward agreement might be made. The summit conference was scheduled for mid-May, 1960, in Paris. Two weeks before the delegates assembled, the Russians downed an American U-2 plane engaged in an intelligence mission over the Soviet Union. This was the seventeenth incident in ten years involving United States planes, most of them flying near rather than over Russian territory. While on earlier occasions the Russians had been satisfied with making diplomatic protests, this time they decided to make a major issue out of American espionage. Premier Khrushchev, in breaking the news of the U-2 incident, saw little hope any longer for the success of the summit meeting. He later warned that he would use rockets against any country that lent its bases to future United States flights over the U.S.S.R. and that such flights would lead to war. American authorities at first denied that they had sent the U-2 plane on its mission but later had to reverse their stand. Such clumsiness cast serious doubts on America's leadership. As a result, predictions about the outcome of the Paris conference were extremely pessimistic.

As it turned out, the summit meeting never really got under way. At its opening session on May 16, 1960, Khrushchev launched into a savage attack on the United States and President Eisenhower who, he said, would no longer be welcome if he came to Russia. Khrushchev demanded that the President apologize for the U-2 incident and that those persons guilty of "deliberate violation of the Soviet Union" be punished. When these demands were rejected, the Russian leader left Paris. The West, in a joint communiqué, blamed the failure of the summit meeting on Khrushchev. The Russians in turn accused the United States of deliberately torpedoing the conference by aggressive actions.

The summit fiasco did not noticeably affect cold-war tensions, which had been running high for several weeks. Khrushchev, having let off steam in Paris, struck a more moderate note on his way home when he told an East German audience that a solution of the Berlin crisis could wait until after the American elections in the fall. President Eisenhower's statement to the American people that the United States "must continue businesslike dealings with the Soviet leaders" was termed as "of positive value" by the Russian premier, who added, "I still believe that the President wants peace." Such moderate Russian statements, however, were balanced by unrelenting attacks against the United States. Soviet Foreign Minister Gromyko, in a vain attempt to have the UN Security Council condemn the U-2 flight as "aggressive," called America's action "provocative," "bandit-like," and "piratical." In early July the Russian delegation walked out of the UN Disarmament Commission in Geneva, charging that the West, and particularly the United States, was not negotiating in good faith. Not long afterwards Premier Khrushchev threatened to use intercontinental missiles if the United States made any attempt to intervene against Castro in Cuba.

The intensity of this new Soviet offensive in the cold war caused anxiety and bewilderment in the West. "I simply do not understand what is your purpose," British Prime Minister Macmillan wrote Khrushchev in a direct appeal to reason. Some Western observers suspected that Khrushchev's new toughness was due to pressure from Communist China. The heavy sacrifices involved in China's "great leap," so the argument went, would be borne more readily by the Chinese people if these sacrifices were felt to be necessary to win the cold war. Peaceful coexistence implied a degree of mutual tolerance between capitalism and communism which was alien to strict Marxian doctrine. Instead, the Chinese Communists during the summer of 1960 advocated a "hard line" policy and asserted that lasting world peace would come only as the result of a class struggle against capitalism and imperialism. Western imperialism was still the favorite target of Soviet and Chinese Communists alike. Soviet actions in backing Fidel Castro in Cuba and Patrice Lumumba in the Congo were defended on grounds of anti-imperialism, as were Communist attempts to undermine America's position in the Far East, especially in Japan.

In June, 1960, President Eisenhower went on a goodwill tour to America's allies in the Far East. With one major exception, he was given a rousing welcome everywhere. Filipinos cheered the President's promise of continued United States aid, and the Nationalist Chinese gave him one of the most tumultuous receptions of his career, even though the Communists used the Eisenhower visit as the occasion to resume their artillery barrage against Quemoy. In South Korea, where the repressive and undemocratic regime of President Syngman Rhee had recently been ousted, the President's support of the new regime was gratefully acknowledged. The Second Korean Republic was officially launched in August, 1960, when John M. Chang took office as premier of Korea's first truly parliamentary government.

America's strongest ally in the Far East for the past ten years had been Japan. It was here that the announcement of President Eisenhower's trip caused such violently hostile demonstrations that his visit had to be canceled. At the root of the trouble was the agitation of a determined, Communist-led minority against a new United States–Japanese security treaty to replace the one signed in 1951. Despite Soviet warnings of "dangerous consequences," the new agreement was finally ratified. Premier Kishi, who resigned in July, 1960, was succeeded by Hayato Ikeda, another supporter of close ties with the United States. Even so, the failure of President Eisenhower to visit Japan was a serious blow to American prestige and a victory for communism.

THE COLD WAR IN THE UNITED NATIONS

In the fall of 1960 the theater of the cold war shifted briefly to the halls of the United Nations in New York. In an attempt to use the United Nations as a forum for his propaganda line, Premier

Khrushchev attended the fifteenth General Assembly which convened in late September. He brought with him several of his minions from the satellites of eastern Europe, and while in New York he found an additional ally in his latest friend, Cuba's Fidel Castro. To present the case for the West, President Eisenhower and Prime Minister Macmillan put in brief appearances. The leading neutralist nations were represented by Tito of Yugoslavia, Nasser of the United Arab Republic, Nkrumah of Ghana, Nehru of India, and Sukarno of Indonesia. Also present were the heads of state of several smaller countries, including most of the new African states. Never before had the United Nations played host to so many illustrious delegates.

For nearly four weeks the spotlight was on the bewildering antics of Premier Khrushchev. Alternating between threats and cajolery, he tried to dominate proceedings by appealing for support of the neutralists. In doing so he treated the Assembly to a series of performances never before witnessed in this decorous body —insulting and heckling delegates, calling the Security Council a spittoon and the Secretary General a fool, and taking off his shoe for use as a gavel. Orderly democratic procedure was obviously alien to the Russian leader.

In the course of these colorful goings-on, some old and several new issues came up for debate. Disarmament again occupied the center of the stage, but no agreement was reached. Khrushchev's attacks on Secretary General Dag Hammarskjold's role in the Congo crisis found little support among UN members and his proposals for the revision of the Secretariat and the Security Council were turned down. The Russians succeeded, however, in pushing through the Assembly a proposal to hold a debate on immediate independence for all remaining colonial territories. It remained to be seen whether the West would inject Soviet "imperialism" into such a debate. On the issue of Communist China's admission to the United Nations, finally, the West won its narrowest victory in history, with 35 per cent opposing, 22 per cent abstaining, and only 43 per cent favoring America's proposal of postponing the question for another year.

All in all, the results of the UN "summit meeting" were a draw, each side having made some gains and sustained some losses. The United Nations had increased its prestige, but hardly its power, and the two superpowers as usual had dominated the proceedings. Nevertheless, the growing number of neutralist states showed signs of drawing together into a "third force" and of using their influence to bring the East and West together in another summit meeting. If successful, these efforts might prove the only positive result of an otherwise puzzling series of events.

Behind the truculence which Russia showed in her dealings with the West during 1960 was a self-assurance that was new in Soviet policy. Its origins can be traced back to 1957 and to the Soviet Union's spectacular triumphs in the race for outer space. Subsequent Soviet economic achievements further strengthened this confidence in the superiority of the Communist system. The result was a cocksureness in which Khrushchev saw nothing incongruous about telling the West to change its ways or get "its knuckles rapped," while at the same time assuring the world that Russia was sincerely interested in peaceful coexistence. Time, the Russian leader boasted, was on the side of communism. A Communist victory over capitalism no longer depended solely on military superiority, it was certain to come as the result of peaceful economic competition between the East and West. One of the most important demonstrations of this competitive coexistence was in the struggle for the allegiance of the world's underdeveloped and uncommitted nations. The main weapon in this struggle was economic aid.

AID TO UNDERDEVELOPED LANDS

The term "underdeveloped" applies not merely to the colonial regions recently liberated from foreign control, but to any area suffering from a low standard of living, including most of Latin America. It does not, furthermore, denote inherent poverty. As we have seen, many of the economically backward nations are rich in resources that, if developed, could bring great profits. Even in their present state the backward nations play an important role in the world's economy by contributing vital raw materials and markets for industrial exports. To help these countries develop their economic potentialities, therefore, is not merely a dictate of political necessity to gain support in the conflict between the free and Communist worlds. It is also a matter of economic self-interest for the more highly industrialized nations of Europe and America.

The need to aid underdeveloped countries has become the more urgent because of the unprecedented population growth since

1945. A UN survey in 1960 estimated the world's total population at 2.9 billion. This number is growing at the rate of 48 million per year, or 85 people per minute. The reason for this "population explosion" is not so much an increase in the birth rate as a decline in infant mortality and the death rate. Official birth-control programs have not been very effective, except in Japan. If present trends continue, the world's population at the end of this century will be twice what it is today. The bulk of this increase will take place in Asia, Africa, and Latin America, whose populations will make up five-sixths of the total. Unless drastic steps are taken to satisfy the economic needs of these vast masses, the poor, quite literally, will inherit the earth.

The development of economically backward regions, in the opinion of most specialists, must be attacked from two directions—through self-help and through outside aid. The first point is sometimes overlooked, but it is very important. Where the will for self-improvement is lacking, no amount of foreign assistance will do much good. The responsibility for giving aid has been borne by all the advanced nations, although the United States has contributed the major share. We have already discussed the initiation of the Point Four Program by President Truman in 1949 (see p. 74). Its basic idea was to give technical assistance supplemented by financial aid. Compared to the billions spent each year on military aid, the funds appropriated to the International Co-operation Administration (ICA) for Point Four were meager. Even so, the accomplishments of the Point Four Program in such areas as public health, agriculture, and education have been impressive. The United States also was a major contributor to the UN Technical Assistance Program, as well as to such regional schemes as the economic projects of the Organization of American States in Latin America, and the development programs of the Colombo Plan nations in South and Southeast Asia.

Aside from technical assistance, the greatest need of underdeveloped countries has been for long-term investment in public works and basic industries. Here, too, the United States has taken the lead, both in such joint undertakings as the International Bank for Reconstruction and Development (World Bank) and the International Finance Corporation, as well as in the purely American Export-Import Bank. But the economic aid given by these bodies, often in collaboration with private investors, tended to go to countries that already had some degree of industrialization, rather than to more backward regions. To help the latter, the United States government in 1957 established the Development Loan Fund. It was designed to make so-called soft loans on easier terms, including repayment in foreign currencies. A similar agency was the International Development Association (IDA), founded in 1960. Its members, besides the United States, were Canada, Japan, and the leading nations of western Europe. America had long been concerned over the failure of some of these countries—notably Japan and West Germany—to share their growing prosperity by shouldering some of the foreign-aid burden. Such a joint effort was needed especially in view of the economic offensive which the Communist bloc had begun to wage in the non-Communist world.

The beginnings of this Communist offensive go back to 1954, when the Soviet Union granted a first modest credit to Afghanistan. Next on the list of recipients were India, Egypt, Indonesia, Syria, and Iraq. By 1960 the rate of Communist aid had risen from 11 million dollars to more than 1 billion dollars per year. The total aid, both economic and military, which the Communist bloc extended between 1954 and 1960 was estimated at 3.8 billion dollars. Compared to the more than 26 billion dollars which the West spent over the same period, this Communist figure looked insignificant. But the effectiveness of the respective aid programs must not be measured simply by comparing the amounts spent by each side. Of equal, if not greater, importance was the way in which the money was spent.

While the Communists were careful to concentrate their aid on a few key countries, the free nations spread their funds thinly over a wide area. Communist aid, furthermore, was usually given in the form of long-term, low-interest loans rather than outright grants. This method seemed preferable to countries afraid of accepting handouts for fear of incurring political or military obligations. Since United States foreign aid tended to favor nations that placed themselves firmly within the Western orbit, such fears seemed justified. The Soviet Union, on the other hand, claimed that its aid had "no strings attached." The fact that Communist strings were nonetheless real for being less visible was usually overlooked. Finally, much of the economic assistance given by the Communist bloc was in the form of trade rather than aid. Through trade the poorer countries hoped to earn needed funds for economic development without becoming subject to "Western imperialism," or "dollar diplomacy." Again this Communist emphasis on "trade, not aid," was deceptive, leading in many cases to the very dependency which the underdeveloped countries hoped to avoid.

Despite such hidden drawbacks, the Communist aid program was able to score some notable successes. To meet this challenge, the United States in 1959 and 1960 revised its own foreign-aid measures. From a past emphasis on military and bilateral aid, America now turned toward funneling more and more economic aid through international agencies like the Inter-American Development Bank, the International Development Authority, and the United Nations. President Eisenhower in his address to the United Nations in September, 1960, promised American support for a comprehensive program of UN assistance in various fields, especially in Africa. Simultaneously, the UN Food and Agriculture Organization embarked on a five-year "Freedom from Hunger" campaign to raise the marginal living standards of more than half the human race. Such multilateral aid programs, since they are free from any political strings, are acceptable to all countries that refuse to join either side in the cold war but prefer to remain neutral. The cost of foreign aid runs high. For the decade of the sixties alone it has been estimated at more than 300 billion dollars. Most of this money could be provided through freer trade; but a substantial share will have to come from aid, grants, loans, and private investment. The world's underdeveloped countries present an immense reservoir of potential friends and economic partners. It is up to the West to recognize the value of trading with them and of investing in their future. If the West fails to do so, the East will.

COMPETITION FOR ARMS AND OUTER SPACE

Competitive coexistence between East and West was found in every sphere, from politics and economics to art and athletics. It was especially keen in the race for armaments and for control of outer space. When the Soviet Union first caught up with the United States by developing its own atomic and hydrogen weapons, it seemed as though a stage had been reached in which the threat of mutual annihilation would serve as an effective deterrent to war. But as each side began developing its defenses against atomic attacks, and as military specialists began raising doubts about the annihilating effects of such attacks, the fear of nuclear war continued as great as ever. "Limited" wars along conventional lines, furthermore, were still possible. To be prepared for any kind of war, therefore, remained the overriding concern of East and West alike.

The comparative military strength of the Communist and free worlds was the subject of much debate. As far as traditional forces were concerned, the picture was fairly clear. With an army of 2.5 million, the Soviet Union held numerical superiority over America's 870,000 men. On the sea and in the air, the picture was more reassuring. Except for submarines, the United States had far more ships than Russia, and until 1960 America was the only country to have nuclear-powered submarines. In October, 1960, the Soviet Union announced that it, too, had developed such a craft. America's more than 35,000 military aircraft exceeded Russia's by about 10,000 planes. The United States was stronger in long-range bombers, while Russia had more fighters, fighter-bombers, and interceptor planes. Taken as a whole, these were the forces that would decide a small "brush-fire" war. The United States in such a war could also count on the support of one or several allies. But American forces were scattered so widely that some critics felt their strength to be insufficient. Failure to prepare for limited wars, these critics held, might lead to a situation where local Communist victories could be prevented only by "massive retaliation," which in turn would bring on full-scale nuclear war.

The main efforts of the United States were spent in preparation for a possible nuclear conflict. It was toward this end that Congress voted more than 40 billion dollars each year. Most of this money was used to close the "missile gap" between the United States and Russia. The extent of this gap again was a matter of controversy. That Russia initially led the field in the development of long-range missiles was generally acknowledged. It was only after the successful launching of its own intercontinental ballistic missiles (ICBM's)—the Atlas and the Titan—that the United States began catching up with the Russians. By 1960 the Soviet Union was still judged ahead in ICBM's as well as in shorter-range rockets for use against America's European allies. The United States had perfected several types of intermediate-range missiles (IRBM's), notably the Jupiter, the Thor, and the Polaris. The successful firing of the Polaris from a nuclear-powered submarine early in 1960 gave America a boost in the missile race. Later in the year, however, the Russians announced that they had developed a similar "invulnerable deterrent."

With the perfection of long-range missiles carrying nuclear warheads, "push-button" warfare had arrived. Because of the element of surprise in such a war, air defense became a matter of foremost concern. The United States tackled this problem from two directions: by setting up early warning systems, such as the DEW line across Alaska and northern Canada, and by anti-aircraft and antimissile defenses. By 1960 America had several surface-to-air missiles, like the Nike-Hercules and the Bomarc, for use against airplanes. The only weapon against ICBM's, however, the Nike-Zeus, was still under development. Little was known about Soviet air defenses other than fighter aircraft. Russia's cities, like those of the United States, were surrounded by anti-aircraft installations. But as for defense against ballistic missiles, Soviet Defense Minister Marshal Malinovsky claimed that it was impossible. Effective protection against long-range missiles might easily become the decisive factor in a nuclear war.

The contest for military leadership between the United States and the Soviet Union was closely related to their competition for the conquest of outer space. The competition began when Russia put its first Sputnik into orbit on October 4, 1957. This feat was followed by America's launching of its first satellite on January 31, 1958. In mid-1960 some thirty-six man-made objects were circling the earth, including satellites, rockets, and parts of space vehicles. In addition, three satellites were orbiting the sun, two of them launched by the United States and one by the Soviet Union. America had put by far the greater number of objects into orbit and had gained more varied and more valuable scientific information from such probes. The Russians, on the other hand, had sent up heavier vehicles and had shown greater capability of recovering them. With manned space flight as the main object of Russo-American rivalry, Russia's achievements were considered the more important.

Russia's leadership in space research was of great propagandist value in the era of competitive coexistence. Not only were the Soviets ahead in rocket power, they also were likely to become the first to make use of outer space for military purposes—reconnaissance, communications, or actual combat. America, on the other hand, was handicapped in its missile and space programs by constant interservice rivalries. The Army, Navy, and Air Force each had their own missiles, while a separate civilian space agency was charged with developing high-thrust rockets for space flights. Soviet missile projects, in contrast, were reportedly concentrated in military hands, thus avoiding unnecessary duplication and expense.

Because of the secrecy surrounding military preparedness, it was impossible to reach any definite conclusion about the comparative strength of the two superpowers. Such a comparison, moreover, had to take into account the forces of the other Communist and free nations. This much was clear, however: both sides had sufficient military power to strike a crippling or annihilating blow against the other; and each side was spending unprecedented sums on arms to the detriment of more constructive peaceful purposes. The resulting "balance of terror" exposed mankind to a degree of tension unknown in any other age. The only possible relief from this tension was through disarmament.

ATOMS FOR WAR OR PEACE?

The question of disarmament, as we have seen, had come up at almost every East-West conference since 1945. The basic problem on each occasion turned out to be the control of nuclear weapons. The United States consistently proposed that disarmament proceed in stages, each stage accompanied by careful international inspection. The Soviet Union, with equal consistency, called for a complete ban on nuclear weapons, to be followed by some unspecified form of control. The need for disarmament, meanwhile, became more urgent as both Great Britain and France joined the ranks of the atomic powers. Britain exploded its first atomic bomb in 1952 and its first hydrogen bomb in 1957; France followed suit with its first atomic bomb in 1960. With technological development lowering the cost of atomic weapons, the outlook was for other powers to join the "atomic club" in the not-too-distant future.

The leading agency concerned with disarmament since 1952 was the UN Disarmament Commission. Its last session ended in June, 1960, when the Soviet delegation walked out of its Geneva meeting. By that time the two sides had reached tentative agreement on some minor details, although the basic difference over control remained unresolved. Later in 1960 the disarmament issue was brought before the UN General Assembly, in two resolutions which summarized the Western and Soviet positions. The West again called for step-by-step disarmament, accompanied by inspection and controls. The Soviet Union demanded complete disarmament, including the abandonment of overseas bases, followed by negotiations on controls.

There was one aspect of the atomic race which posed a serious threat even in time of peace. As leading scientists the world over warned against the dangers of radioactive "fallout" from atomic tests, the United States and Russia in 1958 agreed to a temporary suspension of such tests. In subsequent negotiations the two powers, together with Great Britain, tried to find ways of making this test ban permanent. The stumbling block, as in the disarmament talks, turned out to be the issue of inspection and control, especially of underground explosions. If, nevertheless, atomic tests were not resumed, the main reason was the pressure of public opinion, especially among the neutrals. Even a permanent test ban, however, would not free the world from the nightmare of nuclear war; it would merely prevent scientists from devising still more horrible means of destruction.

Compared to the time and money spent in preparation for a nuclear war, the efforts to develop the peaceful uses of atomic energy have been negligible. A first step in this direction was made with President Eisenhower's "atoms for peace" proposal in 1953. The United States subsequently offered to contribute fissionable materials to an international pool if other nations would follow suit. In addition, America began making atomic fuels available to more than twenty-five countries. In 1956 both England and France started their first atomic power plants and the six nations of the European Economic Community established the Euratom agency for the common development of atomic energy (see p. 62). The Soviet Union, meanwhile, began sharing its own atomic knowledge with its satellites and with Yugoslavia and Egypt.

In October, 1956, a UN "atoms for peace" conference in New York established the International Atomic Energy Agency (IAEA) with headquarters at Vienna. Its purpose was to make available to less developed countries fissionable materials and nuclear equipment for peaceful projects, such as the construction of atomic power plants. The fissionable materials were to be contributed by those countries that could spare them. To make sure that these materials were used for peaceful purposes only, a system of inspection was to be set up. "We have done something," the American delegate to the "atoms for peace" conference said, "that makes it more likely that we and our children will live out our lives in peace."

As it turned out, this statement was much too optimistic. The IAEA initiated some programs of research and nuclear information and drafted some health and safety rules for the use of nuclear fuels. When it came to setting up a pool of such materials, however, difficulties soon arose over the safeguards necessary to assure that recipient nations would not divert atomic materials to military purposes. The Russians and some neutrals objected to inspection as an infringement of national sovereignty. The United States and the other Western powers, on the other hand, refused to allocate any nuclear materials until some system of inspection had been agreed on. Like disarmament, the use of the atom for peaceful purposes thus hinged on the crucial question of control.

THE FUTURE IN PERSPECTIVE

As the year 1960 drew to a close, the fear and distrust generated by more than a decade of cold war was stronger than ever. Again and again the neutral members of the United Nations urged that "constructive steps" be taken to reduce world tensions. But it was difficult to see how such a reduction of tensions might be achieved. Premier Khrushchev continued his vacillating tactics of threats and promises, expressing hopes for a summit conference while in the same breath delivering ultimatums on Germany and disarmament. These two issues—Germany and disarmament—had been fundamental to the cold war from the very beginning. They were no nearer solution in 1960 than they had been in 1950.

Looking back over the recent past, the future at the end of 1960 certainly looked dark. If, nevertheless, this did not cause a wave of pessimism, it was because people had grown used to living in a climate of fear. There were those even who predicted that men in time would adjust to the constant dread of annihilation by moving underground! "A broad and significant habit pattern will be introduced and accepted," this prognosis ran, "one grotesquely different from any we have known for thousands of years—that of adjusting ourselves to the idea of living in holes" (from a report issued by the Center for the Study of Democratic Institutions). To brighten this gloomy picture, we do well to remember that while the cold-war years had brought despair to some, they had brought deliverance to others. More people have gained political freedom since 1945 than in any comparable period in history. To help these people stand on their own feet while maintaining their newly-won freedom is the major challenge before the free world today. Unless it is met with boldness, imagination, and generosity, victory in the cold war will surely fall to the Communists.

Epilogue: Grave New World

IN ONE OF HIS MOST FAMOUS SPEECHES during World War II, President Roosevelt described the "Four Freedoms" that he believed every man should have a right to enjoy—freedom of speech, freedom of worship, freedom from want, and freedom from fear. It was felt at the time that the defeat of Fascist authoritarianism would open the door to the world-wide realization of these freedoms. But as we now know, this view was overly optimistic. It was based on the assumption that there were fundamental differences between the totalitarianism of the right (fascism) and the totalitarianism of the left (communism). There were differences in the ideologies of each system, of course. But in their suppression of individual liberty and in their desire for territorial expansion, the Soviet Union and Communist China today prove themselves worthy heirs to the oppressive and aggressive policies of Germany, Italy, and Japan. Actually, the area in which the basic freedoms of speech and worship are enjoyed today is smaller than it was before World War II.

The picture looks somewhat more hopeful with regard to the third ideal for a better world—freedom from want. The economic rise of both the Eastern and Western worlds from the ruins of World War II has been spectacular. In many countries a higher standard of living is enjoyed by more people today than at any other time. This improvement does not mean that the problem of economic want has been solved, however. The majority of the world's population still lives on a level barely above subsistence, and the scourge of famine has by no means been eliminated. For the first time in history, however, there now exists a general awareness among the more highly developed and prosperous nations that not only humanitarianism but also self-interest demands that they help the underdeveloped and poverty-stricken regions of the world to raise their economic level. While there is just cause for concern over the world's rate of population growth, the infinite energy unlocked by atomic research promises to provide the means of ultimately insuring a decent living to all mankind.

But the eradication of economic misery, despite such hopeful beginnings, has been retarded by our failure thus far to achieve the fourth of President Roosevelt's ideals—freedom from fear. There exists in the world today an all-pervasive fear that has become so much a part of our lives that we find it difficult to remember what it was like to live without it. When President Roosevelt spoke of "freedom from fear," he advocated "a worldwide reduction of armaments to such a point and in such a thorough fashion that no nation will be in a position to commit an act of aggression against any neighbor—anywhere in the world." It was the fear of war, then, from which the American president hoped to free the postwar world. But it is doubtful that he envisaged, at the time he made his speech, the proportions that this fear would assume after World War II. People have always feared wars; they certainly did so during the years between the two world wars. Since war in our atomic age promises to be so infinitely more horrible, fear of war has become more intense than ever before.

Much of world history since 1945 can be explained in terms of this fear of a third world war. Russia's expansion immediately after World War II certainly had many causes; but prominent among them was the desire to prevent the recurrence of the terrible experiences the Russians had gone through during the German invasion. As far as the West is concerned, the chief motive behind the strengthening and consolidation of its forces since 1947 has been the fear that Communist aggression might unleash another major war. At first the race for preparedness between the East and West proceeded on the assumption that weakness invites intervention and thus leads to war, while strength serves as a deterrent to aggression and thus helps keep the peace. More recently, however, this policy of "peace through strength" has been overshadowed by a new concept of "peace through fear." It is the horrible chaos envisaged as the result of an atomic war that in the last few years has proved to be the most effective restraint on hasty actions that might lead to mutual destruction.

Preparedness in the atomic age imposes a heavy economic and psychological strain. To call a halt to such preparedness would be a major step toward achieving freedom from both want and fear. Yet to relax this armed watchfulness requires first and foremost the generation of genuine trust between the East and West. And to achieve such trust has thus far proved impossible. Yet somehow, it seems, ways and means must be found to break the vicious circle of large armaments leading to mutual suspicion, and mutual suspicion leading to still larger armaments. Disarmament, in other words, will require a twofold process, psychological as well as military. For that reason it will be very slow and often discouraging. We may derive some comfort from the fact that the crisis of the cold war, had it occurred at any other time in history, might already have flared up into a major explosion. The fact that the cold war has not yet caused such an explosion justifies some slight hope that it may not do so in the future.

The course of world history since 1945 has been unique in other ways. To realize the uniqueness of the period, we need only consider the vocabulary we use in discussing everyday developments. Expressions like "iron curtain," "cold war," "containment," "coexistence," or "missile gap," while not necessarily new, certainly have taken on a special meaning unknown before the end of World War II. Some historians feel that to gain the right perspective on the world in which we live, we should not go too far in stressing the uniqueness of our age. There have been other periods in history, they point out, when the world was split between major factions and ideologies warring against each other. A world that survived the drawn-out struggle between Christianity and Islam, for instance, may well survive the present struggle between communism and democracy. Yet this argument overlooks the one element in our current conflict that has no precedent in the past—the thermonuclear bomb. It is an axiom of military thought that any weapon will in time find its match in a new means of defense. But if we believe our scientists who tell us that man now has within his power the annihilation of the very planet on which he lives, then even the deepest cave will give no shelter.

It is often held that the best means of avoiding world destruction would be the creation of an effective world government. There are, of course, the beginnings of such an organization in the United Nations. Although the United Nations has fallen short of the expectations of its creators, it still has rendered valuable services in settling some minor international crises and in making its moral weight felt in some major ones. But the United Nations is still far from being a true world government. As long as self-interest continues to be the guiding principle of nations, and as long as the stronger powers are unwilling to create a world organization commanding greater strength than they do, an effective supranational government remains a pious hope. Apart from this continued hold of nationalism, the ideological split between the East and West makes the formation of a world state still more difficult.

It is sometimes pointed out that we tend to overemphasize the role of the two superpowers, Russia and the United States. We must not forget that together they include only about one-seventh of the world's population. Certainly the gradual emergence of the former colonial regions, whose peoples constitute a majority in the world, may profoundly alter the present picture. But it would be wishful thinking to expect the influence of this potential "third force" to be necessarily for the better. The position of neutralism taken by so many of these new nations is often defended as impartial and benevolent. Yet such a position is more often dictated by weakness and by the needs of the moment. It is not suggested that the colored peoples of the world will some day stand against the white peoples. The fear of such a possibility, often voiced in the past by defenders of colonialism, will prove unfounded unless the white nations are shortsighted in their dealings with the less highly developed peoples. But the nationalism shown in recent years by Arabs and Africans, as well as by some Asians and Latin Americans, does not hold much promise that the emancipation of the colonial peoples will bring us any closer to the ideal of world government.

The inability of people, then, to solve their differences through some form of supranational government, and the possibility that these differences, if unresolved, may result in a major catastrophe are the main reasons why our present world is such a fearful place to live in. It would be false optimism to assume that this situation will improve within the near future. But such an environment does not mean that we cannot at least try to lessen the dread in which we are forced to live. Most people make the mistake of viewing the world's problems far too narrowly and rigidly, ignoring or excluding alternatives and overlooking the possibility of a middle course. We live in an age in which the word "compromise" is under suspicion as being synonymous with "appeasement." But compromise need not be regarded this one-sidedly. Only through a process of give-and-take can misunderstandings gradually be eliminated and fears made smaller. Such lessening of tensions will be slow work, requiring imagination, patience, and good will, while at the same time calling for continued watchfulness. To ignore the possibility of thus gradually reducing the differences that today divide the world would be a fatalistic admission that man no longer has control over his own fate.

INDEX

Acheson, Dean, 73, 75, 77
Adenauer, Konrad, 25, 38, 52 ff., 173
Afghanistan, 119, 185
Africa, 157 ff., 184, 186
Albania, 25, 30, 107, 108, 122, 127
Algeria, 47, 48-49, 50, 152, 155, 161
Angola, 157
Ankara Treaty, 111
ANZUS Treaty, 34, 166, 167
Arab League, 34, 152
Argentina, 89, 92
Aristov, Averki A., 115
Asian-African conferences, 161 ff.
Assembly of Captive European Nations (ACEN), 108
Aswan High Dam, 153-54
Ataturk, Mustafa Kemal, 151
Atlantic Charter, 5, 9, 20
Atomic bomb, 13, 15, 31, 32, 49, 54, 168, 189, 196
Atomic disarmament, 31, 168, 173, 189 ff.
Atomic tests, 2, 190
"Atoms for peace," 2, 31, 168, 170, 190-91
Attlee, Clement, 13 ff., 41

Index

Australia, 34, 44, 149
Austria, 17, 20, 60, 64; peace treaty with, 60, 113, 172

Baghdad Pact, 153, 161
Baltic States, 18, 105
Bandung Conference, 161
Baruch, Bernard M., 31-32
Batista, Fulgencio, 92, 96
Belgium, 28, 58-59, 159. *See also* Congo (Belgian)
Ben-Gurion, David, 31
Benelux countries, 28, 58-59, 61-64
Beneš, Eduard, 28
Beria, Lavrenti P., 112
Berlin crises, 7, 24, 176, 180
Berlin Conference (1954), 171
Bermuda Conference, 170
Bessarabia, 17
Betancourt, Rómuló, 92
Beveridge Report, 41
Bidault, Georges, 46
Bled Alliance, 111
Bolivia, 92, 93
Bonin Islands, 34
Bourguiba, Habib, 155
Bradley, Omar, 77
Brazil, 92, 93
Bricker amendment, 169
British Commonwealth of Nations. *See* Commonwealth of Nations
Brussels Treaty, 28-29, 54, 61
Bucovina, 18
Bulganin, Nikolai A., 103, 112, 114, 122, 172, 174, 176
Bulgaria, 6, 17-18, 25, 27, 30, 107 ff., 121, 122, 127
Bunche, Ralph, 4
Burma, 143, 144, 145-46
Byelorussian Republic. *See* White Russian Republic

Camargo, Alberto Lleras, 92
Cambodia, 47, 144, 147-48
Camp David meeting, 177-78
Canada, 29, 44, 87-89, 94, 149, 185
Caracas Conference (1954), 94
Carpatho-Ruthenia, 18
Casablanca Conference, 6
Castro, Fidel, 92, 96-98, 181, 182
Castro, Raul, 97
Central Treaty Organization (CENTO), 138, 153, 155, 166, 167
Ceylon, 44, 133
Chang, John M., 181
Chen Yun, 140
Chiang Kai-shek, 8, 35, 139, 142, 171-72

China. *See* Communist China, Nationalist China
Chou En-lai, 140, 141
Chu Teh, 140
Churchill, Sir Winston, 5 ff., 8, 13, 26, 41, 42, 44, 65, 72, 168, 170, 171
Clay, Lucius, 23, 24
Colombia, 89, 92
Colombo Plan, 148-49, 184
Colonialism, 44, 131; opposition to, 44, 131-32, 143, 161, 175, 179
Cominform, 24, 28, 109, 122
Common Market. *See* European Economic Community
Commonwealth of Nations, 8, 44, 64, 88, 89, 133, 145, 148, 156, 158, 159
Communism in Africa, 160; in Asia, 76-78, 134, 181; in China, 139, ff.; in eastern Europe, 25 ff., 106 ff., 121 ff.; in France, 25, 28, 45 ff.; in Germany, 53; in Italy, 25, 28, 57-58; in Latin America, 92, 94, 97; in Middle East, 120, 149 ff., 157, 173; in southeast Asia, 145 ff.; in United States, 74-75. *See also* U.S.S.R.
Communist China, 10, 35, 98, 134, 138, 139-44, 171, 193; and Korean War, 36, 76 ff., 111, 139, 142; and United Nations, 36, 142, 182; and United States, 35, 142, 171-72, 176; and U.S.S.R., 35, 143, 180-81
Congo (Belgian), 11, 59, 159-60
"Containment," 26
Council for Mutual Economic Assistance, 27, 109
Council of Europe, 65
Council of Foreign Ministers, 15, 17
Cuba, 89-92, 96-98, 119, 180
"Curzon Line," 7, 19
Cyprus, 44, 155-56
Czechoslovakia, 18, 25, 27, 28, 107 ff., 121, 125-27, 173

Damascus Pact, 153
Denmark, 29, 60, 64
Desegregation, 80, 85
Development Loan Fund, 185
Dewey, Thomas E., 73
Diefenbaker, John, 88
Disarmament, 5, 31, 168, 172-73, 174, 176, 178, 182, 189 ff., 194
"Disengagement," 176
Dominican Republic, 89
Dobruja, 18
Dudintsev, Vladimir, 117
Dulles, John Foster, 80, 170, 173
Dumbarton Oaks Conference, 8, 9

Dunkirk Treaty, 28
Dutch-Indonesian Union, 146

East Prussia, 14
East Germany, 22, 24 ff., 51, 54, 107 ff., 109-10, 125-27, 173
ECSC. *See* European Coal and Steel Community
Ecuador, 94, 95
EDC. *See* European Defense Community
Eden, Sir Anthony, 9, 43, 172
EEC. *See* European Economic Community
Egypt, 119, 152 ff., 173, 185, 190
Ehrenburg, Ilya, 117
Eisenhower, Dwight D., 29, 79 ff., 96, 98, 131, 138, 164, 170 ff.
"Eisenhower Doctrine," 154, 161, 175
Elizabeth II, 43, 89
Erhard, Ludwig, 51
ERP. *See* European Recovery Program
Estonia, 18
"Euratom," 62-63, 190
European Coal and Steel Community (ECSC), 62-63
European Defense Community (EDC), 54, 64-65
European Economic Community (EEC), 62-63
European Recovery Program (ERP), 27, 74
European union, 46, 55, 60-66
Export-Import Bank, 184

Faisal II, 155
Far Eastern Commission, 15
Farouk I, 153
Faure, Edgar, 172
Federation of Rhodesia and Nyasaland, 158
Finland, 15, 17-18, 27, 28, 106, 173
Food and Agriculture Organization (UN), 12, 186
Formosa, 34, 35, 77
"Four Freedoms," 193
France, 10, 17, 20, 28, 40, 45-50, 65-66, 149, 161, 189; and colonies, 47, 48-49, 132, 133, 159; and Germany, 7, 22, 46-47, 50, 54, 55-56, 64-65; and Indochina, 47, 147
Franco, Francisco, 59
Free Trade Association, 64
French Community, 50, 159
French Union, 47, 148
Frondizi, Arturo, 92

Gaitskell, Hugh, 43
Gandhi, Mohandas K., 132, 133, 135
Garcia, Carlos, 145
Gasperi, Alcide de, 57
Gaulle, Charles de, 38, 45 ff., 56, 178
Geneva Conference (1954), 171
Geneva Conference of Foreign Ministers (1955), 174
Geneva "meeting at the summit" (1955), 172-73
German Democratic Republic. See East Germany
German Federal Republic. See West Germany
Germany, 6, 10, 13 ff., 17, 21 ff., 40, 50 ff., 60, 65-66, 170, 193; denazification of, 23, 56; eastern frontier of, 7, 14, 53, 173; occupation of, 7, 13 ff., 20, 22 ff.; rearmament of, 54; reparations from, 6, 14, 22-23; reunification of, 23-24, 53, 172, 174, 177. *See also* East Germany, West Germany
Gerö, Erno, 124
Ghana, 44, 159
Gheorghiu-dej, Gheorghe, 127
Goa, 133
Gold Coast. See Ghana
Gomulka, Wladyslaw, 111, 123, 126
Gottwald, Klement, 28
Great Britain, 6 ff., 10, 17, 20, 22 ff., 26, 28, 29, 30, 40, 41-45, 64-65, 149, 153, 157, 189; Conservatives, 42-43; Empire, 43-44, 157, 158; Labor, 41-42, 43. *See also* Commonwealth of Nations
Greece, 6, 17, 21, 24, 26-27, 29, 30, 111, 128
Gromyko, Andrei, 176, 180
Grotewohl, Otto, 109
Guevara, Ernesto "Che," 97-98
Guinea, 159
Gursel, Cemal, 151

Haiti, 89, 93
Hammarskjold, Dag, 4, 12, 159, 182
Herter, Christian, 98
Hirohito, Emperor, 34
Hiss, Alger, 75
Hitler, Adolf, 13, 19, 30, 61
Ho Chi-minh, 147
Hungary, 6, 17, 18, 25, 107 ff., 122, 127; revolution, 11, 114, 120, 123-25, 138, 175
Hydrogen bomb, 44, 82, 168, 189

Iceland, 29
Ignatov, Nikolai G., 115
Ikeda, Hayato, 181
India, 132-33, 143; Union of, 30, 44, 119, 133, 134-38, 179, 185
Indochina, 47-48, 113, 147, 166, 171
Indonesia, 11, 30, 59, 119, 144, 146-47, 179, 185
Inter-American Development Bank, 186
International Atomic Energy Agency (UN), 31, 190
International Bank for Reconstruction and Development. See World Bank
International Co-operation Administration (ICA), 184
International Court of Justice (UN), 12
International Development Association (IDA), 185, 186
International Finance Corporation, 184
International Labor Organization (UN), 12
Iran, 29, 151, 153, 157
Iraq, 152 ff., 155, 185
Israel, 11, 30, 149; and Arabs, 31, 152, 154, 161
Italy, 15, 17, 29, 40, 56-58, 111, 193

Japan, 8, 15, 33 ff., 149, 170, 184, 185, 193; peace treaty, 34, 167; and United States, 15, 33 f., 167, 181
Jinnah, Mohammed Ali, 132, 138
Johnson, Lyndon B., 87
Jordan, 153, 154, 176

Kadar, Janos, 125, 127
Kasavubu, Joseph, 160
Kashmir, 11, 30, 133-34, 138
Kassem, Abdul Karim, 155
Kefauver, Estes, 78
Kennan, George F., 26
Kennedy, John F., 68, 69, 87
Kenya, 158, 160
Khan, Mohammed Ayub, 138
Khrushchev, Nikita S., 86, 98, 101, 112 ff., 164, 172, 175, 176 ff.
Kishi, Nobusuke, 181
Konev, Ivan, 121
Korea, 10, 15, 35-36, 171. *See also* North Korea, South Korea
Korean War, 11, 33, 75-78, 88, 111, 113, 139, 166

Kostov, Traicho, 111
Kozlov, Frol R., 115
Kubitschek, Juscelino, 92, 93
Kurile Islands, 8, 34

Ladoga, Lake, 18
Laniel, Joseph, 170
Laos, 47, 144, 147-48
Latin America, 89-98, 183
Latvia, 18
League of Nations, 10, 12, 20, 30
Lebanon, 11, 153, 154, 176
Libya, 155
Lie, Trygve, 12
Lithuania, 18
Liu Shao-chi, 140
London Conference (1947), 24
Lumumba, Patrice, 159, 181
Luxembourg, 28, 58

MacArthur, Douglas, 15, 33, 76-78
Macmillan, Harold, 43, 178, 180, 182
McCarran-Walter Act, 169
McCarthy, Joseph, 75, 81, 169
Magsaysay, Ramón, 145
Makarios, Archbishop, 157
Malaya, 44, 144, 148
Malenkov, Georgi M., 103, 112, 113
Manchuria, 15
Mandates, 12, 30, 34
Mao Tse-tung, 35, 140 ff.
Marshall, George C., 23-24, 27, 73, 75
Marshall Plan, 27, 42, 47, 48, 59, 61, 73
Masaryk, Jan, 28
Matsu, 142, 172, 176
Mayer, René, 46
Mboya, Tom, 160
Menderes, Adnan, 151
Mexico, 92
Michael, King, 13
Middle East, 149 ff.
Middle East Treaty Organization (METO). See Central Treaty Organization (CENTO)
Mihailovich, General, 110
Mikoyan, Anastas I., 113, 115, 177
Mindszenty, Cardinal, 108
"Missile gap," 86, 187-88
Mobutu, Joseph, 160
Moch, Jules, 46
Mohammed V, 155
Molotov, Vyacheslav, 9, 103, 112, 114, 122, 123, 173
"Molotov Plan." See Council for Mutual Economic Assistance

Monnet, Jean, 45, 62, 64
Morgenthau, Henry, 6
Morocco, 152, 155
Moscow Conference (1944), 6; (1947), 23
Mossadegh, Mohammed, 151
Mountbatten, Lord Louis, 133
Mozambique, 157

Nagy, Imre, 124-25
Nasser, Gamal Abdel, 153-54, 175, 176, 182
Nationalism, 132, 196; Africa, 157 ff.; Asia, 132 ff.; Europe, 40-41; Middle East, 149 ff.; Americas, 88, 89 ff.
Nationalist China, 10, 15, 35, 77, 95, 142, 171-72, 181
NATO. *See* North Atlantic Treaty Organization
Ne Win, 146
Nehru, Jawaharlal, 132 ff., 179, 182
Nepal, 143
Netherlands, 28, 30, 58, 146
"Neutralism," 11, 33, 128, 132, 133, 135, 144, 148, 157, 160, 183, 196
New Guinea, 59, 146
New Zealand, 34, 44, 149
Ngo Dinh Diem, 148
Nicaragua, 89, 94
Nigeria, 44, 130
Nixon, Richard M., 83, 87, 92, 96, 177
Nkrumah, Kwame, 159, 160, 161, 182
North Atlantic Treaty Organization (NATO), 29, 49, 54, 59, 61, 74, 88, 166, 167, 172, 175-76, 177
North Korea, 36, 76-77, 143
North Vietnam, 143, 144, 145
Norway, 29, 60, 64
Novotny, Antonin, 127
Nyasaland, 44
Nyerere, Julius, 160

Oder-Neisse line, 7, 14, 53, 173
Ollenhauer, Erich, 53
Organization for European Economic Cooperation (OEEC), 27, 61
Organization of American States (OAS), 95, 98, 167, 184
Outer Mongolia, 8, 143

Pacific Charter, 149
Pahlevi, Mohammed Riza, 151
Pakistan, 30, 44, 133, 138-39, 149, 153

Palestine. See Israel
Panama, 92
Paraguay, 89
Paris Conference (1946), 17
Paris "meeting at the summit" (1960), 179-80
Paris treaties (1954), 54-55
Pasternak, Boris, 117
Pauker, Ana, 111
Perón, Juan, 89
Peru, 89, 95
Pescadores, 171
Petersberg agreement, 25
Petsamo, 18
Philippines, 34, 144, 145, 149, 181
Pieck, Wilhelm, 109
Pleven, René, 46
"Point Four," 32, 74, 184
Poland, 6 ff., 13 ff., 21, 25, 27, 107 ff., 121, 126; boundaries of, 7, 14, 53, 173; revolt in (1956), 114, 123
"Population explosion," 1, 83, 93, 134, 144, 183-84
Porkkala, 18, 173
Portugal, 29, 59, 64, 132, 133
Potsdam Conference, 13 ff., 35
Punjab, 134

Quebec Conference, 6
Quemoy, 142, 172, 176, 181

Rajk, Laszlo, 111
Rakosi, Matyas, 124
Rapacki, Adam, 176
Republic of China. See Nationalist China
Republic of Korea. See South Korea
Rhee, Dr. Syngman, 36, 181
Rhodesia, 44
Ridgway, Matthew, 78
Rio Treaty, 94
Rokossovsky, Konstantin, 123
Romania, 6, 13, 17-18, 25, 27, 107, 122, 127
Roosevelt, Franklin D., 5 ff., 9, 13, 70, 82, 193
Russia. See U.S.S.R.
Ryukyu Islands, 34

Saar, 56
Sakhalin Island, 8, 34
Salazar, Antonio de Oliveira, 59
San Francisco Conference, 8, 9 ff.
Satellites: Axis, 17 ff.; Soviet, 106 ff., 121 ff.
Saudi Arabia, 152, 153
Schumacher, Kurt, 53

Schuman, Robert, 46, 55, 62
Schuman Plan, 62
SEATO. *See* Southeast Asia Treaty Organization
Slansky, Rudolf, 111
Socialism in France, 45; in Germany, 53; in Great Britain, 41-42; in Italy, 57-58
South America. *See* Latin America
South Korea, 36, 76-77, 171, 181
South Vietnam, 47, 145, 148
Southeast Asia, 144 ff.
Southeast Asia Treaty Organization (SEATO), 138, 149, 166, 167
Space probes, 1-2, 86, 175, 188
Spain, 59, 167, 170
Spychalski, Marian, 111
Stalin, Joseph, 6 ff., 13 ff., 21, 81, 101 ff., 115-16
Stalinism, 102-6
Stepinac, Cardinal, 108
Stettinius, Edward, 9
Stevenson, Adlai, 79, 81
Sudan, 155
Suez Canal, 152, 153; crisis (1956), 11, 43, 89, 125, 153-54, 175
Sukarno, Achmed, 132, 146-47, 165, 182
Suslov, Mikhail A., 115
Sweden, 60, 64
Switzerland, 10, 60, 64
Syria, 153, 185

Taft, Robert A., 71, 73, 74, 75, 76, 79, 80
Taft-Hartley Act, 72, 74
Tanganyika, 158, 160
Teheran Conference, 6
Teng Hsiao-ping, 140
Thailand (Siam), 144, 145, 149
Thanarat, Sarit, 145
Tibet, 138, 143, 166
Tito, Marshal, 110-12, 122, 127-28, 182
"Titoism," 110, 121, 122, 123
Toynbee, Arnold, 170
Transylvania, 18
Trieste, 17, 58, 110, 111
Truman, Harry S., 13 ff., 26 ff., 32, 70 ff., 82, 184
Truman Doctrine, 24, 27, 73
Tunisia, 152, 155, 157
Turkey, 15, 26-27, 29, 111, 128, 151, 153, 157

U Nu, 146
Uganda, 158
Ukrainian Republic, 9
Ulbricht, Walter, 109, 126
UN. *See* United Nations

Underdeveloped countries, 32, 183 ff., 194
Union of South Africa, 44, 157, 158, 160, 161
United Arab Republic, 153, 154
United Nations, 6, 8, 9 ff., 29 ff., 36, 76, 95, 134, 152, 154, 159, 162, 175, 181 ff., 186, 189, 196; Charter of, 9 ff.; Disarmament Commission of, 31, 168, 174, 180, 182, 189; Economic and Social Council of, 12; Educational, Scientific, and Cultural Organization of (UNESCO), 12; General Assembly of, 8, 10-11, 30, 32; Membership of, 10, 59, 60, 122, 161, 162, 182; Secretariat of, 12, 182; Security Council of, 8, 10-11, 17, 30, 32, 182; Technical Assistance Program of, 12, 32, 184; Trusteeship Council of, 12; veto in, 8, 11, 29, 32
U-2 plane incident, 179-80
United States of America, 1, 10, 69-98; economic aid to foreign countries, 12, 27, 32, 35, 42, 48, 51, 74, 87, 95, 128, 135, 138, 146, 149, 151, 184 ff.; Eisenhower administration, 79-87; elections, 72, 73, 79, 80, 81-82, 87; foreign relations, 6 ff., 13 ff., 20 ff., 26 ff., 44, 59, 71 ff., 76 ff., 80 ff., 85 ff., 119, 165 ff.; military power, 187-89; Truman administration, 70-79
U.S.S.R., 1, 5 ff., 10, 98, 101-28, 193; and eastern Europe, 7, 21, 25, 27 ff., 106 ff., 121 ff.; economic policy, 102, 104 ff., 113, 116; foreign relations, 5 ff., 13 ff., 20 ff., 25 ff., 29 ff., 106 ff., 113, 119 ff., 165 ff.; Khrushchev era, 115-21; military power, 187-89; Stalin era, 101-12

Vandenberg, Arthur H., 71, 73
Vasilevsky, Alexander M., 103
Venezuela, 89, 92
Vietnam, 10, 147
Vyshinsky, Andrei, 103

Wallace, Henry, 72, 73
Warsaw Pact, 121, 123, 124, 172, 177
Western (European) Union, 28, 61, 65
West Germany, 24 ff., 29, 50-56, 173, 185
White Russian Republic, 8-9
Willkie, Wendell L., 169
World Bank, 12, 184
World Health Organization, 12
World War I, 1, 30, 39; peace settlement, 17

World War II, 1-2, 5 ff., 104; peace settlements, 5 ff., 16 ff., 34, 60
Wyszynski, Cardinal, 108, 123

Yalta Conference, 6 ff., 14, 35
Yemen, 152
Yugoslavia, 6, 17-18, 25, 27, 30, 58, 107 ff.; and U.S.S.R., 110-12, 122, 127-28, 190; and West, 111, 128, 167

Zhdanov, Andrei, 103
Zhukov, Georgi K., 112, 114
Zionism, 30

PRINTED IN U.S.A.